Neil Archer is Lecturer in Film Studies at Keele University. He is the author of *Studying Hot Fuzz* (2015), *The French Road Movie: Space, Mobility, Identity* (2013) and *Studying The Bourne Ultimatum* (2012), and co-editor of *Adaptation: Studies in French and Francophone Culture* (2011). His most recent book is *The Road Movie: In Search of Meaning* (2016).

'An excellent book, well-written and authoritative, with a strikingly fresh agenda.'

Charles Barr, Professor, School of Art, Media and American Studies, University of East Anglia

BEYOND A JOKE

PARODY IN ENGLISH FILM AND TELEVISION COMEDY

NEIL ARCHER

BLOOMSBURY ACADEMIC
LONDON • NEW YORK • OXFORD • NEW DELHI • SYDNEY

BLOOMSBURY ACADEMIC
Bloomsbury Publishing Plc
50 Bedford Square, London, WC1B 3DP, UK
1385 Broadway, New York, NY 10018, USA
29 Earlsfort Terrace, Dublin 2, Ireland

BLOOMSBURY, BLOOMSBURY ACADEMIC and the Diana logo
are trademarks of Bloomsbury Publishing Plc

First published in Great Britain by I.B. Tauris 2017
Paperback edition published by Bloomsbury Academic 2021

A catalogue record for this book is available from the British Library.

A catalog record for this book is available from the Library of Congress.

ISBN: HB: 978-1-7845-3663-3
PB: 978-1-3502-4244-9
ePDF: 978-1-7867-3090-9
eBook: 978-1-7867-2090-0

Series: Cinema and Society

Typeset by Jones Ltd, London

To find out more about our authors and books visit
www.bloomsbury.com and sign up for our newsletters.

Contents

Preface: Repeat Performances

Halfway through *The Trip to Italy* (2014), the film and BBC series directed by Michael Winterbottom,[1] actors Steve Coogan and Rob Brydon, playing fictional versions of themselves, are enjoying a drink in Rome. Coogan laments the invasion of the Italian capital by tourists, in the spirit of his literary hero Byron, whose footsteps the two men are following on their trip. Brydon reminds him that they are themselves embodying the democratisation of modern travel. Aren't they, Brydon asks, merely doing the same thing that E. M. Forster's Europhile protagonists were doing a century previously?

> EMMA (COOGAN'S PA): Yeah, look at *Room with a View*...
>
> COOGAN: With Daniel Day-Lewis, who used to be posh, before he became Irish.
>
> BRYDON [ADOPTING 'ARISTOCRATIC' ACCENT]: 'Ah, Miss Honeychurch, I wondered if you might allow me the privilege of joining you for dinner on the palazzo this evening...'
>
> COOGAN: Why are you doing Hugh Grant?
>
> BRYDON: I'm not doing Hugh Grant; Hugh Grant would be, 'Ah, gosh, Miss Honeychurch, I-I-I wondered if you might, uhh, as it were, join me, uhh, this evening...'
>
> COOGAN: It sounds a lot like your Day-Lewis, only half an octave up.
>
> BRYDON: And a little bit taller; I went taller as well, I straightened my back...
>
> COOGAN [ADOPTING 'NORTHERN IRISH' ACCENT]: 'I spent fifteen years of my life in prison for something I *didn't do*! I saw my father – *die* – in prison, for something he *didn't do*!'
>
> BRYDON: 'Daniel Day-Lewis is Ronan Keating in: *Boyzone: The Movie!*'
>
> COOGAN: That was Gerry Conlon, from the Guildford Four...
>
> BRYDON: Was that after Westlife?

This sequence encapsulates what happens in *The Trip to Italy*, as its two mimics drive and eat their way around the country, reeling off as they do a host of impersonations – Marlon Brando, Al Pacino, Woody Allen, and of course Hugh Grant, to mention only a few – linked at best tangentially to Italy, but who are all connected by cinema: cinematic performances that have been repeatedly watched and listened to, preserved in the mind, then re-performed with (mostly) consummate mimetic skill by two British comics on holiday. But it also, in turn, sums up what Winterbottom's film is really about: the fascination with other films, and other voices; the impossibility of escaping these voices as they take over our own words; what it means to talk about being original in a world where everything, it seems, has been done, seen and screened.

What is so unexpected, though, about *The Trip to Italy* is that we haven't seen much like it on film before. There are plenty of films, English ones included, that look and sound like ones we have seen already. Critics and analysts of film often call this style pastiche; a concept to which we will turn at more length later. What is different in *The Trip to Italy*'s cinephile borrowings is that they are never subsumed into a consistent and coherent narrative and style. When Coogan and Brydon chat in the style of Batman and Bane from *The Dark Knight Rises* (2012), competing to see who can be least intelligible, they remain a pair of comic actors and impressionists, imitating two frankly ridiculous voices, sitting in a restaurant somewhere between Genoa and La Spezia.

When the subject of imitation is as clearly marked as it is here, we move towards the comic mode most frequently identified as *parody*. As this book will explore, parody is a key practice in English film and television comedy, with *The Trip to Italy*, in fact, being just one of the more recent examples. Impersonation can be a form of parody in the way it highlights the excesses or peculiarities of a particular voice: Pacino's huskily mannered line deliveries; the weirdly sonorous inflections of Roger Moore; Day-Lewis's chameleon leaps from Edwardian aesthete to imprisoned Ulsterman (*In the Name of the Father* [1993]) to US President (in *Lincoln* [2012]). It can in this respect be cruel or mocking, as in the unsparing comic assault on Tom Hardy's gagged, gas-masked villain in the Batman film. But imitation, as the saying goes, is also a form of flattery, requiring as it does that the performer literally *impersonates*; in other words, that they take in or assume the character of their subject, whose uniqueness usually motivates their imitation in the first place. To impersonate is also, in this way, to love – even Bane.

The Trip to Italy is also, in this way, unsparing of Coogan and Brydon themselves, hopelessly unable as they are to speak in their 'own' voices. But this is both the dilemma and the pleasure of the film itself, which can never escape its dependence on other films. Echoes of past films acknowledged by its travellers and occasional companions – *The Godfather* (1972), *Roman Holiday* (1953), Roberto Rossellini's *Voyage to Italy* (1954), Federico Fellini's *La Dolce Vita* (1960) – haunt *The Trip to Italy*, just as the gestures and voices of actors present and past ghost their way through the performances of Coogan and Brydon.

In the end, it is this knowingness about its own place in cinema history that makes *The Trip to Italy* so interesting; especially as it is also self-questioning about its place as a 'national' work of film and television. As much as its own dynamic duo take inventive comic shots at the superhero blockbuster, its comic targets, and its own frames of self-reference, include – as shown above – such archetypal English products as *A Room with a View* (1985), arguably the defining film of the so-called Merchant-Ivory film line. Coogan and Brydon's continuity with Forster's travelling English also marks *The Trip to Italy*'s own perpetuation of this same tradition: English films for English audiences about the English abroad, but which – as is also the case with *The Trip to Italy* – is also a local film *for a global audience* that enjoys watching the English, especially when they are dressed in their Edwardian finery. A global audience that, judging by the limitless exportability of *Downton Abbey* (ITV, 2010–), has hardly dwindled in recent years. But of course this is not another *Room with a View*, nor even a *Downton Abbey*. The finery on display here consists of three-quarter length trousers and Birkenstock sandals; the manners are not polished to perfection, and the accents (Mancunian and South Wales) some miles from the cut-glass tones of drama-school Received Pronunciation. And the actors themselves, as much as they spend most of both *Trips* thinking they should be in the movies, are still best known, in their home country at least, as stars of English television.

Parody of Hollywood; parody of English costume drama; parody, as much as anything, of itself: *The Trip to Italy* is all these things at once. It is at once a film in the form of a BBC television series for many of its viewers; for others, specifically its cinematic audience, it is a television series squeezed into a film, starring an English and a Welsh actor who are well known without, let's face it, being *that* famous. It is about how they see others, and consequently, how others see them; but ultimately, in its tendencies toward self-parody, it is about how they see themselves – as performed for the benefit of others.

I would also say, and with due respect to Welshman Brydon as *The Trip to Italy*'s gently mocking presence, it is a very English film, though not because it is preoccupied with England. Its 'Englishness', if we can call it that, lies in its preoccupation with everything else, its relation to the bigger world in which this not-very significant Italian holiday takes place. In many ways, *The Trip to Italy* encapsulates the characteristics of English film and television comedy in light of its global audience. Defining these in more detail is the aim of this book.

Acknowledgements

My acknowledgements first and foremost to everyone at I.B.Tauris for bringing *Beyond a Joke* to fruition, especially to Tom Stottor and Sophie Campbell for their editorial care and enthusiasm. When I started writing this book, I could not imagine it would be coming out in the context of a national referendum on Britain's place in Europe, nor in light of a significant and continuing discussion about the United future, or otherwise, of this Kingdom. While I was not able in this book to broach these latter contexts at any length, the meaning of 'Englishness' in a globalised world, and its representation and construction in media, are possibly as keenly contested and important as they have ever been. My own feelings on the matter, and how I see these issues explored in various film and television texts, are perhaps obvious from the contents of these pages. I leave the reader to take my arguments as a departure for further discussion: in any event, this book could not have come out at a more appropriate time.

Thanks to my various colleagues and students at Keele for making it such a great place to work, and for contributing to some of the conversations informing this book's key ideas; and to the Faculty of Humanities and Social Sciences, for the period of research leave that helped me get it all together. Special thanks to Joe Andrew, Susan Bruce, Beth Johnson (now at Leeds), Tim Lustig, Helen Parr and Nick Reyland. Thank you also to John Atkinson and Yoram Allon, for letting me write other books in the meantime that just couldn't wait around.

A shorter and slightly different version of Chapter 4 was previously published as ' "The Shit Just Got Real": Parody and National Film Culture in *The Strike* and *Hot Fuzz*', in *Journal of British Cinema and Television* 11/1 (2016), pp. 42–60. Many thanks to the editors for permission to reuse material for this book.

For entertainment and inspiration: Lewis, Rory, Andy; to Stevie G for lessons in commitment and determination; to Leslie Nielsen, Will Ferrell and Cary Grant for lessons in comedy; and to Michael Palin, for lessons in being great. To Aaron Sorkin, without whose dialogue the world would be less brilliant; to LEGO, without whose products the world would be less interesting; to Microsoft, without whose software (let's admit it) this book would still have been written, just a lot less easily.

Love and dedications, lastly, to my family: to Steve and Mags Archer for indulging both my childhood predilection for Playmobil and *Star Wars*, and my somewhat meandering approach to educational and career trajectories; to Matthew 'Tuds' Archer, self-confessed comedy snob, for Highgate-Road TV and *Tiger Woods* – not to mention the *Spaced* and *Garth Marenghi* DVDs which pretty much got this particular ball rolling; to Giulia Miller, who does not always share my interest in parody, but who does share both my life and my fondness for *Lost*, for which no little mercies I am extremely grateful; and of course to Noa, who has long worked out the comic benefits of parody, if not necessarily in theory, then certainly in practice.

List of Illustrations

List of Illustrations

General Editor's Introduction

For as long as there has been popular entertainment there has been parody. The Victorian stage saw parodies of every aspect of culture: Greek myths, fairy tales, English history, Arthurian legend, the Arabian Nights, grand opera, popular melodrama, Shakespeare, Scott and Dickens. Parody only works if the audience recognises the nature, themes and characters of the work being sent up. While parody exaggerates and deploys incongruity to mock the essence of its subject, at the same time it celebrates that subject as something that is worth this kind of attention. Neil Archer's theme is parody in British film and television and he delivers a multi-layered and richly nuanced study establishing parody as a much more complex phenomenon than many critics have allowed. Inevitably Hollywood is the principal target but paradoxically British screen parodies of Hollywood genres and blockbusters had the effect of projecting British film and television into a global context. Golden Age Hollywood figured regularly in the parodies that were an integral part of such much-loved television series as *The Morecambe and Wise Show* and *The Stanley Baxter Picture Show*. The *Carry On* series regularly turned to Hollywood for its subjects, parodying Westerns (*Carry On Cowboy*), horror films (*Carry On Screaming*), historical epics (*Carry On Cleo*), Empire melodramas (*Carry On Up the Khyber*) and eighteenth century naval dramas (*Carry On Jack*). Along with a series of close readings of a wide variety of film and television texts, among them *Hot Fuzz*, *Shaun of the Dead*, *Monty Python and the Holy Grail*, *The Hitchhiker's Guide to the Galaxy*, *Royal Flush* and *Ripping Yarns*, Archer examines the opportunities and limitations of parody and addresses the subjects of national identity and global appeal, intertextuality, the production context, audience reaction, visual style and genre aesthetics. The whole study adds up to a serious exploration of the world beyond the joke.

Jeffrey Richards

Introduction: Why Parody, and Why Now?

Close-up: A young man and woman are standing by the window of their flat, looking out onto the illuminated North London night. The man speaks into a child's walkie-talkie. 'See you at the rendezvous'. A muffled yawn comes down from the other end, revealed as another man at the wheel of a transit van. 'OK, Tim' he replies. Back in the flat, the woman leans in to pass her own message: 'Good luck'. Now in long shot, we see the camouflage-painted van heading off, as the swooning strains of John Williams' score from *The Empire Strikes Back* (1980) fill the soundtrack. We see the young couple from behind, the night sky before them: the door to their sitting room closes in the foreground, creating an improvised horizontal wipe: finally, with a climactic burst of Williams' famous theme, the credits appear on a background of stars.

Elsewhere: A milk float is crawling down a rural village road just above walking pace. With the float now going over four miles per hour, a bomb beneath it has been activated, set to go off should the speedometer dip back below this mark. The young priest at the wheel has just managed to avoid a pyramid of cardboard boxes placed carefully in the left hand lane, thanks to the quick thinking of Father Crilly, who had time to rebuild the pile on the other side. 'Keep driving!' the Father instructs his young friend, as he speeds off to devise a solution. Cut to a phone conversation

1

I.1 Hollywood in Craggy Island: a Mass comes to Dougal's rescue in the 'Speed 3' episode of *Father Ted* (1998)

between Crilly and his colleague Father Beeching. 'We have to help him', implores the former. 'We need to do something practical!' Cut back to the road, the milk float and the sound of a not-too-distant chugging engine. A Roman Catholic altar, pulled by a tractor, glides into view alongside the milk float, with Fathers Crilly, Beeching and a third colleague in the middle, who speaks out: 'Mass is being said today for Father Dougal McGuire, who finds himself in a trying and unfortunate situation. We pray God will protect him from harm at this time, and deliver him to safety'.

The first sequence described above comes from 'Dissolution', the penultimate episode of *Spaced*: a sitcom, produced by LWT and the Paramount Comedy Channel for the UK broadcaster Channel 4, which ran for two seasons in 1999 and 2001. The second is from 'Speed 3', part of the third and final season of *Father Ted*, again produced for Channel 4 between 1995 and 1998. In 'Dissolution', the background to this concluding scene is the betrayal and consequent disappearance of Tim and flatmate Daisy's alcoholic landlady, Marsha, the object of their friends' search. 'There are over a hundred off-licences in this area', Daisy reflects. 'She could be in any one of them'. The bomb in 'Speed 3', meanwhile, has been placed there in revenge by Pat Mustard, the priapic local milkman, father to multiple lookalike 'hairy babies' throughout Craggy Island, whose morning deliveries are halted by Ted Crilly and Dougal McGuire's detective work.

Explaining these sequences in narrative terms is to some extent secondary to their other function as *parodies*. Given even a passing familiarity with the texts to which these shows refer, it is difficult not to read both sequences doubly: as at once operating in their own coherent and contained comic world, but also drawing attention to, and reflecting upon, the other texts influencing them. In a move very typical of *Spaced*, the end of 'Dissolution' employs an almost identical editing pattern, soundtrack and choice of mise-en-scène to the last scene in *The Empire Strikes Back*, only with nocturnal London standing in for the vastness of space, and a transit van for the Millennium Falcon. 'Speed 3', as its title helpfully reminds us, derives its milk-float plot from the film *Speed* (1994) (which was followed by *Speed 2: Cruise Control* in 1997), where the bomb was on a school bus travelling at 50, rather than four, miles per hour. While the milk float's trundle affords the other priests time for a Mass, breaks for tea and even a screening of *The Poseidon Adventure*, 'Speed 3' also replicates many aesthetic characteristics of the original blockbuster: fast-edited movements between driver and his point of view; extreme close-ups of speedometers and the grinning mouth of the taunting bomber; a long tracking shot showing the packaged explosives along the underside of the float.

I have chosen to start this book with these two examples because both encapsulate the central aesthetic practice analysed in this book; namely, the incorporation, relocation and reworking of predominantly American texts, more often than not *cinematic* ones, to comic effect. In this instance, both *Spaced* and *Father Ted* take Hollywood and put it in a place where it apparently does not belong. Not only do both shows, as sitcoms, construct their own local settings in which to place their other-worldly inter-texts; in their status as television shows, and within terms of Channel 4's practices of production and reception, they are already shaped and determined by a media aesthetic within which the 'big-screen' character of the Hollywood blockbuster can never be entirely at ease.

Beyond a Joke is about English film and television comedy (*Father Ted's* brief presence here a slight, though not complete, aside),[1] and the function of parody within them. This is potentially a rather broad subject, though the above examples illustrate the more specific focus for this book: the relationship of English comedy, both in film and television, to the globally dominant modes of big-screen entertainment. Television comedies like *Spaced* work by bringing the scale of Hollywood filmmaking down to a 'domestic', small-screen size, which offers room for considering the respective characters of English and Hollywood production. In this sense, television shows can themselves be understood as specifically engaging with cinema, or even constituting part of the national 'film culture' itself. Indeed, and as I will discuss at a later point, part of the appeal of a show like *Spaced* was the way it tried to encapsulate a particularly *local experience* of global popular culture – and my personal response to the series relates significantly to my own experience as an English consumer of Hollywood cinema, mainly in a domestic *televisual* context.[2] Here, as elsewhere, this relationship is explored through modes of parody. As this book will explore, examples of parody in English film and television afford a similar, though complex, reflection on English film culture in light of Hollywood's globally dominant forms.

Exactly what this relationship is, however, is not always straightforward. This is a book about parody, though one of my motivations for writing it is a sense that 'parody' often seems an inadequate theoretical term for what it describes. A journalistic form of critical shorthand might identify the sequences from both *Spaced* and *Father Ted* as parodies, or 'spoofs', of *The Empire Strikes Back* and *Speed*. But does our critical task end at the point of recognition? Surely not, if parody is indeed going to mean anything beyond simply acknowledging a source of textual influence. To say more broadly that in a parody text A is parodied by B (where, let us say, A is American movies and B is English film or television) is often taken as a self-sufficient statement. But with what implications?

Defining Parody

One way to begin approaching this question is to consider in more detail what actually goes on in a parody text. Dan Harries' *Film Parody*, which goes further than any other existing text in establishing a theoretical method for analysing such movies, provides a lucid definition from which to start:

> I define parody as the process of recontextualising a target or source text through the transformation of its textual (and contextual) elements [...] This conversion – through the resulting oscillation between similarity to and difference from the target – creates a level of ironic incongruity with an inevitable satiric impulse.[3]

As Harries' terms indicate, parody relies significantly on the idea of *incongruity*. In comedy theory, incongruity's humorous effect relies on the setting up and subsequent undermining of expectations: the humour, as Brett Mills describes it, arises 'from the disparity between the ways in which things are expected to be and how they actually are'.[4] Also adopting the line of incongruity, Linda Hutcheon outlines parody in terms of 'transcontextualisation', where textual components – the structure and motifs, say, of a specific genre or familiar text – are placed in a different time and place where they no longer 'fit'.

This form of 'repetition with difference'[5] allows us to view the aesthetic and ideological operations of texts through the prism of other contexts: hence the potential for 'satiric impulse' Harries identifies. Mills' sustained point is that the incongruous in comedy rests on a cognitive, rather than emotional, response, reliant as it is on the viewer identifying expectations and norms, and in turn recognising the deviation from them.[6] Incongruity consequently offers surprise but also pleasure in demonstrating 'the tenuous and artificial nature of social norms' and 'undermining their supposed transparency and obviousness'.[7] In the case of the above sequences, putting Hollywood genre in the contexts of an English or Irish everyday locale, and also the contexts and aesthetics of a television sitcom, lays bare the incongruity between the representations of the cinematic blockbuster and the world in which both *Spaced* and *Father Ted* take place.

While Harries focuses mainly on parody within the American tradition, the tropes he defines through his analyses underline the potential significance of cultural difference, and the movement across cultural contexts, in the work of parody texts: the 'reiteration' or 'quotation' of elements from a target text or texts 'to create an association between the prototext and the parody as well as to establish conventional narrative expectations'; the 'inversion' of signifiers in order to suggest 'an opposite meaning from [...] the target text'; 'misdirection', in which 'conventional elements are evoked [...] and then transformed to deliver an unexpected turn'; 'literalisation', in the form of 'visual, aural and textual' puns that self-reflexively '"literalise" the film-making process'; 'extraneous exclusion', where '"foreign" lexical units' are inserted 'into a conventionalised syntax'; and 'exaggeration', which involves taking elements of the source text and 'extending them beyond their conventionally expected limits'.[8]

Looking at 'Speed 3', then, we can see how the episode sets up via reiteration expectations drawn, in this case, from our (assumed) knowledge of the movie *Speed*, by specifically 'quoting' the film in its narrative, editing patterns and mise-en-scène. 'Speed 3' then playfully inverts the pre-established generic norms, but also (negatively) exaggerates them, by having the float travel so slowly, before the eventual and misdirected pay-off in the form of the travelling altar, pathetically revealed to us as it drifts into Dougal's point of view. In a later scene, striving to find a way to get Dougal off the float without detonating the bomb, Ted scribbles furiously on an unseen blackboard in front of the gathered priests. Turning to them, he states his plan: 'We put the brick on the accelerator!' – only to reveal, in the following, literalising shot, these exact same words written on the board. The pay-off shot in both sequences exemplifies the show's varied markers of incongruity with relation to Hollywood cinema's generic norms; though with the added transcontextual point that the whole episode, within the parameters of *Father Ted*'s world, represents its own form of extraneous inclusion. In turn – as this form of parody theory suggests – the 'transparency' of structures and motifs as usually deployed in genre cinema, but also their rootedness in specific cultural and filmmaking contexts, are both exposed and undermined.

There is quite a bit more to it than this, as I will suggest below, though this brief analysis suggests some of the specific aims and functions within parody, especially here in a national context. Parody, in short, is never just a fact: it always implies something else, which then becomes an accompanying object of analysis. Enjoying parody involves recognition, and specifically, the recognition of difference. Identifying what parody really does can therefore explain much about why and how, for example,

Hollywood-targeting parody emerges in specific national contexts. Parody is rarely, if ever, accidental; it is always deliberate, and frequently responsive in character. Working out why, when and in what way parody surfaces in English film and television comedy is the task of this book.

Does Parody Matter?

With the exception of *Film Parody* and Wes Gehring's *Parody as Film Genre*,[9] film parody as a type of practice has not been widely covered in full-length academic studies. In-depth treatments of parody in the non-Hollywood context, moreover – Geoff King's chapter on parody in his *Film Comedy* being a notable exception[10] – are even scarcer. This lack of academic attention is quite surprising, given the significance of parody as a form within late twentieth- and early twenty-first century cinema.

The relative lack of critical interest afforded parody emphasises its reputation as a supposedly minor cultural form. This is possibly related to the historically 'negative assessment', on the part of critical theorists, 'of the worth of comedy',[11] and its accompanying dismissal of the parodist as 'merely a mocker of other texts'.[12] Because parody film is usually dependent on one or often more prior texts (the 'source' or 'target' texts), and can lend itself to a limitless range of generic models, parody theory has had difficulty establishing itself as a textual practice or category.[13] Related to this, parody is almost never connoted within the traditionally approved terms of film authorship or 'quality'. With a few exceptions, probably because of its dependence on other texts, and therefore its implicit lack of originality, parody does not provide us with many *auteurs* in the familiar sense of the term, or the kind of films that feature in critics' lists or prestigious award ceremonies.

Parody is also difficult to pin down ideologically. While parody more broadly is often seen as essentially 'polemical' in its re-presentation of cultural texts or practices,[14] parody cinema in particular is as frequently associated with the commercial imperatives of popular filmmaking. Scholarship on parody film, focusing mainly on Hollywood, has emphasised the ways in which parody's relative cheapness and ready-made models for imitation have made it a convenient form for studio exploitation,[15] though emerging recent work on European cinema[16] has also recognised how the parodic recycling of earlier motifs and genres is a domestic (though not always exportable) model for commercial production. Within the high-turnover, saturation strategies of contemporary film exhibition, parody offers the promise of decent returns in its reworking of familiar popular forms. For some, this cheapness of production may also point towards a poverty of imagination, if not a broader crisis in cultural production more generally.

The above example from *Spaced* offers a case in point. Here, the visual and musical elements of *The Empire Strikes Back* are recreated – reiterated – in a way clearly designed to evoke recognition. The viewer aware of the reference might take pleasure from this, acknowledging this formal nod to the earlier film. The framework within which the action of *Spaced* takes place – its North London setting, and its replacement of the various accoutrements of the *Star Wars* universe with toys and old motor vehicles – provides the marked inversion of norms, the extraneous inclusion and acknowledgement of difference central to the workings of parody texts. Here, though, the detailed effort to reiterate the comparative scene from *The Empire Strikes Back* potentially overwhelms any intent to expose or undermine the latter film's 'norms'. If anything, the systematic use of such tropes within the preceding 12 episodes of *Spaced*, and the perennial quotation of the *Star Wars* films, allows this sequence from 'Dissolution' to sit quite comfortably within its established fictional world, in which pop-cultural reference points effectively replace the 'real world' from which they are only notionally distinct. This begs the question where parody in *Spaced* begins and ends, as well as asking whether parody can accommodate such apparent devotion to the supposedly 'targeted' source text.

Similarly, viewers alert to reiterations of *Speed* in *Father Ted* will acknowledge their insertion within the world of Craggy Island. But in acknowledging this, what kind of actual pleasures are we talking about here? Beyond our ability to identify the object of reference in these instances, is there actually any narrative, reflective or affective *point* to such shows' use of quotation? Any discussion of parody as cultural production of the late twentieth and early twenty-first century, then, needs to consider the ways in which culture in this era is best understood. Inevitably, given its privileged status within discussions of this period, this means situating parody within the terms of the 'postmodern'.

Parody, Pastiche and Postmodernism

Fredric Jameson's work on the emerging discourses of postmodernism, gathered in his 1991 book *Postmodernism: Or, the Cultural Logic of Late Capitalism*, gave new impetus to the study of parody. For Jameson, as Simon Dentith explains, ' "consumer" or "late capitalist" […] society [is] a world without cultural hierarchies: a depthless world in which the recourse to nature, or the past, or "high" culture, as ways of getting the measure of the world, has been abandoned'.[17] A significant implication in Jameson's discussion is that parody in its widely familiar sense of 'mockery' or 'spoof' can no longer hold. Parody here elides into what Jameson calls 'pastiche': 'blank parody… a neutral practice of such mimicry, without any of parody's ulterior motives, amputated of the satiric impulse';[18] a mode characterised by the nostalgia film, identified by Jameson in the form of *American Graffiti* (1973), or through the recycling of genre tropes, such as those of film noir in *Chinatown* (1974) and *Body Heat* (1981). Rather than 'get the measure of the world', then, such practices merely reflect (again and again) the victory of capitalism and the reduction of artistic products to commodities.

While we should take Jameson's rather generalised assessment of post-modern cinema with some scepticism, his views have turned out in many senses to be prescient. Regardless of whether or not parody has been effaced by pastiche, Jameson has been proved largely correct inasmuch as the sequel has become the dominant commercial manifestation of con-temporary global cinema. Whether this reflects the cultural logic of 'late capitalism', or more simply the conservative commercial logic of an always-anxious Hollywood (or whether in fact these are one and the same), is too big a question to address here, but to some extent both logics overlap in terms of the marketplace. As Harries has argued,[19] it is the institutional reliance on genre and franchises that has given rise to the development of parody as a sustainable genre in contemporary Hollywood. Because par-ody demands by its own nature recognition on the part of its audiences, it assumes a degree of familiarity with its 'targets' on the part of those same audiences. This means that audiences for films parodying certain genres (for instance, the *Scary Movie* parodies of the horror genre) are also the audience for those same genres: their engagement with the parody text therefore serves as part of the production and maintenance of the genre through both modes, in a process of recognition and reiteration. And while its relocation to the contexts of television adds some nuance to the issue, at one level, the reiteration of both dominant and recent Hollywood franchise movies in *Spaced* and *Father Ted* does little to challenge this idea of parody mostly sustaining its own apparent targets.

In our emphasis on the 'blank' nature of contemporary parody, though, we risk overlooking what Jameson's critique reminds us; namely that parody *in principle* has a 'satiric impulse' and reflects upon other texts. Indeed, the subtlety in Harries' assessment of recent Hollywood is to identify the maintenance of dominant genres *within* the apparently derisive or critical terms of their parodies, suggesting in turn that genres evolve through forms of reflective criticism. Like other theorists looking at parody at the turn of the millennium, such as Dentith, Harries is alert to Jameson's conflation of parody and pastiche within a 'neutral' form of mimicry.[20] Implicit in Harries' reading of contemporary Hollywood parody is the centrality of viewers' knowledge about other films. Harries therefore identifies the ways parody films are predicated on the film literacy and critical awareness of their prospective viewers. What Harries calls the condition of 'ironic supersaturation'[21] underpinning recent parody obviously cuts both ways, begging the question what meaningful difference there is between parody and 'straight' filmmaking. Yet we may at least see it as symptomatic of a more conscious and engaged viewing practice than might otherwise be supposed.

While Hutcheon specifically opposes Jameson in her *Politics of Postmodernism*,[22] her earlier *A Theory of Parody* emphasises the critical dialogue introduced between past (the context for the parodied text) and present in which we critically receive the parody. Hutcheon's argument is interesting in the way that, against the more traditionally 'mocking' tones of parody, such practices indicate a position with regard to past representations that does not imply superiority, but simply historical, cultural or political distance. But because Hutcheon's examples pertain on the whole to the fields of classical music, literature and the fine arts, it is not clear how this argument would deal with the parodic reworking of low or popular genre forms, such as the action movie (in *Hot Fuzz* [2007]), the sci-fi movie (*The Hitchhiker's*

Guide to the Galaxy [2005]), or gory horror fiction and 1980s hospital drama (*Garth Marenghi's Darkplace* [Channel 4, 2004]); nor, in its emphasis on past and present, does it account for the fact that most contemporary parody, as Harries notes, engages with extremely recent texts. In fact, an important point made by Dentith is that the contemporary dominance of parody needs to be understood in relation to the increasing dominance within postmodernity of *popular culture*, rather than a form of critical dialogue across and within the 'high' cultural fields. Postmodernity, best characterised by the medium of television, gives us 'a raucous and multivocal culture, in which the traditional cultural hierarchies have broken down'.[23] For Dentith, then, the emergence of parody as a cultural form may reflect more broadly the validation of popular culture's 'longstanding parodic energies',[24] rather than providing another means for the critically established arts to maintain their status.

Redefining Parody

Let us go back then to the question of what parody is really doing. As noted, part of my motivation in undertaking this study was a dissatisfaction with the kinds of terms frequently used to describe films I liked: words such as 'parody' itself, but also 'spoof', 'mockery' and 'lampoon'. If there were an obvious way to avoid these terms I would probably not need to write this book. We should nevertheless look briefly at some of the problems inherent to these definitions of parody as a critical term.

In *Cult Cinema*, for example, Jamie Sexton and Ernest Mathijs use the phrase 'loving mockery' to describe certain parody films, such as the legendary 'mockumentary' *This is Spinal Tap* (1984).[25] On the one hand, such ambivalent phrases capture the difficulty in describing a film that is at once highly knowing about its reference points, dismantling at every turn the pretensions and pomposity of its subjects. Yet the film is also at some level a *celebration* of these subjects, as confirmed by the status of *Spinal Tap* as a 'cult' text appropriated, re-watched and effectively performed by viewers worldwide, who in some instances went on to watch the 'band' perform in live concerts, and bought the soundtrack album from the film.

This discussion of parody films within the terms of Sexton and Mathijs's wider project points to one of parody's key paradoxes: that the notional critique of its target text(s) is offset by the fact that its audience is often one and the same. But this in itself is as much a logical as an empirical observation, as it would make little sense for audiences to watch parody film purely for the instructional purposes of deconstructing 'bad objects' of film. From my perspective, the enjoyment of a film like *Hot Fuzz* is hardly due to me not liking the type of action movies it looks to parody: far from it, in fact. In much the same way, my interest in the television and film versions of *The Hitchhiker's Guide to the Galaxy* is consistent with my wider regard for science fiction, and not because I dislike the genre. 'Loving mockery', in other words, even in its ambivalence, does not really do justice to the highly complex significance of parody film.

Richard Dyer, meanwhile, has provided a set of viable working definitions of parody that enable us to distinguish it from other modes, such as pastiche, with which it is often improperly equated. Dyer notes a frequent overlap between pastiche and parody in the sense that both modes, as much as they can be clearly defined, use techniques of imitation. Dyer nevertheless distinguishes the two modes in terms of 'attitude, but also by the nature of their relation to that which they imitate'. As Dyer explains: 'while it is always possible to misread both pastiche and parody as straight imitation, it is much easier to do so with pastiche because it remains formally closer to that which it imitates'.[26] Yet the implied 'distance' of parody is not always so easy to delineate, given the point that parody, for reasons already outlined, involves 'both nearness and opposition'.[27] Dyer concludes that, unlike in much pastiche, parody's own complicity with its source is problematic: 'Perhaps parody is theoretically distinct from pastiche chiefly because it minds being inexorably implicated in that from which it seeks to distance itself and that is why it is so hysterical – so angry, so mocking, so unkind – about it'.[28]

Dyer touches on the idea here that parody's critical dimension 'implies a sure position outside of that to which it refers, one of secure judgement and knowledge'.[29] This is possibly what underpins the type of quick, 'self-evident' critical responses to parody texts I alluded to at the beginning of this introduction; the critical shorthand that merely sees parody as a negated version of something else. For Dyer, parody's marking of the textual deviation from its souce inevitably signals a 'negative evaluation',[30] one which logically restricts the possibility of complex readings or ambiguity (something which Dyer values in pastiche as an alternative model). I suspect that the 'sure position of knowledge' and 'evaluative' viewpoint inferred from the parody text have enabled parodies to assume such a 'given' function within our discussion and analysis of films. Within this restrictive logic, there is no need to critically elaborate on the parody text, the meaning of which is apparently obvious. But what if this is not so clear-cut? What if, contrary to Dyer's claims, we can read parody outside this logic? If parody is no longer secure in its judgement, more ambiguous in its evaluative character, does it stop being parody, or is it the case that we need to rethink what we sometimes mean when we use this term?

To return briefly to our earlier examples, is it so obvious that *Father Ted*'s use of parody is necessarily *at the expense of* the film from which it draws its comic inspiration? By its own nature as a parody, 'Speed 3' is consistently aware of the aesthetic and narrative conventions it reworks, evoking them, to the best of its televisual abilities, with devotion and attention to detail. The obvious relish with which such generic tropes are displayed in the show, and my own pleasurable response to them, suggests that at some very significant level I am a willing participant in the pleasures of a genre film like *Speed* (which, in fact, I like very much). Granted, enjoying this through the framework of an episode of *Father Ted* implies certain ironic and reflexive viewing positions, but it would again seem like bad faith to hide the pleasurable effects of the show's generic allusions completely behind the veil of 'mockery'. As we will see throughout this book, whether in *Monty Python's Life of Brian* (1979) or Morecambe and Wise's television shows, up to the various genre parodies of the *Wallace and Gromit* film series, we should constantly take into account our own investment and pleasure in the very genres and motifs that are the object of parodic intent.

Indeed, Harries' point that there is no significant distinction between the fans of a film genre and the audience for its parody would suggest that, for whatever particular reasons, we need to rethink some of the more critical, evaluative and above all negative assumptions about parody: assumptions that are all too easy to uphold when discussed in terms of national cinemas and their notionally oppositional take on the globally dominant forms of Hollywood. In what ways, then, can a parody hold up an imitated text to apparent critical distance *and also love it*, not in spite of this critical distance, but *as a process of it*? On the face of it, this seems a difficult and counter-intuitive question to answer, but this is nevertheless one of the aims of this book.

Questions of Scale: Globalisation, the Global Audience and Englishness

As already noted, a main focus in this book is the ways that both big and small screen English comedy engage, via parody, with the dominant global imaginary of popular – and mainly Hollywood – cinema. By introducing the role of television as a constituent part of an English *film* culture, I am already acknowledging the significance of *scale* to discussions of English parody. Our analysis is not limited to television, of course; yet some comparative idea of scale, of the relevant 'smallness' of English film, as well as television, especially in the face of Hollywood's global production and marketing machine, plays an inevitable role when we come to look at parody texts. While I will touch on some important exceptions, as well as production circumstances that complicate the simplistic reduction to 'English' film and television, any discussion of the latter must acknowledge the specific economic contexts in which it is made. English film, for example, and indeed English television, is typically produced on a smaller scale, and on a much lower budget, than its American counterparts. This sense of scale is in fact reinforced by the frequent links between television production and film, with many films under discussion in this book – the *Monty Python* series, *Shaun of the Dead* (2004), *Wallace and Gromit: The Curse of the Were-Rabbit* (2005), *The Hitchhiker's Guide to the Galaxy* – strongly connected to their earlier manifestations on the small screen or the television backgrounds of their casts and crew; while others, such as 1988's *The Strike*, a film made primarily for screening on Channel 4, highlight the type of domestic viewing contexts to which such English 'filmmaking' is often limited.

This comparative sense of scale has a key role to play in the broader traditions of English comedy (as I will outline in Chapter 1), and is exploited to great effect in a number of the films and shows considered in this book. We should nevertheless be wary of deducing from these contexts any simplistic assumptions about the 'smallness' or 'realism' of English film and television, its repudiation of a dominant large-scale aesthetics, and the idea that parody somehow demonstrates these notions as fact. Such attitudes are overly cosy in their recourse to a technologically and economically all-powerful other, against which England's little world bumbles along in its comically under-equipped, though consequently more 'authentic' fashion: a sort of Hobbit-like perspective, pitting the honest Shire of English production against Hollywood's evil Mordor. The perpetuating of such archetypes of English identity, moreover, both in spite and because of its willingness to uphold a kind of specific and different national character, runs into more problems than it avoids. As Andy Medhurst writes in *A National Joke*, 'How can an account of national identity avoid endorsing nationalist politics? [...] Haven't the forces and trajectories of globalisation made the idea of national identity irrelevant?'.[31] This problem of 'endorsing' a national cinema within the apparently post-national contexts of globalisation is a central one informing this book.

Medhurst goes on to sketch and debunk two opposing positions in the globalisation/national debate: on one side, the post-national 'cosmopolitan' world view, with its foundation in economic privilege and mobility;[32] on the other, 'the Three Little Pigs of authenticity, organicism and community', rose-tintedly and reductively defended against Ronald McDonald's 'Big Bad Wolf'.[33] As acknowledged by its similar title to this earlier study, *Beyond a Joke* endorses Medhurst's view that the national, or to use the less loaded term, the local, does still have a significant role to play within globalisation, though without needing to be pulled into the antagonistic and divisive orbits of nationalism or resistance. Given that globalisation has often been seen as little more than a euphemism for the 'McWorld' of US cultural and economic imperialism,[34] and because Hollywood as an institution remains at least economically central to this conception, the idea of national or local cinemas and television as countering this dominance has obvious political mileage. At the same time, such opposition risks collapsing into limiting, protectionist discourses that essentialise ideas of the national, and ignore the potentially productive impact of globalisation on our traditional conceptions of national and local identities.

One of Medhurst's designated aims is therefore to 'uncouple the national from the nationalistic':[35] to work out a way of discussing the national, or in this case Englishness, without falling prey to the prescription of a specific type of identity. The importance of such a project has not, in fact, been lost on filmmakers and producers. Andrew Higson has recently talked about what he calls the 'packaging of Englishness' in recent film production, and in particular the drive within certain strains of recent film production to make 'culturally English films'.[36] Higson consequently shifts the focus from more traditional though overly broad conceptions of 'British national cinema' towards the mobilisation of certain *ideas of England* and Englishness in late twentieth- and early twenty-first-century filmmaking. The main factor underpinning Higson's argument is that the putative conditions for a 'British cinema', or even an English one, no longer exist, at least in the way they might formerly have done: Higson's studies indicate the extent to which even something as apparently straightforward as 'English film' has become an extremely complex term, given the increasing reliance on international – and more often than not American – investment. As we will see, in 'English' films as diverse as *Royal Flash* (1975), *The Hitchhiker's Guide to the Galaxy* and *Hot Fuzz*, trying to locate these films in clear national terms proves more difficult than at first appears.

Asking whether these circumstances are desirable for English filmmaking overlooks not just the economic realities of film production, but the shifting sands of a globalised culture. As Higson puts it, his book *Film England* 'is in part an attempt to think through national cinema in the era of accelerated globalisation – and to do so by focusing on the possibility of English cinema'.[37] What does it mean, in other words, to discuss English cinema within the terms of an 'accelerated' global culture, and an increasingly transnational cinema, which in theory undermines the potential for specifically 'local' cinemas to exist? But at the same time, as Higson's book testifies, the accelerated globalisation of film culture is also paradoxically the means through which 'culturally English' film, a selling point of which is its appeal to certain types of Englishness, can be constructed for a global audience. This is partly a consequence of the increased global dissemination of cinematic product, but it is also a by-product of globalisation's shrinking of the knowable world. The circumstances of such 'culturally English film-making' in fact highlight the ways that national or local cinematic identities are frequently shaped and documented precisely through their emergence as globally identifiable concepts, and as differentiated cinematic products, and are not simply some pre-existent reality such films bring forth.

Parody, as this book argues, becomes one way through which English film and television comedy sells itself to the world, as well as domestically. It is of course easy to read the 'packaging of Englishness' described by Higson as little more than a specialist business strategy,[38] for films that both play up and play with the idea of Englishness in ways that may attract overseas audiences. The unprecedented American success of *Four Weddings and a Funeral* in 1995 fuelled a line of films – Working Title productions such as *Notting Hill* (1999), *Bridget Jones's Diary* (2001), *Love Actually* (2003) – tailored for both domestic and international audiences, in their shared projection of attractive (mainly) English settings and characters. Easy as it is to see these as fantasy projections of an idealised national character, selling an 'inauthentic' idea of the country, this would overlook the fact that ideas of England or Englishness are always already culturally constructed, not to mention the fact that the films above are themselves, to a significant extent, playing parodically with established archetypes of English place and character (most prominently, in the form of Hugh Grant's 'flustered twit'[39]). More importantly, it would fail to recognise the ways in which the very forces and flows of globalisation have already reshaped what it means to be English in the first place.

Criticising the supposedly 'inauthentic' nature of these 'global' films, then, underestimates the degree to which such films represent new configurations of Englishness within globalisation. To take the example of *Hot Fuzz*, in a defining gesture of recent English parody film, we see the relocation of Hollywood generic elements to a 'culturally English' context: here, predominantly, the genre of action cinema within a more rural setting familiar from the 'heritage' strains of English film and television. The film's climactic face-off sees an array of generic expectations and norms systematically turned around, the potential for generic realism and effect deflated by incessantly incongruous elements. Simon Pegg and Nick Frost's country coppers leap into a waiting police car, ready to chase their escaping adversary, supermarket owner Simon Skinner (Timothy Dalton). 'PUNCH – THAT – SHIT!' yells Pegg's Sergeant Angel, punctuating a series of crash-zooms showing seat-belts fastened, pedals pressed and tyres skidding; following which, as the car races off, a 'Village of the Year' banner slowly unfurls and falls behind a trio of visiting judges. The chase winds up at a model village, where Angel and Skinner – in a scene encapsulating English parody's engagement with scale – slug it out amongst towers and buildings half their size, before Skinner finds his jaw grotesquely impaled on a miniature church spire. The fleeing, corrupt police chief, meanwhile, making a break for it in his car, finds himself unexpectedly acquainted with the film's perennially escaping swan, and the physical barrier of a well-placed tree.

A simplistic reading might see this purely in terms of an oppositional critique at the expense of the action genre's systems of representation, and its ideological value within the cultural economies of Hollywood and its global dissemination. But this would overlook the way in which parody's incongruities – in the case of *Hot Fuzz*, the way the film weighs up apparently irreconcilable elements to comic effect – is also a means of interrogating what these different elements actually signify. To suggest that *Hot Fuzz* 'mocks' the Hollywood action movie is largely to miss its point. Rather, the film asks what it is that designates one system of representation as 'Hollywood' and one as 'English'. *Why* are they, or why *should* they be, incompatible? What are the limitations of an 'English' context, within which the translation of Hollywood generic elements is supposedly so incongruous? In the above example, couldn't we equally suggest that the source of humour is not so much the incongruity of Hollywood's stylistic motifs, but the inadequacy of the film's setting and context to cope with the demands of action movie aesthetics? And given the binary extremes of scale and register within which such sequences operate, how simple is it to designate the 'real' and the 'fantasy', the supposedly 'authentic' England on one side, and Hollywood's artifice on the other?

I therefore pursue Higson's suggestion that we think of national cinema as a 'textual process' of representation through which 'national identity is constructed'.[40] Parody, in the view of this book, is central to this process, because of the way it mediates between representations: between the 'fantasy' *and* the 'real'. Neither side is allowed within this particular mode to cohere within either term, as this would imply a stable and prescriptive notion of identity from which to speak. Parody can be seen in this sense not as a capitulation to the logic of the Hollywood machine, but as a mode that negotiates the presence of Hollywood within the national culture; and above all, as a form that is playfully resistant to making *any* representation – national or otherwise – feel true and authentic.

Parody and the 'Glocalisation' of British Film Comedy

In the context of globalisation, then, parody becomes one way through which the local re-emerges, but is also reconfigured, within the global. Parody's essentially dialectical practice is well suited to the terms of what Roland Robertson has called 'glocalisation':[41] the point at which the local, in a form of hybrid interaction, meets the global to produce new, often self-consciously mixed, playful forms. Such a view rejects the assumption that globalisation implies the bland homogeneity of 'McWorld'. As Ulrich Beck argues, the defence of local specificity within globalisation, and indeed the 'framework in which the meaning of the local has to establish itself',[42] needs to be rethought in dialectical rather than simply oppositional terms, insofar as 'local specificities [within globalisation] are globally relocated and […] *conflictually renewed*'.[43]

An implication of this for understanding parody is the way it reverses the terms of criticism. When the 'Speed 3' episode of *Father Ted* parodies *Speed*, there are actually two competing trajectories of reflection at work, in a similar way to the later *Hot Fuzz*. On one side, as we have seen, the episode's use of parody highlights the incongruity of Hollywood's generic system within the world both of Craggy Island but also television sitcom. But on the other side, the absurd inversions of the parody, its combined emphasis on diminished scale and inappropriate response, also points toward the inadequacies of Father Crilly's colleagues to encompass the expectations of a Hollywood action-movie aesthetic. When the combined minds of Craggy Island's clergy initially decide that the best way to save Dougal is to have a mass, the terms and trajectories of the parody are flipped around onto that world, and not that of the Hollywood blockbuster. *Speed*, as Tom Shone remarks, with its systematic progression of tasks and obstacles, 'provide[s] an almost abstract distillation of [blockbuster] thrills'.[44] If the over-determined nature of such movies underpins the absurd humour of 'Speed 3', though, so does its opposite, in the form of procrastination and vacillation, as the priests dither between the choice of 'biscuit or cake' with their tea. As if to underline this point, after the mobile mass, and following a smoke-filled montage of fervent discussion and planning, Ted announces incredulously the conclusions of the other priests: 'So that's your best option, is it? "Have another mass"?'

Methodology and Structure

As we have seen, adopting a shorthand approach to the discussion of parody affirms only what the parody text *is not*. But such a model hardly tells us much about the specific work of parody, or indeed its more ambiguous function, within the terms of the viewing experience. As the above examples indicate, we need to be alive to the various, complex and above all *productive* ways parody may be read.

By definition the methodology and focus of this book is comparative. Parody's gift to the film historian and theorist is that it insists on such an approach: we cannot really make sense of parody without looking at the way parody texts reference and re-work other texts, and to what effect. This involves more, though, than just identifying a set of prior texts upon which a parody has drawn. What I call the 'tick-box' approach to parody – the identification and listing of quoted texts – may be a common feature of DVD extras, and a great game for film and television fans, but has obvious limitations as a critical method. It tells us little to nothing about the contexts and motivations for such references within the text; nor does it inform us about the specific effects of such quotation on the text and our relationship to it. It also ends up reiterating the cultural centrality of these same reference points, thereby ironing over any other intent parody may notionally have. Identifying the target texts and reference points of parody is consequently just the first part of an analytical task. Our main concern is to work out what motivates these particular points of reference at a particular time, and to what effect. But we also need to ask the broader question of why parody as a mode becomes significant at a certain point. What is it, in other words, that makes certain films and television shows at a certain historical juncture turn to parody, rather than other narrative forms?

One of the aims of this book will consequently be to explore the contexts – technological, institutional and cultural – contributing to the development of parody in English film and television. An added and central issue here is the extent to which parody in English film and television culture is somehow readable in terms of what, for the moment at least, we will call English 'character'. There is an intriguing chicken-and-egg type of discussion to be had here. Is the English character predisposed to parody? Or is the assumption of such parodic English character derived retrospectively from the types of cultural production we have come to understand as English?

A main discussion point in this book, then, is the extent to which our idea of English identity is informed through a process of dialogue, as much as it is attributable to any putative idea of national character. Important recent work on English and wider British comedy[45] has been useful in its willingness to balance, in its readings of national comedy traditions and their evolution, immediate questions of cultural context with broader historical factors. The first chapter will trace some of these developments, establishing the foundations for the parodic tradition in English screen comedy. I will also use this first chapter to explore some of the texts and contexts that lie outside my primary area of focus. What earlier forms of English comedy can we see as a precursor to more recent examples of parody (for example, the longer traditions of music hall and popular English traditions such as the *Carry On* series)? What traditions in film genre, aesthetics and performance style (character-comedy films, for instance, and comic actors' movements from small- to big-screen comedy) have shaped our sense of a 'typical' English filmic identity? I will also look at the relationship between English television comedy and Hollywood film during this period (focusing especially on *The Morecambe and Wise Show* and the comic duo's unsuccessful venture into feature films). I then conclude with a look at the franchise that has most succinctly distilled the longer history of English screen comedy, and also challenged the putative divisions between small and big screen entertainment, as well as our understanding of the global and the local: Nick Park's *Wallace and Gromit* series.

The second chapter focuses on the film work of the Monty Python group, especially *The Holy Grail* (1975) and *Life of Brian* (1979). While very well known, and much documented in terms of their production and reception, the Monty Python films have not received a great deal of close critical analysis. In part because of a received notion of what the group does as a comic team, but also because of a resistance to fully dealing with parody as a mode, these films have frequently been limited to their status as genre spoofs. Drawing on some of the recent film-historical work on the 1970s,[46] but also revisiting a number of earlier debates in film theory, I argue here that both films are worth reappraising in terms of their commitment to a type of realism. As I suggest, the work of parody in a film like *The Holy Grail*, far from merely serving to debunk genre, contributes to a wider discussion of representation, economics and class, while *Life of Brian* explores not so much the ideology of religious belief as the construction of verisimilitude in the biblical epic. As I will explore with regard to both films, in ways that will inform many of the analyses in this book, much of their parodic humour is founded on our own awareness of, and complicity with, the emotional and ideological power of cinematic genre.

This ambiguous aspect to parody, the way it frequently involves a level of complicity with its notional 'target', is a main area of focus in the third chapter. While concentrating mainly on three texts – the films *The Charge of the Light Brigade* (1968) and *Royal Flash* (1975), and Michael Palin and Terry Jones's television series *Ripping Yarns* (BBC, 1976–79) – this chapter looks more broadly at some of the cultural, political and economic circumstances of the late 1960s and, more specifically the 1970s, and how these find themselves explored through various parody texts. In particular, I consider the significance of decolonisation, and the wider diminishing of Empire and influence, on these texts, from *Follow that Camel* (1967) to *The Spy Who Loved Me* (1977). Moving beyond the somewhat limiting model of historical 'reflection' criticism, though – the idea that such films can somehow mirror the time and place of their production and reception – I ask what it is that makes parody the apt mode during this period for exploring our relationship to the imperial past. This chapter, then, aims to tease out some of the key texts' complexities; most notably, the way that such texts frequently use modes of stylistic address – aspects of historical realism, emotive composition and mise-en-scène, a lushness of period detail in both sound and visuals – that cut across their apparent critique, rendering potential viewing positions less clear cut.

As a related line of enquiry, I locate the aesthetics of these works within specific industrial and institutional contexts. As such, I consider the parodic, ostensibly Empire-bashing mode of both *The Charge of the Light Brigade* and *Royal Flash* within the terms of transnational film production, the respective crises in English and American filmmaking, and the tendencies of genre taste. Equally, I look at the (again, under-analysed) series *Ripping Yarns* from the viewpoint of contemporaneous film and television production in Britain. I consequently look to question some of the more received attitudes around Palin and Jones's show by making links between *Ripping Yarns* and the subsequent tendencies of 'heritage' film and television in the 1980s. As I show, a thorough understanding of *Ripping Yarns* requires us to acknowledge its implication, and consequently our own, in the aesthetics and ideologies of Empire.

Chapter 4 takes a more detailed look at the implications of parody for our understanding of national cinema, especially within the recent contexts of globalisation. Central to this chapter is a comparative analysis of two films across two filmmaking contexts: Channel 4's *The Strike* and Working Title's *Hot Fuzz*. As I discuss in this book, both films work through modes of parody to express specific points of view regarding the aesthetics, ideology and cultural influence of Hollywood genre cinema. I argue, though, that these superficially similar representations are pointedly inflected by very different contexts and discourses of national cinema. As I suggest, it is important to view both films against the backdrop of distinct historical moments and perspectives: in the case of *The Strike*, within the terms of 1980s English filmmaking and the controversial contexts of American-style production practices; in the case of *Hot Fuzz*, in light both of Working Title's globalised production remit, but also changing theorisations of our relationship to local and global cinemas. I therefore consider the possible limitations of *The Strike*'s critical model for parody, in turn, looking to *Hot Fuzz* (and, as the third collaboration between writer-actor Simon Pegg and director Edgar Wright, the pair's earlier work in *Spaced* and *Shaun of the Dead* [2004]) as the model for a productive and viable form of English cinema for the globalised cinematic economy.

Chapter 5 will build on the findings of Chapter 4, addressing the issue of parody and its relationship to questions of taste, culture and 'canons' in late twentieth- and early twenty-first century English culture. Central to this chapter is the idea of 'parody without parody'. As I explore here, much parody within these contexts blurs the traditional critical divide between the parody and its source. Such texts encourage us to rethink the idea of the parody as a mode of distinction and critical distance. Parody in this instance does not assume a negative position but becomes instead a way of articulating particular viewing positions with regard to certain types of film and genre, and especially, serves as a means of illustrating authorship in the climate of DIY filmmaking. Returning briefly to both *Shaun of the Dead* and *Hot Fuzz*, and looking in more detail at the television shows *The League of Gentlemen* (BBC, 1999–2002) and *Garth Marenghi's Darkplace*, I explore their relationship to the horror genre. As I discuss, the appropriation of horror motifs in these works (from *The Wicker Man* [1973] to the 1980s 'video nasty') is not in a bid to anachronistically repeat them, but rather to articulate the viewer's – and perhaps more pertinently the *fan's* – particular experience and enjoyment of such texts; while in some instances – the appropriation, for example, of James Herbert's horror prose style in *Garth Marenghi's Darkplace* – parody is used in an unexpected way to heighten or enhance a 'low' and derided style. As this indicates, rather than reinforce them through mockery, such uses of parody may serve to reconfigure discursive boundaries of 'high' and 'low' culture. As I conclude here, such texts invite us to rethink the traditional form and dominance of cultural canons, shifting attention to a significantly more non-hierarchical idea of cultural value.

In the final chapter, I use as a case study the parody traditions in English science fiction film and television. As I consider here, science fiction is an especially pertinent area for the practice and discussion of parody, because of its connection to the dominant economies and technologies of global film (and increasingly, television) production. The prevalence of spectacular science fiction cinema within the era of 'post-' or 'neo-classical' Hollywood makes the genre an obvious target for parody amongst wider global film cultures. As I discuss in this chapter, the discourses of English film and television science fiction are poised curiously between an anti-Hollywood rejection of spectacle and image, in favour of a notionally more 'ideas-led' approach, and a more ironic, and consequently parodic, reflection on the differences of scale and technology between American and English production. In the first section, I focus on the respective television (BBC, 1981) and film versions of *The Hitchhiker's Guide to the Galaxy*, looking at their production circumstances and aesthetic differences. Looking firstly at the BBC series, I analyse the ways the show has been pulled in different and often antithetical critical directions. Questioning, via the evidence of its production, its status as self-parody, and even its possible parody of contemporaneous Hollywood sci-fi, I argue for the series' more engaged attempt to create science fiction within the terms both of comedy and effects-driven television. As I suggest, the series is significant not for any rejection of sci-fi aesthetics, but rather for its reworking of the terms of science fiction itself through parody – to the extent that parody becomes a type of science fiction. This apparently counter-intuitive logic, I go on to discuss, is central to the later (Hollywood-produced) film adaptation, in its partially successful efforts to parody sci-fi tropes while also functioning as a big-budget sci-fi movie. Following this, I go on to look at two recent films that, in a similar way to the film of *Hitchhiker's Guide*, exploit and invert the conventions and traditions of science fiction cinema, in order both to critically reflect on the genre and create a distinctive kind of parody science fiction. In *Paul* (2011), written by and featuring the stars of *Hot Fuzz*, the logic of sci-fi film is turned on its head, as the motifs of sci-fi are seen to shape recent American history, culture and geography. In *Moon* (2009), meanwhile, a study in isolation free from historical markers of time and place, the over-familiar tropes of sci-fi cinema come to make up the horizons of the film's world, and for that of its unfortunate protagonist. *Moon*, in this way, and in a neatly concluding way for the book as a whole, comes to reflect upon the colonisation of experience by prior films, and is therefore a suitable representation of our 'postmodern' experience taken to absurd lengths.

1

Cricklewood vs. Hollywood: The Roots and Routes of British Parody on Screen

Running through my head as I have written this book are a number of sequences encapsulating the parody tradition in British film comedy: Wallace and Gromit battling with a Cyborg sheepdog; Graham Chapman's King Arthur skipping along to the accompaniment of coconut shells; Simon Pegg and former James Bond Timothy Dalton slugging it out in a model village; the destruction of the Earth by the bureaucratic, poetry-loving Vogons to make way for an inter-planetary bypass. Such images, across a range of contexts, provide a neat visual summary of a certain type of film. We might easily recognise this type of film as 'English'. My interest in this chapter is to work out where this idea comes from, why, and what exactly it means.

What, we might ask, is so 'English' about parody? A study concerning itself with the relevance of parody to English film and television will need to address this important initial question. Sequences like those above may seem 'typically English', but in understanding this notion we get into a circular argument. Does English film and television comedy take this form because this is what 'Englishness' is about? Or do we only define this idea of Englishness in light of these particular representations?

It should be clear, one hopes, that these apparently very similar ideas are two very different frameworks for understanding film and television. To talk about parody as playing a role in constructing a national culture is not

26

the same as saying parody is inherent to that culture itself. But the potential eliding of these two notions is symptomatic of a pitfall in national film or television studies, where the effect is taken for the cause; where what is in truth a specific form of *dialogue* – the main focus and argument of this book – is taken as a form of *natural speech*, unproblematic and assumed. As I will discuss, such assumptions about what is 'essentially English' overlook a wide range of factors – economic and political, as well as cultural – underpinning parody's use within English comedy.

While comedy and realism are often seen as antitheses within English film and television culture, both types are often marked in critical discussion as oppositional to some notion of a dominant global cinema, usually Hollywood. Within this discourse, the qualities of realism are nationally specific, partly because of their focus on particular regional or class contexts (especially those outside the dominant social and economic strata), but also because their settings, narratives and aesthetics mark them as distinct from other dominant types of cinema. Arguments for realism as somehow native to wider British film, for instance, are numerous, giving rise in fact to the established generic category of 'British social realism'. But what does it really mean to say that such film practices, within a medium so relatively new and already international as cinema, have some sort of claim – in the case of realism, for some advocates, an almost *moral* claim – on our sense of cultural identity and our ideas about what film is supposed to do? And what, in this case, underpins the claims of one type of film or television to speak for 'us', over and above those other types existing alongside it?

As we will see, parody has itself been incorporated into this prevailing discourse of realism-as-English, in its putative oppositions to Hollywood illusionism. Such arguments identify the way certain texts exploit or foreground the discrepancy between the contexts of English film (its settings and its economic realities) and those of Hollywood. Implicitly or otherwise, though, such arguments also acknowledge the dominant imaginary of Hollywood's powerful 'other' as a structuring factor in these representations. Moreover, they risk a prescriptive line of thinking once they presuppose that there is an inevitably distinctive, 'authentic' Englishness behind such parodic tactics; or in their tacit assumptions that realism is the inevitable and 'natural' state to which these same texts should eventually devolve (a subject I will pursue in more detail in Chapters 2 and 4).

For the sake of argument, though, to what extent can we identify a type of national character in the study of comedy cinema? Geoff King lucidly outlines the problems inherent to any attempt to define 'national' as a characteristic of cinematic output:

> The problem of seeking to isolate distinctive 'national' comic traits is complicated from two directions: from both inside and outside the particular national context involved. To demonstrate that particular aspects of the comedy produced in one nation are uniquely characteristic of that country is extremely difficult, given the number of potential counter-examples that would have to be taken into account [...] We can [however] move away from broad claims about the nationally-representative-or-otherwise qualities of particular forms of comedy, to consider the question at the level of industrial strategies of audience-targeting.[1]

King's insistence that formal characteristics of national film comedy are hardly unique to that one cultural context, and that we understand the national in 'relative rather than absolute' terms,[2] are views this present study shares. In pursuing this line, though, we must be wary of overlooking the longer representational and institutional histories that may inform the shape and content of these 'industrial strategies'. Whether or not we believe (and I do not) that types of English parody emerge as naturally as waters from some eternal spring, we can still make sense of how, when and why certain forms of film emerge; as well as understanding why, at particular points, modes of parody acquire different kinds of discursive value. I will therefore start with a consideration of one of English parody's most immediate predecessors: music hall, and its related cinematic output. I will then see how this tradition finds different embodiments through different contexts in British film and television, identifying the form and discursive function of these varied outputs. In doing this we can start to identify certain recurring types of practice, aesthetics and performances of parody. This chapter will therefore sketch the movement of some of these recurring tropes through to the present day, and in turn, consider their applicability to a type of 'parodic imaginary' in English film and television.

Music Hall, Character Comedy and Parody Performance

Andy Medhurst has identified the ways that the traditions of music hall prescribe an English space of popular humour and community, in ways that, as we see, finds its distinctive way into both film and television. The specifically working-class contexts of the music hall, from its Victorian origins through to and indeed beyond the twentieth century, imbue it with a particular kind of political, collective identity. The typically profane, ironic and knowing laughter of the music hall is, Medhurst writes:

> a laughter that is communal, collective, resigned, blunt, basic, a way of getting by, of alleviating the depressing limitations of low horizons [...] Music hall was often vibrantly vulgar, testing the limits of censorship and questioning the stranglehold of 'decency', so often a code word for attempts to foist the constrictions of middle-class propriety on to working-class lives [...] The halls, in effect, became the primary cultural space in which...alternative values were articulated, and the articulation took concrete, collective shape in the punchy, combative performance styles of the singers and comics and in the audience's active participation.[3]

As this type of entertainment for a particular *people*, in an etymological and evaluative shift, becomes identified with the *popular*, this comic 'spirit' of the music hall comes to be associated with a type of culture that – depending on your perspective – is either the 'low' culture of mass entertainment or, conversely, an oppositional culture rejecting 'the constrictions of middle-class propriety'.

Music hall is therefore instructive for the way it is at once debasing and, potentially, political in its vulgarity and lampooning of bourgeois traditions and dominant representations. As Medhurst notes, possibly the earliest parody films in the English tradition were those (now mostly lost) starring comedian Dan Leno, which poked fun at the 'overwrought melodramas' popular at the time.[4] There were also the satirical 'Pimple' films, as performed by Fred Evans, which played with topical subjects and even legendary episodes of British history: titles included *Pimple's Battle of Waterloo* (1913), *Lieutenant Pimple's Dash for the Pole* (1914) and *Pimple's Charge of the Light Brigade* (1914). What is noticeable even in the titles of these short films is the way they position themselves so parodically alongside national discourses and even films of the time: *Pimple's Battle of Waterloo* was even produced as a specific response to *The Battle of Waterloo* (1913), one of the earliest feature films to appear, with significant hype and fanfare, on British screens. In the positioning of the ridiculously-named Pimple alongside evocations of history, adventure and the epic, these films clearly look to undermine the pretensions and grandeur of national myth-making, and shape the emerging role of a popular cinema itself in this process.

The form of the 'Pimple' films also reminds us of the importance of 'character comedy' to parody cultures, and emphasises the importance of performance, personality and communication to the parodic imaginary. The incongruous placing of Fred Evans' character in an almost endless succession of nominally grandiose contexts encourages the type of identification with an 'everyman' figure that King sees as central to the character-centred comedy film.[5] We need only to look at the success of Rowan Atkinson's effectively silent 'Mr. Bean' character, both on television (ITV, 1990–95) and in two cinematic outings (*Bean* [1997] and *Mr. Bean's Holiday* [2007]), to understand the continued appeal of this type of character comedy. In terms of the economics and profile of English production, the *Bean* brand, as well as the other Atkinson vehicle *Johnny English* (2003)/*Johnny English Reborn* (2011), give support to King's assertion that character comedy 'has proved extremely successful in a range of national, regional and international markets'.[6] King is not of course limiting his discussion to non-Hollywood production, referring to the broader production practices and reception of the comedian vehicle; and as much as we might wish to see Mr Bean as an English phenomenon, his is in many respects a type played out across any number of national and Hollywood contexts.

Given that Mr Bean distils a rich and broader tradition of physical character comedy, stretching back into the silent era (via Jerry Lewis, Jacques Tati and Peter Sellers amongst others), his identification as a specifically

English figure – culminating in his guest performance at the London 2012 Olympics opening ceremony – may owe therefore to the particular narrative contexts of his adventures, as it does to Atkinson's wider association (most prominently, through the various *Blackadder* series [BBC, 1983–89]) with English comedy film and television. The incongruities of character comedy, and its narrative potential for chaos, owe a substantial amount to the way its comic figures are located; both within terms of the genre in which they find themselves, but also as removed from their familiar locale. While the character comedy of the *Bean* and *Johnny English* films may eventually conform to the structural tropes of the Hollywood film, in which the protagonist successfully brings about narrative resolution, these same tropes are also frequently parodied by virtue of the same protagonist's obvious incongruity; the clear evidence that they are the wrong person for the task (even, or especially, if they don't themselves acknowledge this discrepancy).

Music hall – or more specifically, the film stars to have emerged from its later contexts – once again offers a precedent here, insofar as it is often identified with a particular type of narrative, performance style and audience engagement. In his analysis of the Gracie Fields vehicle *Sing As We Go* (1934), Andrew Higson looks for clues as to the film's frequent associations with a type of Britishness: a Britishness which Fields, the music-hall star who at the time was also one of the highest-paid actors in Britain, was often seen to embody. The narrative of *Sing As We Go* centres on Field's adventures as a newly-redundant mill worker seeking employment, and getting into unexpected adventures, in the seaside resort of Blackpool. Fittingly, it is to some extent the incongruity and comic spectacle of the actual Fields body, always slightly chaotic, comically never quite at ease with its surroundings, to which Higson attributes much of the film's national associations. The motifs of character comedy are central to this process:

> There is something of a tension between Grace, the narrative character, and Gracie Fields, the attraction. The tension is true of all stars, but in Fields's case [...] it seems to be accentuated [...] She clearly does inhabit a relatively autonomous imaginative world, but it is not a world (a diegesis) where space and time are rigorously organized by narrative requirements.[7]

Higson's analysis in effect answers the concerns of Medhurst, in his own consideration of the music-hall film star, when he highlights 'the central problematic of the 1930s variety star film – how to accommodate such performers within existing cinematic genres'.[8] Since performers such as Fields or George Formby established their popular performance personae through their engagement with their audiences, with the confidentiality and community that come with it, how – if at all – could this 'be fitted into the demands of the ninety-minute narrative film?'[9] Higson's argument is that it does not need to be. *Sing As We Go*'s tendency toward spectacle, in the form of musical or comic numbers, but also in Fields' engagement with a putative audience beyond the camera – a camera she, like Formby in his films, often addresses[10] – becomes the real point of the film. The consciousness of Fields herself as a performer, rather than a fully-integrated character within a diegetic story-world, and the sense in which the film suspends narrative development to the promotion of performance as an event, works to create a sense of film as participatory, speaking to an 'implied live audience'[11] beyond the camera. An aesthetic of interaction, communication and community, in other words, descended from the same type of music-hall performance to which the film owes much of its content and form.

While we are not describing parody as such here, we are dealing with a mode of performance that is to a significant extent disruptive, knowingly so, of the conventions of dominant narrative cinema and its tendency toward verisimilitude. Just as importantly, these spectacular disruptions are, via the performers who embody them, enacted and marked with very specific cultural connotations and identifications. The audience that laughs and sings with Fields and Formby is also positioning itself alongside these stars, and by implication, on the other side of all those things that stand in their way. Participation through a type of reflexive film practice; identification with a central performer; opposition to everyday authorities, be they diegetic (the bosses, the police) or meta-diegetic (the 'laws' of narrative film itself): all these are elements frequently seen in English film comedy.

Such types of participation through performance are hardly limited to the broader styles of physical character comedy, though. The various parody performances of actor-writer Simon Pegg (discussed in Chapter 4) frequently revolve around the incongruities of Pegg's English everyman, in its evolving guises, finding himself dealing with unlikely generic contexts or inter-textual interruptions: be it *Shaun of the Dead*'s electrical goods salesman, barely registering and then barely repelling a zombie invasion; or *Hot Fuzz*'s pedantic Met Officer converting himself into a fully tooled-up Angel of Retribution. Pegg's performance implicitly encourages forms of audience recognition and interaction, in the way we identify the disjuncture between character and situation. A similar approach is taken in Steve Coogan's character vehicle, *Alan Partridge: Alpha Papa* (2013), which has Coogan's preening Norfolk DJ pitched into the unlikely role of police negotiator, when Partridge's sacked former colleague takes his radio station staff hostage. In spite of his vanity and idiocy, and despite his best efforts not to, Partridge manages to save the day, providing in turn a showcase for Coogan's appallingly well-observed character comedy.

Here and There (and Back Here)

As hinted at above, the idea of the 'wrong man' (or woman) in character comedy also potentially implies the importance of the 'wrong place'. Both Medhurst and Higson have identified the importance of holidays, especially at English seaside resorts such as Blackpool and Brighton, both to the audiences of much British comedy and the films' own narratives. The 'holiday' film setting functions as a form of cinematic 'carnivalesque',[12] a suspension within, and inversion of, the quotidian order of social life. But it can also work in an ideologically doubled way, allowing its audiences both to enjoy the unfamiliar and at the same time reaffirm what is recognisably 'ours'. Medhurst identifies this tendency as most prominent in the *Carry On* series of films (1958–92), particularly in the way these films offered a series of changing settings (both geographical and historical) while being built essentially around repetition and recognition, 'of actors, the echoes of jokes and the consistency of tone'.[13] Like many film series, the appeal or otherwise of *Carry On* is this promise of continuity within difference. The core ensemble of actors in these films (Kenneth Williams, Joan Sims, Charles Hawtrey, Sid James amongst others), after their initial entry into the series, rarely offer anything more than the reiteration of a comic persona with familiar tics: 'Most of these had one act which they stuck to, or which stuck to them …never straying far from the droll chunk of personality'.[14] It is important to understand the particular pleasures and meanings produced by this stubborn insistence on performance continuity. The significance of the films to this book is in the way this consistency of style and attitude, with regard to constantly renewing locations and genre contexts, establishes a fixed point of identity that – rightly or wrongly – plays a role in constructing an idea of cultural Englishness within the contingency and fluidity of global change.

The more specific focus on holidays in the series (especially in *Carry On at Your Convenience* [1971], *Carry On Abroad* [1972] and *Carry On Girls* [1973]) owes something to the earlier Fields and Formby films, and has indeed set something of a template for more recent films – most notably the two movies (2011 and 2014) based on the television series *The Inbetweeners* (E4, 2008–10), both of which, in the transition from small screen to big, revolve around holidays abroad. Yet these physical relocations are possibly less interesting for our present purposes than the way these films suspend reality via excursions to different film genres. If the holiday films derive some of their jokes from cultural difference, a trope that also finds its way into some of the more racially-inflected parodies (*Carry On...Up the Khyber* [1968] most particularly), what we see in the cycle of genre-targeting films – *Carry On Cleo* (1964), *Carry On Cowboy* (1965), *Follow That Camel* (1967) and *Carry On Henry* (1971) – is also the play of cultural difference at the level of the film text and its associations. Here, the immovable block of the series' core cast and values comes up against a flow of ever-changing generic contexts: the Roman epic (*Cleo*), the western (*Cowboy*), the foreign-legion adventure (*Camel*) and the historical film (*Henry*).

Like genres themselves, performers come with their own set of motifs and expectations. As Dan Harries points out, the regular appearance of Leslie Nielsen in numerous parody franchises (the *Airplane!* movies [1980, 1982], television's *Police Squad!* [ABC, 1982] and the *Naked Gun* film series it inspired [1988–94]) meant 'his star image [became] intertwined with parodic discourse'.[15] Nielsen's handsome yet highly expressive face, his genial combination of B-movie earnestness and actual cluelessness, pre-empt the intervention of parody within the generic framework, arguably to the point that his presence *in itself* unhinges any potential 'belief' in the film. Nielsen's own presence is therefore a kind of spectacle, denying the possibility for the film to assume any type of verisimilitude or realistic narrative coherence. Similarly, the ubiquity and inflexibility of the *Carry On* performers in the series, along with the frequent use of extraneous references and embedded topical allusions, automatically undermines the possibility of genre narrative to function in the usual credible terms.

A difference though is that Nielsen is a veteran actor of American film and television working mainly within parodies of this same American tradition. Without ever leaving England, though, both practically (the whole series, one trip to Wales apart, was filmed there) and symbolically (in the form of the familiar 'domestic' cast), the *Carry On* films are happy to move beyond their native generic reference points to embrace – or make fun of – wider international, and more specifically American, film types. Once more, we see how *Carry On* maintains an older film tradition, identified in the early 'Pimple' films, in which the familiar English character-performer is placed, incongruously, wrong-headedly and also stubbornly, in the 'wrong' genre. In fact, as much as their assertions of taste and cultural politics, as well as their specific content, may distance them from the often dubious values of the *Carry On* series, we can see a very similar kind of pattern in the films made by the Monty Python team (the subject of the next chapter), or once again, in the recent cycle of genre parodies written by and starring Simon Pegg.

While noting that the type of community represented in the *Carry On* series is very different from the collective spirit of music hall, Medhurst goes so far as to suggest, albeit rather enigmatically, that the films represent 'the last cinematic flourish of "us" humour'.[16] While Medhurst probably does not mean this, what might rightly or wrongly be understood here is that this collective 'us' is also not 'them' – whoever 'they' may be. At its most divisive, in fact, 'they' in the *Carry On* films are whoever does not fit within the white, gendered, 'English' norms embodied by the films' stars. But more generously, in its cycle of genre parodies, 'us' humour is also identifiable as a particular attitude and spirit with regard to the dominant cinematic modes and fashions of the time. 'We' – 'the English' – are hence defined in an over-determined way as the opposite of that which is grandiose, excessive, and above all, too serious for its own good. Parody's own practice of puncturing inflated senses of importance, in this English cultural context, marks Englishness as the antithesis of the big, glossy and dominant cinematic mainstream.

Medhurst's comment of course begs the question of where 'us' humour has gone, and why. The rest of this book is in some respects a sustained answer to this question: what will be clear is that this collective 'us' changes significantly across time, for very particular reasons. To illustrate this, I would like, in the remainder of this chapter, to consider two very prominent examples of the way a collective comic imaginary – one notably linked to the formative traditions of music hall – persists within the mainstream of English popular culture. As we will see, though, these examples also highlight the evolving contexts through and against which we may read the types of imagined communities constructed through these works.

From Hollywood to Cricklewood and Back Again (Though Not Via Pinewood): Morecambe and Wise on Television and on Film

It is notable that the demise in the late 1970s of the *Carry On* series as a cinematic institution was followed by its maintenance, through perennial repeats of the films on broadcast TV, as a popular *televisual* institution. Unless we take a careful contextual look at the dire circumstances in which English cinema, during the 1970s and 1980s, tried to get itself made and seen, we might overlook this possible cultural paradox: one in which a comic institution both gave up the ghost *and* persisted within the popular imaginary. It is a paradox that has at its roots specific relationships to the respective big and small screens of film and television during this time, revealing in turn the place of both media in the construction of an English film culture.

The television work of Eric Morecambe and Ernie Wise, especially during their decade-long tenure as the BBC's biggest light-entertainment draw (1968–77), is especially instructive in this respect. Both in the series *The Morecambe and Wise Show* and in their hugely popular BBC Christmas specials (the last of which, in 1977, drew an estimated 28 million viewers), the duo established a familiar comic repertoire based around their engagement with each other, with their audience (both live and beyond the camera), and with the various guests that came on the show, all this in front of a theatrical curtain (a throwback to their origins in variety theatre) constructed specifically for the television studio. This network of communication between the duo and the audience, often with the guest as the willing butt of their jokes – or indeed, as the active exponents of their own self-parody – extended frequently into a series of film or genre parodies: comic inversions of classic MGM musicals, for example, or verbal and visual takes, not in a dissimilar vein from the aforementioned *Carry On* films, on Hollywood genres. In a superficial way these televisual performances of genre parody perpetuate a type of differentiated, national collective imaginary, though one in which the institution of television itself – as a traditionally 'intimate' medium, a smaller screen with inevitably reduced production values, though at the same time capable of mass(ive) broadcast appeal – plays a significant role. At a time when there were only three channels on British television, where the notion of broadcast (before VCR, 'niche' channels and on-demand television) still referred to a genuinely wide public audience, *The Morecambe and Wise Show*, at the peak of its 1970s popularity, *was* television itself. It could therefore make a claim to represent, within the terms of television's intimate *and* wide-ranging address, a dominant imaginary of its cultural time and place. By inference, televisual parodic performances of Hollywood cinema, played out communicatively via the living rooms and collective national address of live television viewing, inscribed a sense of national specificity: a smaller-scale comic sensibility counter to the grandiosity and pomposity of dominant cinema.

Seductive as this may sound, this might be a bit far from the truth, failing as it does to account both for the wider circumstances behind Morecambe and Wise's work, and the actual nature of the shows in question. The duo's work in their series both for the BBC and Thames Television frequently revolved around a studio mock-up of a flat, in which the pair worked, bickered and slept (usually, like Laurel and Hardy, in the same bed). As a spatial reflection of my own childhood viewing contexts, then, *The Morecambe and Wise Show* felt for the most part grounded in the domestic and the everyday; only to then take off into unexpected and often lunatic, grandiose flights of fancy. Like my experience of watching the *Carry On* films on television in the late 1970s and early 1980s, my sense of any cinematic points of reference was limited (a point to which I will return in a later chapter); prescribed, even, by the parameters of *The Morecambe and Wise Show* itself. Whether or not my younger self saw where its genre parodies were coming from, what was clear from the show – and in the Christmas specials above all – was that these excursions into the unfamiliar were distinctly *out of the ordinary*. And indeed, as much as a pre-video and pre-on-demand TV show epitomises the notion of a national television event, what these shows also had was a sense of *scale* within the otherwise confined space of the television format.

Perhaps more clearly, though, what distinguishes these 1970s performances both from the *Carry On* parodies and their successors in BBC comedy (in shows by the likes of Lenny Henry, (Dawn) French and (Jennifer) Saunders, and Harry Enfield, to name just a few) is their very obvious collusion with the markers and producers of taste and cultural status they are only superficially deriding. When the duo invite prestige stage and film actors such as Peter Cushing, Vanessa Redgrave or Diana Rigg onto their stage, the communal work of self-deprecation is counter-balanced by the fact that such guests still function as glamorous star turns, who in turn help sustain the cultural kudos and prominence of *The Morecambe and Wise Show* within a broader (and notably less class-confined) taste culture. Good taste, moreover, is inextricably bound within the duo's performances, which, while drawing on the motifs of classic music hall and variety (which by the 1970s had arguably, through its status as 'classic' and nostalgic, already shed some of its specific class connotations), worked largely through the clever verbal debunking of dialogue to intricately bathetic effect.

When, then, the Oscar-winning actor Glenda Jackson appears in a skit on the film *Cleopatra*, Jackson's largely unprecedented willingness to send up her own distinguished persona, giving Royal Shakespeare Company resonance and diction to Ernie's (or rather writer Eddie Braben's) beautifully bad dialogue – 'All men are fools, and what makes them so is having beauty like what I have got!' – is also a reiteration of Jackson's high-cultural status and glamour at that time. In a similar way, the perennially hollow or incomplete *trompe l'oeil* sets – styrofoam steps that get punctured and dragged off by singer Shirley Bassey's stiletto heel, or a grand staircase that Jackson climbs, only to disappear over the back of – serve comically to emphasise the unreality, the illusion of glamour and grandeur best associated with the films, genres and styles the show targets. And yet these empty sets, makeshift appropriations from the Hollywood dream factory, also suggest the potency of these same worlds, the aspiration to them which forms the platform for the show's bathos.

What in fact makes Morecambe and Wise so intriguing as an English institution, an almost literal part of the national furniture, is that their identification as English derives so consistently from their complex relationship to America. Graham McCann's biography of Morecambe and Wise is alert to the way that America is far from the spurned cultural and geographical 'other' to the duo's music-hall world. It was, rather, the place and iconography with which they and many of their peers identified, and to which they aspired – hence their incessant, but ultimately fruitless, efforts to break the US market between 1964 and 1968, primarily through their appearances on *The Ed Sullivan Show*.[17] Exactly why they did not make it across the Atlantic can only remain the stuff of conjecture: McCann points both to Morecambe's reticence and lack of confidence outside the British comfort-zone, and to the more tangible issues of cultural specificity, accents and comprehensibility. One of the notable aspects of Morecambe and Wise's huge success in England, though, and as suggested above, is the way it was founded not on the rejection of American cultural models, but on their incorporation within the television format the duo exploited so successfully.

This is seen more forcibly in the skits based around Hollywood musical numbers, the title song from *Singin' in the Rain* being a key example. In this sketch from the 1976 Christmas show, Wise assumes the Gene Kelly role, giving his own version of Kelly's ebullient umbrella dance – with the difference that here, there is no rain to be singin' in. Morecambe is here the bemused policeman, constantly looking to correlate Wise's behaviour with the actual weather. While the assumption may be to see these skits as 'spoofs', with their distinctive inversions – most obviously in this case, the absence of rain – these comic inversions worked alongside an exacting attention to the design and mise-en-scène of the original films, as well as their dance steps. As McCann notes, the success of such sequences derives from an inherent tension within the Morecambe and Wise pairing: between Morecambe's insistence that 'Life isn't Hollywood, it's Cricklewood', and Wise's determination to emulate the Hollywood idols of his youth, such as

1.1 Fantasy confounds realism: Singin' without the Rain in *The Morecambe and Wise Show* (1976)

Mickey Rooney and Fred Astaire.[18] The result is a type of comic set-piece that is at once affectionate in its recreation of MGM musical atmosphere, yet also consistent in its (or rather, Morecambe's) efforts to keep its fantasy in check, drawing attention to its artifice.

We are once again drifting dangerously close to the terrain of 'loving mockery', which as I have already suggested, is an inappropriate way of describing parodic performances. The *Singin' in the Rain* sketch, for example, is not really interested in debunking the conventions of the musical form, focusing more on its romance, as Wise performs Kelly's routine, umbrella and all, the absence of rain notwithstanding. Morecambe draws attention through his visual commentary on Wise's performance, but never at the expense of Wise himself, who dances on regardless. Wise's dry run of Kelly's routine is in this sense both generous to the original film but also touching in its commitment to form and feeling, and the insistence that it *is* raining in spite of evidence to the contrary. Notably, it is the realist

40

Morecambe, and not the fantasist Wise, who is the butt of the jokes, as he consistently gets drenched by random water sources – a drain pipe, a bucket emptied from a window – wherever he moves.

Morecambe's insistence that life is Cricklewood rather than Hollywood turns out in itself to be indicative of the duo's style. His epigrammatic one-liner works through the phonic closeness of the two places, together with the incongruity of their imaginary juxtaposition (at least to anyone who knows Cricklewood); but contained within this gag's bathetic fall is also a pathos: the sense, in other words, that the imagination *is* Hollywood. This romance, unrealisable as it may ultimately be, colours the content and shape of Morecambe and Wise's most memorable work; and in their musical sketches above all, it becomes a defining element of their brand of popular comedy. These of course are performances for a mass audience, taken from other works of global mass entertainment, with which the huge domestic audience was presumed to be familiar.

There is plenty of speculation as to why most English comedians coming up through stage and television fail to convert successfully to feature film, and while this isn't the place to answer this question, the example of Morecambe and Wise may at least shed some light on it. The kind of music hall-derived films discussed by Higson, such as *Sing As We Go*, demonstrated the potential for a type of popular film addressing viewers it knew and understood, but in a way that made no concession to any other audience. This was a form of product differentiation on the part of a British film industry that, at the time, was alternately producing films with an eye to international markets: as Higson notes, 'the cultural specificity of [films like *Sing As We Go*] renders them virtually inexportable, and indeed few of the British examples of this sort of work had any international circulation'.[19] This kind of domestically-entrenched policy sustained for the most part traditions such as the *Carry On* series, as well as the cycle of sit-com spin-off films produced in the 1970s;[20] indeed, the remarkable success of the recent *Inbetweeners* movies, which challenged Hollywood at the domestic box-office but barely registered outside it, shows a recurrence of this same tradition.

The three Morecambe and Wise vehicles produced in the 1960s by the Rank Organisation – *The Intelligence Men* (1965), *That Riviera Touch* (1966) and *The Magnificent Two* (1967) – were nevertheless rather different entities, and reveal the changing contexts and connotations of national cinema during this period. Though produced relatively cheaply by Rank during a period of uncertainty and transition, and initially incorporating en masse the production team for comedian Norman Wisdom's series of films,[21] their titles and subject matter reflected the increasingly transatlantic nature of British cinema culture. Hence *The Intelligence Men*, in which the pair end up foiling an international crime organisation called SCHLECT, nods obviously to the recent success of the emerging Bond series, and especially *From Russia With Love* (1963); while *That Riviera Touch*, with its glamorous South-of-France crime plot, seemed designed to appeal 'both to those who hankered after the kind of "sophisticated" [Hollywood] screen comedy[…] that had fallen out of fashion, as well as to those who preferred the kind of self-consciously cosmopolitan "caper" movies […] that were currently in vogue'.[22]

These are unusual and uneven films to watch now, to a large extent because they seem unsure how to properly integrate their stars into their narrative world. The pair are consistently situated within the role of unlikely heroes (*The Intelligence Men*), unassuming heroes (*That Riviera Touch*) or mistaken-for heroes (*The Magnificent Two*). As such, they cannot ever be taken for 'straight' characters, but in the process they also become frequently clueless subjects to the vagaries of the films' plots. Perhaps more surprisingly, a few moments aside (Morecambe's maraca-shaking waiter at the start of *The Intelligence Men* being a case in point), they are rarely allowed to physically impose themselves on the films' construction of narrative space. As King discusses, comedian- or character-comedy performance 'can be quite tightly integrated into the narrative and into the diegetic space, but retains a license to break the rules'.[23] At its most successful, such comedy allows for the spectacle of the performer's routine to almost break the boundaries of the film's diegesis. In many of the earlier Hollywood films Morecambe and Wise both admired and aspired to emulate, such as those featuring the Marx Brothers, performance effectively exceeds diegesis altogether, consistently disrupting – verbally, physically, musically – any remnants of narrative coherence and verisimilitude. This, as we have seen earlier, was one of the effects of Gracie Field's 'spectacular' bodily performance and effective audience address in her successful cinematic outings. But this is rarely if ever the case in the Morecambe and

Wise films, intent as they are to work within the generic frameworks they only notionally spoof.

As McCann notes, the films are largely unsuccessful (at least from the viewpoint of the duo's fans) because they fail 'to convey more than the merest hint of the very thing that had made Morecambe and Wise special as a *double-act*'.[24] Interaction and control – either through disruption, or passivity in the face of lunacy – is a hallmark of Morecambe and Wise's work. As is, most importantly, the aside, the wink, the improvised remark: in other words, those things that the intimate aesthetics and reception framework of television allowed them to exploit and communicate with their audience. This inability to find a fit within the formal demands or expectations of the feature film may be one reason why, traditionally, English television comedians have rarely converted their small-screen popularity to big-screen success. But as the example of Morecambe and Wise suggests, it is as much the particular contexts of English film culture in the mid-1960s as the specifics of film aesthetics that influence this tendency.

To target the films in themselves as somehow failing the duo, then, without understanding the context in which they were made, overlooks the changing nature of national film production and film taste. *The Intelligence Men* was possibly the wrong sort of film in which to place Morecambe and Wise, but the specific choice of that project reflected the increasingly *global* nature of film viewing, and the wider imaginary (though not necessarily ambition) of national film production during that time. By a similar token, the cinematic (if not televisual) demise of *Carry On* and 'us' humour at the end of the 1970s may not coincidentally relate to the resurgence of Hollywood film at the end of that decade, and the confirmation of its commercial and imaginary hold on English cinema culture. As I will explore at later points, this tension between a collapsing or threatened institution of national cinema, and the intent to negotiate or even challenge Hollywood's dominant modes, informs film parody throughout the subsequent decades.

Television comedy such as *The Morecambe and Wise Show* in this regard works to claim for itself a cultural-imaginary space that cannot be so easily forged within the field of cinematic production. Such a show can claim, with substantial reason, to be as near to a national cultural institution as television can produce. Dominated increasingly as it was in the 1960s by international (and predominantly American) co-production, and with an eye on international markets, national film production of this period could not expect to have the same institutional quality. Morecambe and Wise have a distinctive historical value inasmuch as they embody the transition through and from different kinds of viewing communities and cultural imaginaries. Though linked biographically and to some extent formally to the traditions of music hall, the duo and their work also embody the cosmopolitanism and transatlantic cultural contexts increasingly significant during the 1960s and beyond.

Nick Park, Plasticine, and the Paradox of the Local

Changes in the respective production and reception contexts of both film and television over recent decades have to some degree altered the framework for understanding both media, and their often mutually-influencing nature. Possibly the best example of this is the series of films featuring the duo of Wallace and Gromit, created by writer-director Nick Park and produced by the Bristol-based Aardman Studios. The original trilogy of short films made by Park – *A Grand Day Out* (1989), *The Wrong Trousers* (1993) and *A Close Shave* (1995) – prove quite allusive in our efforts to place them institutionally. All were premiered on the BBC during the Christmas period, as was the later *A Matter of Loaf and Death* (2008), yet their status as *films*, rather than television programmes, is trebly underscored; by their material status, having been shot on film; by their stand-alone status as individual works; but also by their wider reception within the contexts of film production – most notably, by their nomination (for *A Grand Day Out*) and later triumph (for *The Wrong Trousers* and *A Close Shave*) in the Best Animated Short Film category at the US Academy Awards.

The Wallace and Gromit series exemplifies a type of culturally English product with its imaginary clearly positioned in the longer traditions of music hall and English comedy film; and yet, an imaginary that is also very specifically located at a meeting point of varied, apparently competing contexts. As with our analysis of Morecambe and Wise, it should be clear that the 'English eccentricity' and 'cultural sense of difference'[25] frequently seen as central to this other Northern duo's appeal need to be understood in a much broader dialogic and relational sense. Parody is central to the production of this apparently intrinsic English character, but it is also indicative of a much less stable sense of national identity.

First and foremost, all the films are identifiable as forms of genre parody, whether this be types of English science fiction (*A Grand Day Out* echoes the Wellsian science-fiction adventure of *The First Men on the Moon* [1964], with its improvised space ship-cum-drawing room), the 'caper' movie (the jewel-heist plot in *The Wrong Trousers*), the horror film and the thriller (Wallace's 'framing' in *The Wrong Trousers* being itself a variant on the 'wrong man' narrative familiar from Alfred Hitchcock's films), and last but not least, film noir. *A Close Shave*, for example, highlights its affinities with the latter genre through its initial use of bold, canted titles, its foregrounding of a nocturnal urban setting, and the photographic use of long, expressive shadows and fragmented glimpses of low-key lit faces (in this case, those of the sheep-rustler Wendolene and her dog Preston). This is simply one instance though of a varied and eclectic borrowing, which sees the film veer towards British World War II movies (as Gromit, in a flying sidecar, attacks Preston with a mounted porridge gun), and finally toward sci-fi, as Preston, trapped and shaved within Wallace's Knit-O-Machine, emerges – in a specific nod to the conclusion of *The Terminator* (1984) – as a murderous metal-lic Cyber-Dog. This variety of parodic targets stops both this film and the other Wallace and Gromit shorts from cohering within any obvious generic terms.

This generic blurring has an impact on what we might understand by these films' location and cultural identity. In his appraisal of the Aardman feature films (the production collaboration with Hollywood studio DreamWorks, beginning in 2000 with *Chicken Run*), John Fitzgerald is keen to identify the 'idiosyncratic sense of Englishness'[26] that for him characterises the studio's earliest outings. But what exactly is this Englishness? One cultural framework for these films, besides the visual invention and knockabout humour of long-running comics like the *Beano* and *Dandy*, is an idea of 1950s Lancashire, and much of its specificity – and indeed, its comedy – derives from the uses of this location and its accents. Wallace and Gromit, in other words, channel some of the same North-West English attitude that informs much of the development of English comedy, and a specifically *popular* (and hence political) idea of humour at that.

Interestingly, in Wallace and Gromit's only venture into feature film territory, *Wallace and Gromit: Curse of the Were-Rabbit* (2005), which Park co-directed with Steve Box, this sense of regional comic character is to some degree further emphasised. Very much in the spirit of *Carry On*, the film manages to get a surprising amount of *double-entendre* into its generally family-friendly format: Wallace, for one, holding over his naked midriff a box with the words 'contains nuts'; a lady holding to her chest two chewed cauliflowers, which, as her husband explains, were 'ravaged in the night'. Yet here, as in the earlier films, this type of local embedding, both in the form of old-school comedic inflections and a setting apparently based on 1950s Wigan, jostles with a wider framework of global references. In this film, for instance, allusion is made to the broader, already transnational traditions of Hollywood monster movies; from the classical (the locals' hunting of Wallace at the end, pitchforks in hand, echoes Universal's 1931 film of *Frankenstein*, as well as RKO's 1933 *King Kong*) to the modern, with Wallace's transformation into the monstrous, muscular Were-Rabbit neatly referencing both *An American Werewolf in London* (1981) and the more recent *Hulk* (2003). Somewhere between these, of course, are the most obvious precedents for Park's mixture of spectacular science and the monstrous: Hammer studio's reworking of the horror movie through the prism of the English Gothic, in such films as *The Curse of Frankenstein* (1957) and especially *The Curse of the Werewolf* (1961).

Given this particular mix in the Wallace and Gromit franchise, we might ask why Park's creations have been so consistently championed as representations of *national* film. This might seem an odd question to ask, yet it is an important one, touching as it does on the way we evaluate local and global elements within contemporary cinema. On one side, the apparently parochial and nostalgic nature of Wallace and Gromit's world demands analysis in itself, as it is precisely these same points of British comic reference that had over time fallen out of favour. The work of film and cultural historians to locate the importance of music hall, its related cinematic output, and series such as *Carry On* is itself a way of rethinking and re-evaluating types of cultural product formerly disregarded by criticism, and increasingly consigned to the archive of forgotten performances and unwatched films. As Lawrence Napper has discussed, the early

1.2 Channelling the spirit of Hammer and *The Hulk*, Wallace transforms in *Wallace and Gromit: The Curse of the Were-Rabbit* (2005)

traditions of British comedy up to World War II were consistently marginalised by the discourses of British film criticism, favouring as it did the 'serious political and ideological project' of social realism.[27] As Napper argues, referring most specifically to *Observer* film critic C. A. Lejeune's criticism of working-class comedy, 'the problem was not so much that British films failed to represent the working classes, but that they failed to represent them *in the right way*'.[28] For Lejeune, the type of carnivalesque comedy embodied by Gracie Fields and films like *Sing As We Go* were clearly the 'wrong' type of representations.

Moreover, and as already noted, *Curse of the Were-Rabbit* is already a transnational film by virtue of Dreamworks' investment and input into the production. While this may superficially imply a form of compromise with dominant commercial aesthetics, it notable that Park's films have mostly avoided these kinds of negative connotations: just as its apparent representational parochialism has not been the obvious target of criticism. In fact, while it may reflect a more pragmatic and commercial agenda in the discussion of English film, as 'idiosyncratic' expressions of 'Englishness' the Wallace and Gromit brand has even accumulated some form of counter-hegemonic value. These films, with their cosmic trips to find cheese, showdowns with robo-dogs and face-offs with jewel-thief penguins are as far removed from English film's historical 'realist project' as we might imagine;

and yet, they are not only mobilised as a nationally-specific alternative to Hollywood, but have also been praised, in a way that echoes the 1960s realist agenda, for the way they 'challenge hegemonic constructions of Englishness [through] regional accents';[29] or, as Fitzgerald notes, the way they invoke through the character of Wallace, especially in his tussles with an aristocratic villain (Victor Quartermaine) in *The Curse of the Were-Rabbit*, a consideration of class representation in recent British cinema.[30]

This is quite an achievement; though the films are also symptomatic of the way 'English film' is rarely restricted to any specific ideological and aesthetic project, but rather, and especially within the circumstances of globalisation, involves a complex negotiation of representation, iconography and history, mobilised for both economic and ideological reasons. Wallace and Gromit are in this sense an example of what I call the 'paradox of the local' within global culture, and one which parody's comic juxtapositions are well suited to highlight. The Wallace and Gromit films are curiously split between their location within the traditional stomping grounds of English realism (the working-class North), as well as music hall (ditto), *and* the type of nostalgic, rose-tinted construction of Englishness that many critics – most notably Higson, in his work on the so-called 'heritage' dramas of the 1980s and 1990s – see as endemic of a conservative cinematic view.[31] How the films manage to reconcile otherwise conflicting cinematic perspectives owes much, of course, to their status as animation, of which more below. But our (or more specifically, my) ability to digest what is in some senses an entirely parochial and backward-looking representation is because it is positioned alongside and within the representational framework of a contemporary, globalised film economy. When, for example, Preston the Cyber-Dog reveals himself as such, the incongruous humour relies to a large extent on our recognition of the generic tropes of science fiction cinema – and for many viewers, the awareness precisely that it is a graphic allusion to *The Terminator* – or, at least, the recognition that this moment is not 'naturally' readable within the traditional contexts of English cinema.

In fact, much of the parodic humour of the films relates to what James Christopher, in a review of *The Curse of the Were-Rabbit*, calls 'the perishable traditions of British film',[32] as much as it does to Hollywood. Both the gaudy traditions of Hammer Horror and *Carry On* in the latter film,

Battle of Britain films in *A Close Shave*, and the aforementioned H. G. Wells adaptation in *A Grand Day Out*, are just some of the frames of reference within which Park's films can be understood. Wallace's consistently inventive ways of getting out and about, moreover, delivered by chute onto his motorbike as the garden opens up to release him, is itself most obviously indebted to the inventiveness of shows like *Thunderbirds* (ATV, 1965–66); Gerry Anderson's 'supermarionation' series that, though a British production, incorporated a more transatlantic approach (international locations, American accents) in acknowledgement of the potency of an American imaginary, and in a bid to sell the show to the US.[33] In this instance, then, the circulation of domestic, as well as American, cinema and television becomes part of a network of global inter-textual allusions within which the 1950s North West is in effect just one more historical *image*, no more grounded or 'real' than any of the others.

But in a move that proves highly significant for understanding the *global appeal* of these films, these archetypes of 'idiosyncratic Englishness' are also some of the means through which Wallace and Gromit, and other Aardman productions such as *Chicken Run*, can themselves be re-functioned as exotically 'foreign' objects of consumption for the international market. But this can only be done because their Englishness is integrated within globally identifiable and exportable genre frameworks or motifs (such as the *Great Escape* [1963]-style prison-bust narrative of *Chicken Run*). In fact, given that the murderous mob at the end of *Curse of the Were-Rabbit* is made up of that very bastion of traditional, rural English life – attendees at a village fete, in the grounds of a country house – and that the innocent Wallace takes on the form of the Hollywood monster, the most obvious parodic target of the Wallace and Gromit series may more accurately be these 'perishable traditions' both of English cinema, and also of Middle England more generally, rather than its putative global opposition: a similar parodic inversion, as we will see, to that of *Hot Fuzz* in 2007.

We ought therefore to be wary of the ideological and national inflections that cluster around the Aardman films, in spite of their evident self-positioning within the wider terms of global genre cinema. Park's signature use of the stop-motion animation procedure known as clay animation or claymation – a process central to early Hollywood special effects in films such as *King Kong*, though now rendered an eccentric stylistic option

1.3 Redirecting the object of parody: English villagers literalised as 'angry mob' in *Wallace and Gromit: The Curse of the Were-Rabbit* (2005)

in light of modern developments in CGI – is one further way in which his films seem to cohere within an alternative, anti-Hollywood type of stance. However, besides overlooking the mutually beneficial investment of a Hollywood studio in Aardman's move into feature production,[34] and the enormously labour-intensive and expensive process of making such films,[35] emphasising the status of stop-motion and Plasticine models overlooks their specifically filmic possibilities: in this case, the way that Park's approach works to actually heighten his films' parodic use of cinematic quotation. Animation's inherently non-realist aesthetic is already emphasising its potentially parodic qualities. As Jonathan Gray observes in his work on *The Simpsons* (Fox, 1989–), 'when [an animated film] takes *any* visual trope from live action [it] removes that trope a few steps from us, potentially allowing us to see the trope with fresh eyes, defamiliarized.'[36] As in *The Simpsons*' various allusions, this defamiliarising is at once also a re-familiarising, as the animated allusion brings the content and form of the parodied text into greater relief.

In this way, to see inter-textual allusion in Park's films is also implicitly to study and enjoy other texts and styles, to become aware of their form and function. On the grounds that viewers are rarely so uniformly aware of filmic reference points, in fact, attention to such detail in Park's work can actually *enhance* our awareness of the notionally 'parodied' text, or even teach us about it: an aspect of parody which, as I will discuss in Chapter 5, is as common as it is apparently counter-intuitive. Largely because of the increased control and significantly more reduced depth of filming in miniature, the Wallace and Gromit films afford a much more precise exploration of traditional cinematic, and more particularly cinematographic, effects. We are potentially well positioned not only to enjoy the parodic relocation of film noir aesthetics in *A Close Shave*, but in fact to learn about them, because of the heightened sense of generic quotation at work in the film. Park elsewhere achieves striking, dramatic uses of classical devices such as rack focus (the focal movement within a shot between background and foreground objects), 'deep focus', and even Hitchcockian manipulation of looming foreground objects for expressive effect: my favourite instance in *The Curse of the Were-Rabbit* shows Victor, awaiting the arrival of the monster, eye a shaking tea-cup looming large in the extreme left foreground of the shot; following which, a reverse shot – in a classic example of both misdirection and literalisation – reveals the 'giant' teacup as precisely that: a teacup-shaped fairground ride.

Conclusion: All in the Details

Couched within the films' apparent rebuff to the dominant styles and motifs of big-budget genre cinema, then, is a tacit fascination with, and awareness of, this same cinema. In this respect, the temptation to assume a divisive or negative character to parody within such English films needs constantly to be counterweighed by that which such discussions often disavow: firstly, an implicit reflection on the meaning of English cinema itself, especially in light of the emerging and now dominant global strategies of production; and secondly, and as a corollary of the global cinematic imaginary, a positive, pleasurable engagement with the form and feeling of that dominant cinematic 'other' that is Hollywood.

As I began to explore in the introduction, this global imaginary produced by Hollywood cinema may easily be connoted as the devilish other to English film and television comedy. We also saw earlier that this is both reductive and misleading. As I have argued in this chapter, the devil is not in the detail: the details, in fact, reveal much more sympathy for this devil than might initially seem the case. As we see both here and in subsequent chapters, we can rarely make simplistic and antagonistic distinctions between English and popular American cinemas within a globalised culture. Life may be Cricklewood, not Hollywood. But in English parody's efforts to prove this point, it reveals that the two are not so easily separated.

2

Silly, Really: Parody, Genre and Realism in Monty Python's *The Holy Grail* and *Life of Brian*

Though often overshadowed in critical work on Monty Python, a high point of the comedy group's work, for me at least, comes in their 1983 film *The Meaning of Life*. In some Yorkshire of the non-specified though apparently still Victorian past, a newly-unemployed Roman Catholic worker, played by Michael Palin, discusses with his vast family of ragged children the moral evils of condoms. With babies literally dropping out of his wife as he speaks, the children are instructed as to the sanctity of each ejaculation, before eventually breaking into song. Finally, the refrain that 'Every Sperm is Sacred' is taken up by the massed ranks of the family and their neighbours, as in marching celebration they chorus along the street. A full-on musical number joyfully celebrating the refusal of contraception, very much in the style of British composer Lionel Bart – as seen in the 1968 film version of his musical *Oliver!* – the sequence dazzles with its ebullient blend of choreographed verve and sheer incongruity.

Were this to happen in an episode of the television series *Monty Python's Flying Circus* (BBC, 1969–74), it would no doubt warrant a visit from the character known simply as The Colonel: a British Army Officer, played by Graham Chapman, who would perennially come on to interrupt sketches with variations on the same command: 'Stop that! It's *silly!*' Depending on your point of view, The Colonel sums up much of the Monty Python

2.1 'Every sperm is sacred': over-population as musical number in *The Meaning of Life* (1983)

group's particular kind of comedy. He is, on the one hand, a symbol of their anarchic spirit, their disruption of the form and conventions of television comedy.[1] On the other hand, he might also be a puerile, lame excuse for a joke (a joke without a punch-line, in fact), or just…*too silly*. Either way, The Colonel brings into focus a lot of the issues underpinning analysis of the Pythons' work. Perhaps it *is* just too silly, working simply through the confounding of normal order and logic. My suggestion here will be that it is a bit more than this. But in making this argument, it is important to clarify why this discussion is worth having, and also to avoid what Steve Neale and Frank Krutnik call the 'unreflective celebration'[2] that sometimes characterises writing about the Python team. What is it exactly we are really looking at here, then? And more to the point, what is at stake in such an analysis?

The 2014 *Arena* documentary on the Pythons' London reunion show of that year[3] featured a clip from John Cleese's recent one-man tour, in which he screened the 'Fish-Slapping Dance' from series three of *Monty Python's Flying Circus*. The sketch has Cleese and Michael Palin dressed in khaki and pith helmets, standing by the side of a canal. Palin dances to and fro, lightly slapping the immobile Cleese round the face with a small fish, after which, Cleese produces a significantly bigger fish, with which he knocks Palin into the water. When the sketch comes to a close, back on the stage

Cleese quips that a poor media student might be asked to analyse it one day. Cleese may be having a little laugh here about the academic analysis of comedy and the media studies industry (within which we might include both myself and this book), or perhaps, just as likely, he is merely making a joke out of his own sketch's interpretive impenetrability. Either way, his comment touches on the persistent problem of trying to 'explain' something as intractable and frequently abstract as humour, especially in the case of Monty Python's absurdist style.

I am aware of the capacity for comedy analysis to evaporate the spirit of a joke or visual gag, turning into dry equations something premised on its resistance to sense or decoding. Yet comedy can be taken apart in a way that can illuminate, rather than nullify, its workings; more importantly, analysis performs a vital task in teasing out the often dubious ideology underpinning a great deal of humour. This idea that there is no real thing as 'just a joke' is too obvious to need asserting, but I suggest here we do not limit this observation solely to the politically incorrect or to that perceived as 'bad taste'. I am troubled, in this present context, by the idea that the comedic absurd, the 'silly', is somehow out of analytical bounds. In the case of Monty Python, assuming that we cannot nor should not subject their humour to analysis does no one any favours. The radical tenor of this anti-criticism, extolling resistance to sense and logic, here becomes a kind of conservatism, an acceptance of the comic status quo.

I have no desire here to subject either *Monty Python's The Holy Grail* (1975) or *Monty Python's Life of Brian* (1979) to stinging ideological critique, mainly because I don't think they merit one. One of my points in this chapter is that the films are themselves important forms of critique, even if this is not always so obviously apparent. Digging a bit further in terms of the nature and main subjects of humour in both films is important, if only because this humour may either be broadly condemned or, alternatively, uncritically celebrated – a response that, in failing to acknowledge the often complex or allusive nature of the Pythons' comedy in these films, may be no less problematic in its influence.

Being more specific about the aims and meanings of humour in films like *The Holy Grail* and *Life of Brian* also helps us to address some of its criticisms, and to situate the film within its specific time and place. But it also enables us to think about, or indeed rethink, the particular functions of humour in the Pythons' film work. The critic Geoff Brown, in a 1975 review of *The Holy Grail*, dismissed the team as 'mechanical purveyors of the absurd'.[4] As I will suggest, this put-down of Python humour – interestingly enough, a similar kind of dismissal to the kind The Colonel would come on to make – overlooks the more varied, and indeed engaged, nature of comedy in their work.

Moreover, reductive views of the Pythons' work from whatever perspective overlook the specific way that the group explore and address the medium in which they are working. The well-documented care and attention to detail the team brought to these two films, moreover, often within stringent time and budgetary limitations,[5] suggests we should be wary of simplistically allocating an overarching and fixed style to a range of varied works. Gone, for example, in both *The Holy Grail* and *The Life of Brian*, are the continuity announcers and (save a few isolated moments) direct camera address familiar from the television series, as well as their first film, *And Now For Something Completely Different* (1971), made up of sketches from these shows. As Neale and Krutnik show, *Monty Python's Flying Circus* works largely through the 'principles of diegetic and functional overlap [...] and of interruption and intrusion'.[6] The integrity of the individual 'sketch' is rarely respected in the show, which frequently allows the individual elements within each episode to interact with and overcut each other. To this extent the comedy sketch show as televisual institution is the overarching focus of their comedy here. While both *The Holy Grail* and *Life of Brian* play actively with cinematic conventions – the manipulation of the credits, and of the institutional beginning and end of the screening, in *The Holy Grail*; the jokey titles and generic interruptions of *The Life of Brian* – neither film is that active in its efforts to break the 'fourth wall' and thereby undermine the films' fictional worlds. As I will explore here, if *Monty Python's Flying Circus* sought to disrupt the coherence of popular broadcast television, the specific concern in their film work is the illusory reality constructed through the fiction feature film.

As has been discussed elsewhere,[7] *The Holy Grail*, despite the attraction of the Python group at its core, did not benefit from huge economic investment, and can be considered a relatively low-budget film (Palin's production diaries attest to the frequently improvised and strained process in which the film was made[8]). As a film located somewhere between two major movies based on the Arthurian legends – Warner Bros.' *Camelot* (1967), a version of the Lerner and Loewe musical, and the epic *Excalibur* (1981), directed by John Boorman for Orion – it is tempting to see *The Holy Grail*'s economic and technical poverty as a contributing factor to its particular take on the King Arthur story. The idea that economic deficiency underpins parody is an argument that recurs throughout the discussions in this book; and as I will suggest both here and elsewhere, as much as we need to be attentive to the contexts of film economics, we reduce the possibilities of parody if we view it solely as a negative relation to budgetary power. Nevertheless, the economic contexts of the time are at least notionally highlighted by the opening and closing sequences of *The Holy Grail*. As the film begins, we hear the sound of horses' hooves over shots of a mist-strewn landscape. A crowned knight, whom we eventually realise to be King Arthur, appears skipping across the grass, followed by his servant Patsy hitting hollowed coconut shells together. In the final shots, meanwhile, in what has been called 'the ultimate transcendence of realism' within the film,[9] a squad of policemen interrupt the actual filming and put a stop to the cameras' shooting, an ending possibly determined by economic expediency as much as any aesthetic or thematic intention.

To talk about the policeman's intervening hand on the camera lens as 'the ultimate transcendence of realism' may be a move in the right direction, but not necessarily if we take it to refer to some pre-existent real to which the film ultimately reverts. Seeing the film this way may in fact limit our understanding of the preceding 90 minutes, allowing it to signify nothing much more than an inversion of filmic and/or worldly norms. Like another authority figure such as The Colonel, the policeman's firm hand of The Law draws a line beyond which the film – just before its climactic battle between Arthur's army and the massed French – is not allowed to go. Rather than this reinstating realism and a return to a normal or 'natural' state of affairs, though, I suggest instead we see the film's ending as merely the concluding instance within the film's range of mediations, its variety of stylistic options, via which the film is itself exploring the idea of cinematic realism (and not, in fact, simply delaying realism's return).

We should equally consider the possibility that parody may *in itself* contribute to a conception of the real. Parody's obvious rejection of a 'realist' aesthetic, in the sense of a mimetically believable, coherent and yet fictional world, may give mileage to the assumption that it stands apart from the wider 'project' of English realism to which I have already alluded in the previous chapter. Yet this would underestimate the fact that the coherence and verisimilitude of cinematic realism, its fictional representation of mimetic space, is itself ideological in the way it disavows its own artifice and construction. And as Justin Smith has perceptively identified,[10] it is precisely this ideological value of film aesthetics, especially when in the service of powerful national or religious narratives, that parody plays an important role in undermining.

As I will suggest here, then, 'realism' does not lie *on the outside* of parodic discourse, as some sort of point from which all things precede or to which they return. Parody is here not a simple hiatus or holiday within the serious work of representation. Rather, representation is inherent to the performance of parody itself, which incorporates all stylistic claims to representing the real, including so-called 'realism' itself: the illusion, in other words, of mimetically representing the real world.

The Holy Grail

Though largely under-explored since its production, *The Holy Grail* has received a degree of recent academic appraisal. Smith, for example, has briefly discussed the film in terms of its status within British 'cult' cinema,[11] and within a more detailed account of Python's film output up to *The Meaning of Life*.[12] Elsewhere, Smith and Sue Harper locate *The Holy Grail* within what they call the 'cultural ratification of the mysterious', synonymous with the decade's 'revival of interest in alternative mythologies'.[13] Counter-intuitively, though in this respect very interestingly, Harper and Smith place the Monty Python film within the current of early 1970s Arthurian revivalism.[14] *The Holy Grail* also appeared during a time in which the Arthur myth was finding its way onto screens in somewhat different forms from the late-studio era spectacle of *Camelot*, most notably in the relatively low-budget British production *Gawain and the Green Knight* (1973), and in French director Robert Bresson's characteristically austere, though very violent, *Lancelot du Lac* (1973).

In fact, *The Holy Grail* is positioned intriguingly within this transitional decade, in which a suffering British film industry found itself balanced between, on the one side, attempts at Hollywood-style spectacle, and on the other, exploitation of television sit-coms, and comedy franchises such as the *Carry On* movies. But the production accounts of *The Holy Grail* also testify to the impact of contemporary European art cinema, such as Pierpaolo Pasolini's *Canterbury Tales* (1972) – an apparent inspiration for directors Terry Jones and Terry Gilliam – as well as the same director's version of *The Decameron* (1971), and also *Lancelot du Lac*. According to Palin, films such as these provided the model for *The Holy Grail*, and in particular, for a 'style and quality of shooting [required] to stop it being just another *Carry On King Arthur*'.[15]

Palin's comments are important, revealing as they do the uncertain points of contact between the *Carry On* films and the Python movies. Suffice it to say for the moment that Palin indicates an unease with the potential for pure farce in *The Holy Grail*, its reduction to a series of derisive jokes, made – as is typically the case in the *Carry On* series' genre parodies – from a very comfortable, conservative, normatively 'English' ideological perspective. Certainly, the tendencies of cinematography and mise-en-scène in *The Holy Grail* offer evidence for the film's stylistic intent, most notably its desire to capture some sense of period context, of dirt, violence and hardship: hence its frequent preference for long shots over close-ups, placing its characters within often oppressive and barren landscapes, or its characteristic use of muted light, natural shadows and mist to evoke a pre-modern but far from pastoral atmosphere.

We need to ask though how and why such intents work with, or indeed against, the broader comic remit of the film. The disavowal of any possible connection to the contemporaneous *Carry On* genre parodies, and the insistence on a 'dirty', more historically-grounded representation, beg the question of comedy's function within *The Holy Grail*. Given such an insistence on historical verisimilitude, why not simply make a 'straight' version of the myths? The obvious answer is that it is a Monty Python film, and they are meant to be funny. But why work so hard to make it seem otherwise? The disappointing response to the 1974 investors' preview, which Palin recounts as eliciting very little laughter,[16] was blamed for being '20% too strong on authenticity and 20% too weak on jokes'.[17] This gave rise to significant editorial and soundtrack changes, the addition of a library-purchased musical score being the main one. But this may say more about the over-determined expectations of film comedy, rather than indicate a particular 'failure' on the part of the film. It is interesting on this note that Harper and Smith should see *The Holy Grail* so much within the terms of medieval revivalism and the evocation of 'sublime myth',[18] given that this historical aspect seemed part of the problem in the film's initial reception.

This is a tension then in the film, reflected in the ostensibly conflicting critical approaches to *The Holy Grail* in recent work. Smith describes the way the film achieves a 'plausible degree of historical verisimilitude',[19] mainly in terms of its cinematography. Yet he also draws attention to what he sees as the challenges, structured into the film, to this same historical verisimilitude. The coherence of the film's world, he observes, is constantly threatened either by anachronism or the intervention of material reality: in this instance, the very hard, dirty conditions of making the film itself. This may well represent what Harper and Smith mean by 'the ultimate transcendence of realism', or the impossibility, in the end, 'of rendering historical reality on film'.[20]

Key to this idea, though, is a dialogue between the film's narrative and its modes of narration, to which parody is central. The comic imperatives behind *The Holy Grail* do not undermine the film's engagement with period and history. Parody here works in a more dialectical way to challenge and call into question the claims and meanings of historical 'authenticity' or 'verisimilitude'. This is because *The Holy Grail* is to a large extent about the processes and practices through which we read, and take pleasure in, historical narratives, rather than an attempt to 'do' a historical narrative properly speaking.

'Historical Verisimilitude'

There is a fairly obvious ambiguity outlined above in the way the film achieves a degree of 'historical verisimilitude' while also playing on the 'impossibility of rendering historical reality'. But this is less uncertain once we work out what we mean by 'verisimilitude' in terms of representing history. Robert Burgoyne's work on the historical film, and more specifically the historical epic – essentially the genre to which both *The Holy Grail* and *Life of Brian* most clearly refer – has stressed the way such films work through persuasively mimetic and somatic means, frequently combining

massive scale and wealth of detail in the mise-en-scène in order to produce
'a heightened sense of fidelity and verisimilitude', all as a means of 'reen-
acting the past'.[21] As the connotations of the term imply, verisimilitude
(literally the 'likeness of the real') is only ever an analogical mode and
form of content through which an *impression* of reality is offered to us.
But how do we make sense of this in terms of a medieval reality represented through a late-twentieth century technological medium? Burgoyne's
nuanced view is that the inherent sense of re-iteration structured into the
idea of *re-enactment*

> involves a form of double consciousness, a rethinking of the
> past [...] Rather than a simple re-experiencing, as if there were
> no gap between the actual event and its re-presentation, the
> filmmaker and the spectator alike project themselves into a past
> world in order to reimagine it, to perform it, and to rethink it.[22]

If historical films invite us not so much to relive history as to engage in
a kind of 'historical thinking',[23] it also involves thinking about the very
form through which history is narrated: in this case, the medium of
genre cinema itself. As Burgoyne suggests, our reading of the historical
film works through our understanding of generic syntax and semantics;[24]
our relationship, in other words, to the conventions and codes of a genre.
Consequently, our engagement with the historical film is at once a critical
engagement with cinematic representation. Parody plays an important part
here in the way its essentially formal concerns undermine the potential for
belief in the image, making the syntax and semantics of genre – the specific
and familiar relationship of each to the other being the source of a genre's
verisimilitude[25] – the foregrounded focus of attention. The very idea of 'historical verisimilitude', then, the representation of historical reality, is *The
Holy Grail*'s main target, but also its substance. The instability of historical
verisimilitude is already part of the film's structure, rather than something
merely threatened by the (arbitrary) intervention of incongruous elements.

This would actually suggest that the Pythons' film work is located
within the broader concerns and debates around cinematic realism, rather
than being outside them. The discussion concerning realism and its connections to the ideology of film became central to the editorial aims of the
British journal *Screen*, which from the beginning of the 1970s followed the

lead of French theory (and the political repercussions of events in the late 1960s) in taking apart and challenging the aesthetics and inherent meanings of dominant cinema. One of the recurring assertions throughout the 1970s *Screen* debates, particularly in the contributions of (then) editor Colin MacCabe, is that cinematic realism in its classical sense (mostly associated with Hollywood production from around 1930 to 1960) is characterised by its resistance to contradiction. Classical narrative, writes MacCabe, 'involves the homogenisation of different discourses by their relation to one dominant discourse.'[26] For MacCabe, the verisimilitude produced by Hollywood's continuity system, and the specific orientation of the viewer's involvement within the narration, means this narrative discourse is the only one to be 'match[ed] against the realm of truth,'[27] and therefore stands in ideologically for reality itself. As MacCabe suggests in an earlier essay on Brechtian theory and the realist novel,[28] the unquestioned narrative authority of third person narration finds its equivalence in cinema's pure metonymic power of representation. The camera's transparent gaze in this respect becomes the unchallenged authority subsuming all potential contradiction within its display of 'reality'.

Despite MacCabe's slightly reductive schema, the *Screen* debates on realism retain an important contextual value because of their focus on aspects of class representation, and the politics of representation more broadly. Both MacCabe and Raymond Williams take issue with the assumption that merely representing class, by which one tends to mean the *working* class, is a sufficient condition for political realism. Williams, for example, makes the case for realism as a form of dialectic, in Marxist terms, and not as a 'flat external [reproduction] of reality.'[29] Williams' conception of realism here as an aesthetic method aiming to go 'beyond the surface to the essential historical movements, to the dynamic reality'[30] of its represented moment is perhaps an unexpected way to think about *The Holy Grail*, yet I think it is a valuable approach. Notably, *Screen*'s translation in 1971 of 'Cinema/Ideology/Criticism', originally a 1969 editorial in the French journal *Cahiers du cinéma*, targeted the way political films made within the classical (or 'bourgeois') realist mode 'do not effectively criticise the ideological system in which they are embedded because they unquestioningly adopt its language and its imagery'. Yet the editors recognise that popular entertainment cinema – their specific example being the 1960 Jerry Lewis film *The Bellboy* – can serve a political function not so much through its content, but 'through the criticism practised on [the film] through its form':[31] an exposure, in other words, of what narrative film typically does through the manipulation and disruption of its conventions.

In *The Holy Grail*, this formal criticism is largely enacted at the level of incident and mise-en-scène, where convention is turned and exposed as incongruous within the film's particular contexts. Arthur, self-proclaimed King of the Britons, is like his Knights consistently distinguished by his white clothes and cleanliness, while his subjects are permanently covered in filth (as one peasant remarks, he must be the King, 'because he doesn't have shit all over him'). Significantly, many of the King's commands are met not with a rapid genuflection and a pledging of loyalty, but with disbelief ('Pull the other one!') or plain disregard. Robert Stam, reading *The Holy Grail* through Mikhail Bakhtin's concept of the 'carnivalesque', argues such aspects of the film serve to undermine royal and ecclesiastical authority:[32] perhaps they do, but such arguments do little to question the historical and economic bases that both found and sustain such structures of authority in the first place. I think *The Holy Grail* itself resists this trap because of its engagement with representation: firstly, representation of historical reality from the perspective of twentieth-century cinema (the question, raised previously, of historical verisimilitude), and relatedly, through the film's otherwise overlooked interest in questions of language, discourse and power.

See the Violence Inherent in the System!

A case in point is what is often called (for example, in Palin's production diaries) the 'constitutional peasant' scene: the early sequence in which Arthur attempts unsuccessfully to secure the loyalty of Dennis, the titular peasant. The comic effect of this sequence derives from the way Arthur's efforts to maintain the status given to him as King – which is also the status and centrality demanded by the parameters of the *genre* – are persistently thwarted by both dialogue and mise-en-scène. Arthur's efforts to command the attention and response of his people – 'I am Arthur, King of the Britons!' – are met by Dennis's mother with what may be a contextually accurate rebuff – 'Who are the Britons?' Dennis's mother therefore rejects in one swift response the historical narrative embodied by Arthur, and with it, the narrative of nation with which such legendary narratives, from the *Iliad* to the Finnish *Kalevala* to Virgil's *Aeneid*, to the tale of El Cid and Mel Gibson's *Braveheart* (1995), are historically intertwined.[33] When pressed further to explain himself, Arthur tells them that

> The Lady of the Lake [extra-diegetic music begins], her arm clad in the purest shimmering samite, held aloft Excalibur from the bosom of the water, signifying by divine providence that I, Arthur, was to carry Excalibur [music abruptly ends]. *That* is why I am your King!

At which point, Dennis retorts that

> Strange women lying in ponds, distributing swords, is no basis for a system of government. Supreme executive power derives from a mandate from the masses, not from some farcical aquatic ceremony [...] If I went around calling myself Emperor, just because some moistened bint had lobbed a scimitar at me, they'd put me away!

Within the terms of formalist parody theory, what we are seeing here is characteristic both of inversion – Arthur's generically-connoted expectations of loyalty being dismissed and derided – but also 'extraneous inclusion' – 'inserting "foreign" lexical units into a conventionalized syntax'[34] – insofar as Dennis's rhetoric lies many centuries outside the film's target era. Importantly, though, extraneous inclusion is within Harries' terms only extraneous in relation to the highly restricted and pre-determined semantic and syntactic range of genre itself (what Harries, using a term from semiotics, calls genre's 'logonomic system'). Parody's potential conservatism lies in the way extraneous inclusion can reiterate the boundaries of generic verisimilitude: we may laugh at such inclusions from 'outside' the generic field of signification because we recognise its unlikely nature, but this does not really challenge or interrogate the field of signification itself.

Smith is therefore contextually accurate when he argues that Palin's Dennis 'sound[s] like a world-weary Marxist shop-steward, the source of whose condition of alienated labour is precisely in being transplanted into a mythical medieval narrative'.[35] The comedy in this sense works through the incongruity of Dennis's presence and its topicality, in relation to the prominence and media presence of trade unions during this decade. But we can also see Dennis's language and argument within the terms of genre: specifically, within the terms of the way genre establishes frameworks for historical verisimilitude, and therefore its own horizon of representation. We know the peasant is not supposed to speak like this in Arthurian narrative, or even in films based on it – and we would reasonably assume he would not do the same in Arthurian England! But the force of the peasant's rhetoric, because it specifically addresses the 'norms' of representation in the form of the King, goes further here. It asks us to recognise the threshold of the 'generically realistic', as it raises the question of the peasant's actual, historical voice – or rather lack of it. In other words, the unlikelihood of a medieval peasant discussing political theory gives way to the scandal of the peasant's voice, and indeed body, being written *out of* cultural representation, and therefore from history – and in turn, 'historical verisimilitude' – more generally. This is emphasised by the scene's mise-en-scène, which places Arthur's Excalibur speech, unlike the rest of the dialogue, in a long shot: Arthur here, slightly in the background, looks over and upwards to a non-specified point off screen, while Dennis and his mother rake through mud in the foreground. The scene, therefore, places Arthur in a visually dialectical composition, undermining the impact of his mystical vision; just as the abruptly starting and finishing musical score emphasises the artificially constructed nature of the myth.

It is also a reminder that *no* voice within the historical film has any absolute justification to presence or authenticity, merely that the authority of kingship exudes this right through the force of generic convention. Dennis's incongruous disruption of generic norms begs the question of why we are prepared to tolerate English Received Pronunciation as historically verisimilar, but not Dennis's working-class London accent – an observation that extends throughout the history of cinematic and televisual representations of English history – unless, that is, that our cinematic and televisual education, through the contemporary register of a received English accent, has effectively re-written history as the domain of classically-trained or Oxbridge-educated British actors. Intriguingly, it was in a scene from the BBC film *The Rank and File* (1971), directed by social realist *par excellence* Ken Loach, that the shot of a factory worker

65

2.2 Mise-en-scène as antidote to myth-making: Arthur addresses the peasants in *The Holy Grail* (1975)

quoting Marx was censored by its producers, who insisted that the speaker should not be seen. As Loach argued at the time, British film and television had a long history of making the proletarian body an invisible one: or as Loach put it, 'the insistence on the disembodied voice of the proletariat was a characteristic class weapon of the Establishment'.[36] Dennis the Marxist peasant may have found himself in the wrong time and place, but at least here he has found his voice.

See the Violence Inherent in the Fiction!

If this scene, as in Dennis's parting lines, invites us to 'come see the violence inherent in the system!', the following 'Black Knight' sequence reminds us of the violence inherent in the Arthurian narrative itself. The beginning of the scene shows how *The Holy Grail* is adept at moving between competing, though actually overlapping, discourses of chivalry and violence. We see how the passage of Arthur and his servant through the forest, underscored by the jaunty extra-diegetic music, is almost literally ripped into by abrupt cuts of non-scored action, featuring the Knight and his adversary in mid-battle, before giving way to a more extended view of the duel, as observed now by the King. The fight, cued to the hammering sounds of sword on armour and the guttural cries of the antagonists, ends with the Black Knight throwing his sword through his opponent's visor. In a shot that actually echoes the gory limb-loppings and head-crackings of *Lancelot du Lac*, blood sprays and gushes from the knight's helmet as he falls dead. The scene that follows sees the Black Knight succumbing to repeated bloody dismemberings administered by Arthur, as the stumps of hewed-off arms and legs emit projectile squirts of blood, only for the Knight to brush off these wounds with heroic nonchalance: 'Tis but a scratch!'

Once more, these kind of juxtapositions do not so much deride the Arthurian narrative as bring out its latent, or indeed quite obvious, violence, which both layers of time and the vicissitudes of style have perhaps hidden to our twenty-first century eyes and ears. Returning to Thomas Malory's fifteenth-century *Morte D'Arthur*, as the most prominent source for the long and wide proliferation of the Arthur legends, is to be reminded both of the extraordinary savagery evoked in it, but also the ways in which medieval language distils this violence into a distanced historical and aesthetic experience for the contemporary reader. Reading some of Malory's descriptions is in some respects a Pythonesque experience in itself, in which horrifying violence is rendered in a seemingly perfunctory, repetitive and understated way, cartoonish even in its reduction to minimal action. As, for example, in this account of the Knights' battle with the Roman army:

> Then Sir Gawain was sore grieved with [Sir Gainus's] words, and pulled out his sword and smote off his head [...T]hen came Caliburn one of the strongest of Pavie, and smote down many of Arthur's knights. And when Sir Bors saw him do so much harm, he addressed toward him, and smote him through the breast, that he fell down dead to the earth. Then Sir Feldenak thought to revenge the death of Gainus upon Sir Gawain, but Sir Gawain was ware thereof, and smote him on the head, which stroke stinted not till it came to his breast.[37]

In light of this intent to reclaim the violence of Malory's tale, we should recall the 1970s contexts of the film, and in particular, that it was made at the tail-end of the Hollywood production code. If *The Holy Grail*'s main influences are as much from continental Europe as from America, this is hardly surprising, given the way that the much less representationally constrained European art cinemas could traditionally show what Hollywood in its studio heyday could not. That *The Holy Grail* is (in Jones's words) an 'antidote to the Hollywood vision' has become rather a received idea of the film, possibly because its director tells us it is the case. But this belies its more dialogic practices; the way, in fact, a reading of the film's historical 'reenactment' necessarily involves both continuity with, and distinction from, a genre's existing syntactic and semantic norms. If *The Holy Grail* sets up a representational dialogue with films such as MGM's Cinemascope *Knights of the Round Table* (1953), or the Alan Ladd vehicle *The Black Knight* (1954), based loosely on the very bloody Book Seven of the *Morte D'Arthur*, it is partly to fill in what those films, made under the production code, could not include, but also what they had to surrender to the demands both of classical narrative form and (in *Knights of the Round Table* especially) big-screen spectacle.

This is only part of the task, though, as identifying what the classical Hollywood epic left out gives rise to the other side of the equation: namely, what it *left in*, or indeed, what motivates in the first place the multiple adaptations of the Arthurian stories, and their placing within the popular, spectacular economies of the movies. To assume that *The Holy Grail* simply derides the Hollywood vision of legend is to presume that there is no substantial basis for the latter's representations, which hardly explains why such visions are there to parody at all. Moreover, and as Smith has noted, one of the long-term legacies of *The Holy Grail* is the way so much of its dialogue has acquired familiarity through repetition and shared use amongst fans of the film:[38] an important observation in its emphasis on the inherent pleasures and attractions of the film's Arthurian inter-texts. In its rhythms and repetitions, in fact, its uses of both archaic and understatedly delicate language, or alternately its literalisms and redundancies, it is the language of Arthurian legend that holds much of the latter's evocative appeal. Again, as the example below suggests, Malory's text hardly needs the Pythons' parodic touch to distil its potentially comic qualities:

> And as he rode by the way, [Sir Marhaus] met with Sir Gawain
> and Sir Uwain, and so by adventure he met with four knights
> of Arthur's court, the first was Sir Sagramore le Desirous,
> Sir Ozana, Sir Dodinas le Savage, and Sir Felot of Listinoise;

and there Sir Marhaus with one spear smote down these four
knights, and hurt them sore.[39]

The Holy Grail uses parody as a means of exploring violence by juxtaposing
a style of language and performance with a realistic context that cannot
justify this style. The discrepancy is the intended source of humour, but
with this comic understanding comes an implicit awareness of the appeal
of such 'inappropriate' and non-realist aesthetics. In this sense *The Holy
Grail* moves between time and place, inviting us to sample 'history' but
only with the awareness of our contemporary viewpoint; and hence, it
combines the attractions of historical fiction – and in particular, views of
the legendary past – while remaining alert to the problems, representational and political, inherent to these fictions.

In the scenes discussed above, the presence as performer of co-director
Gilliam reminds us of the same director's foiled efforts decades later to
film Cervantes' *Don Quixote* (1605–15),[40] a book which, as in *The Holy
Grail*, features a hero whose 'delusions of grandeur are pitted against base
reality.'[41] Cervantes' novel places its aging protagonist, who also embarks
on his own form of spiritual chivalric quest, against the unforgiving and
physically punishing novelistic setting of La Mancha. *The Holy Grail* is
itself close in its aims and aesthetic approaches to *Don Quixote*, conveying
much of that novel's combined vision of nostalgic romance, violence and
realist critique. But as Stam has argued, *Don Quixote*'s parodic critique is
also ideological: 'Although critics have usually emphasized the comicity of
Quixote's alchemical imaginings, that comicity is sometimes spoken in an
exterminationist language redolent of [...] the *conquista* in the Americas'.
This conquest, significantly, was 'on one level, a bookish enterprise, a clash
of intertexts, shaped... by Roman imperial law and the literature of the
Christian crusade.[42]

Bakhtin, with respect to Stam, turns out to offer an important perspective here, though less in the temporary terms of the carnivalesque. In his
essay 'The Epic and the Novel' Bakhtin identifies the importance of laughter as that which 'destroys the epic'.[43] Importantly, though, this laughter,
this destabilising of the language of myth, also marks the end of the epic
as a viable form and the historical emergence of novels like *Don Quixote*.
This 'hostility to the elevation of the epic' is therefore 'not some abstract

69

generic principle of subversion, but itself springs from active social forces which constantly pull the language away from th[e] national centre'.[44] We can similarly see *The Holy Grail* not as some absurd departure from representation, but a specific phase in our mimetic understanding of history and language. As in Cervantes' novel, its violence emerges not so much in the *gaps* between 'bookish' talk – in other words, that spoken by Arthur to the peasant, or by the Black Knight to Arthur – but as a barely concealed, hysterical aspect of this language in itself. Arthur's claims to divinely-granted Kingship and his insistence on loyalty, after all, is also a similar claim to the one underpinning the Crusades' own brand of 'exterminationist' rhetoric – linked here to Cervantes' novel via such knight-errant romances as *Amadís of Gaul*. *The Holy Grail*'s critical engagement with this type of mythology and its implicit violence makes the film unusually timely and topical for our contemporary age.

As Burgoyne points out, the epic genre can still be, and frequently is, re-worked as a form of 'national self-scrutiny';[45] and in its comic treatment of the idea of 'Britain' both as a symbolic construction and form of ideological power, *The Holy Grail* is very much situated within the terms of the country's national and international decline in the 1970s. Indeed, the power of the Arthur legends to invoke a sense of national 'imagined community',[46] through its nostalgic evocation of a fabled land and people, is presumably part of these legends' abiding appeal;[47] but problematically so. Seeing this in light of the UK's recent referendum on European Union membership, and following a period in which UKIP, based mainly on an anti-immigration, anti-European platform, has made inroads into mainstream political life, it is interesting to be reminded how much of the Arthurian legends focused on the King's essentially nationalist war on Rome,[48] the *casus belli* of which was Rome's insistence that the British pay taxes to its Empire.

Life of Brian

That *Life of Brian* targets idolatry, its problems and inconsistencies, is a widely-held notion in the discussions around this controversial film. Its tale of Brian Cohen being inadvertently taken for the (latest) Messiah – after accidentally dropping onto a prophet's pedestal and finding himself, to escape the attentions of the Roman army, obliged to narrate parables – centres largely around the arbitrariness of idolatrous belief. Notably, the point in the film where Brian begins to gather a proper crowd is when he says nothing: leaving a story suspended in the middle, as he waits to see if his pursuers have passed, he turns back to find his audience suddenly hanging on his next word. Pointedly, then, Brian's conversion from the son of Terry Jones' Mother Mandy to the Son of God is based on an interpretive void, a literal nothing which expectation and the desire for meaning rushes to fill.

The titular joke of combining the epic register with the none-more ordinary name – *Life of Brian*, shown in the credits in Gilliam's huge stone letters, evokes both hagiography and the titles of preceding biblical films – underlines the point that names are themselves arbitrary and meaningless: until, that is, they become marked by association. The point it makes is not that 'Brian' is an inherently funny name, only it seems so within the contexts of a biblical film. A presumably unfunny title like *Jesus of Nazareth*, by contrast, is not in any sense more realistic: it simply makes more *generic* sense from our understanding and knowledge of previous titles. As in *The Holy Grail*, this only begs the question of how the arbitrary becomes naturalised through the conventions of film genre and its aesthetics.

As Bruce Babington and Peter Evans have observed, the Hollywood Christ film to which *Life of Brian* prominently alludes is typically marked by 'formal conservatism'. Not only is its construction of verisimilitude determined by 'Renaissance iconography, heavily moderated by Victorian sacred art traditions'; it is also 'bound into many specific conventions [...] of music, casting, acting styles, language'.[49] It is in fact this specifically *European* visual tradition that informs the one and only appearance in the film of Jesus, whose pale robes, long hair and suppliant stance are clearly drawn from a longer history of pictorial representation. The movement from this fleetingly-glimpsed figure to that of Brian Cohen is not then so much a movement away from historical reality, as another mode of dialogue between historical approaches and representational systems. Just as the presence of Dennis the constitutional peasant called into question what defines normal and why in the medieval mythic film, looking at the representation and fate of Brian in the later film is also to consider how the biblical movie actually *works*. This is where we limit our appreciation of *Life of*

Brian's achievements once we restrict our reading to a critique of idolatrous belief. It is above all a film that uses parody to explore the construction of verisimilitude and ideological belief specifically in the biblical *movie*.

Life of Brian is as equally astute as *The Holy Grail* in identifying the critical and commercial reappraisal of genre. In the context of 1978, when the film was made, *Life of Brian* was poised between parodying a notionally declined genre and exemplifying a recently renewed one. As a form of the historical epic film, the heyday of the biblical genre ran parallel to the decline of the classical studio system in the 1950s and 1960s, also coincidental with the emergence of Technicolor, VistaVision and Cinemascope as technologies of big-screen spectacle. This period saw the remakes (now in full sound, colour and widescreen) of two films originally made in the 1920s: *The Ten Commandments* (1956) and *Ben-Hur* (1959), before the genre ran out both of steam and economic viability with works such as *King of Kings* (1961), *The Greatest Story Ever Told* (1965) and *The Bible: In the Beginning* (1966), a vast portmanteau movie recounting the early books of the Old Testament. As Harries points out, with reference to Thomas Schatz's work on the evolutions of Hollywood genres, until the 1970s the cultural and economic logic of parody film held that genres required a period of initial saturation, followed by a period of 'dormancy', before they could be a suitable subject of parody: a period of 'digestion [...] in which spectators [could] possibly distance themselves from the targeted logonomic system'.[50] Such a logic would in theory back up the success of writer-director Mel Brooks, whose *Blazing Saddles* (1974) and *Young Frankenstein* (1974) both targeted genres in a state of either radical revision or obsolescence (and Brooks would in fact turn to the historical epic in 1981, in *The History of the World: Part 1*).

As we have already seen, though, while parody film more or less by definition requires an established textual or generic framework to pre-exist it, the period of dormancy is no longer seen as a requirement for it to work. Indeed, the relative contemporaneity of a film like *Airplane!* with the 1970s airport-disaster cycle it so effectively parodied suggests that parody's force and topicality lies in its *closeness* to its targets. The possibility that parody should have any critical function, of course, depends on the persisting verisimilitude on the part of the parodied text or genre. *Life of Brian* turned out in fact to be quite timely, following as it closely did on the heels of the epic television mini-series *Jesus of Nazareth*, the Anglo-Italian co-production directed by Franco

Zeffirelli, which was first screened in 1977. It is important to understand the Pythons' 1970s film and television work in light of prevailing trends in British film and television production, and *Jesus of Nazareth*, though filmed for television, was symptomatic of a large-scale, mixed-funding and big-budget approach to film production that was seen by some as the most economically competitive strategy for British cinema at that time. In a significant blurring of the distinctions between the parody and the parodied source, both *Jesus of Nazareth* and *Life of Brian* were shot in Tunisia, with the latter actually employing many of the same locations Zeffirelli had used, and in some cases specially constructed, for his film. Prior to filming, in fact, there was a debate within the Python camp whether or not their film should actually make the connection more specific by being titled *Brian of Nazareth*.[51]

Once again, this highlights the extent to which ideas of verisimilitude were central to the concerns of the film, though we also need to identify the specific ends to which such verisimilitude is employed. *Life of Brian*'s most overt piece of extraneous inclusion is the sequence in which Brian, chased by Roman soldiers and falling to his death from a rooftop, is inadvertently picked up by a passing alien space craft being pursued by another ship. This abrupt intervention of another film genre is in an obvious sense a nod to the recent emergence of the sci-fi genre as Hollywood's dominant spectacle (after the success in 1977 of *Star Wars* and *Close Encounters of the Third Kind*); and therefore, oddly, an assertion of what actually constitutes the big-screen 'norm' at the end of the 1970s. But its incongruity is also strategic, deflecting as it does the fact that the film's eventual return to first-century Judea – when the space ship crashes, and an unscathed but dazed Brian remerges – is not a return to reality, but to another cinematic construction of reality, an artifice that is only realistic within the terms of its specific and differentiated generic system. And it is this system in particular that *Life of Brian* at once exploits and parodies.

Work on the historical epic film since the 1970s has identified the complex ways in which this genre operates: at once critically despised for its 'aesthetic extravagances' and 'bad taste',[52] yet at the same time seen as having a powerful impact on our popular cultural conceptions of history and the past,[53] to the point where, 30 years after *Life of Brian* was made, Burgoyne's study of the genre can begin with the assertion that it 'has played an exceptionally powerful role in shaping our culture's understanding of the past'[54] largely through 'its ability to establish an emotional connection to th[is] past'.[55] Burgoyne is writing here in light of the epic film's renaissance through films such as *Troy* (2004), *The Passion of the Christ* (2004) and above all *Gladiator* (2000), which have revived and re-shaped the cultural importance and reception of the genre. One view would identify developments in CGI, and its capacity to create virtual land- and cityscapes, as a key factor in the genre's re-emergence. But this would hardly account for why the technology should be turned to this particular genre, so long out of favour, unless we accept Vivian Sobchack's earlier, influential claim that it is precisely the 'extraordinary plenitude' of the epic film[56] – the kind of visual scope that CGI has rendered both more practical and affordable to film producers – that enabled it to grasp our popular consciousness and speak to our sense of the historical event.

When *Life of Brian* shows us the Sermon on the Mount, the camera tracks and zooms back from the initial image of Kenneth Colley's Jesus, over the heads of the assembled multitude. This elaborate shot, to follow Sobchack's reading of the genre, seeks a sense of historical magnitude through an equivalent impression of cinematic scale. Likewise, the long shots that precede this sequence, of crowds walking across the barren landscape to the surge of an orchestral score, invoke a sense of historical weight through their impression of effort and vastness. The titles that punctuate this series of shots, beginning with 'JUDEA A.D. 33', evoke what Sobchack calls the 'portentous calligraphy introducing us to History writ in gilt and with a capital *H*',[57] only to be parodically undermined as the 'Historical' significance of this (fairly general) place and time gives way to further specifics: 'SATURDAY AFTERNOON'… 'ABOUT TEA TIME'. Such interventions serve a realist function, drawing attention to the way the contingent and arbitrary moment of the represented past, or in other terms the everyday, comes to stand metonymically for the historical event in itself. Notably, only the intervention of the last two titles here divert what may otherwise fit entirely within the terms of the epic film's generic verisimilitude: the impression, in other words, that the multitude in themselves can express the significance and magnitude of one point in history. The scene that follows continues this approach, when at the end of long shot away from the speaking Jesus, the watching Mandy comes into focus, as she yells at Jesus to 'speak up!' As much as such a gag is targeted at the logistics of addressing a vast crowd in a desert, it is also in turn targeted at the formal logic of the epic crowd scene itself, where sound and visual editing convey the impression of the voice as capable of improbable clarity and scope, binding the audience on- and off-screen within its power and importance.

This representation of the multitude plays a significant role throughout the film. *Life of Brian* appears to mock the collective fervour of messianic belief and, in its compulsions, its inconsistencies (Follower: Hail, Messiah! – Brian: I'm not the Messiah! – Follower: I say you are, my Lord, and I should know, I've followed a few!). It does this through a specifically generic mise-en-scène of the crowd, of the mass, starting with the pursuit of Brian into the desert, and culminating, in a surprise reveal, with the massed throng discovered waiting outside Brian's bedroom window. Brian's point-of-view shot sees a crowd that, while not of thousands, extends to, and in theory beyond, the cinematic frame. As Kristin Whissel has reminded us, such uses of deliberately overwhelming crowds, literally flooding the horizon of the screen, have since the earliest feature films served as a means of 'represent[ing] historical change on a massive scale'.[58] We have already identified the importance of mythic-national figures to a sense of national and historical identity, though here, following Sobchack's lead, the emphasis is on the historical event as cinematic image: as Whissel notes, in films as varied as *October* (1928), *Triumph of the Will* (1935) and *El Cid* (1961), the display of the human multitude embodies, metonymically more than symbolically, 'a renewed sense of national identity' and 'the unification of previously fragmented people and the arrival of a new era of ideological and national consolidation'.[59] It is worth noting, moreover, that in their intended viewing circumstances such films might also invoke a strong sense of collective belonging amongst the public gathered in the cinema to watch the film.

The specificities of the film's compositional elements here, its attention to a type of generic verisimilitude, remind us once more how *Life of Brian*'s critical parody is less some mode of generalised 'real world' attack, than it is a specific targeting of the modes of cinematic realism and its consequent ideological value. In the 'dialogue' between the multitude and, respectively, Mandy and Brian, the rather pointed joke about mass consciousness (Brian: 'You're all *individuals*!' – The Multitude: 'YES. WE'RE ALL INDIVIDUALS') is secondary to the bigger, cinematically reflexive joke concerning the improbability of the unified mass and its collective voice.

2.3 The parodic mise-en-scène of historical verisimilitude: the faithful multitude in *Life of Brian* (1979)

Much of the comedy in this scene comes from the way this voice gradually assumes the language and inflections of an intimate duologue, prompting and responding on cue with an absurd precision (Mandy: 'Do you promise?' – The Multitude: 'WELL…OKAY'; Brian: 'I've got a couple of things to say' – The Multitude: 'TELL US! TELL US BOTH OF THEM!'). Eventually the incongruity of this perfect back-and-forth dialogue is underlined by its descent into the call-and-response rhythms of English pantomime (Mandy: 'Oh no he isn't' – The Multitude: 'OH YES HE IS!'). Typically for this film, though, and in a similar way to *The Holy Grail*, the more obvious gag, and its highlighting of the incongruous and absurd, only reiterates the point that the context is *already ridiculous*. If we do not initially laugh at the ability for this gathered throng to speak as one voice, it is possibly because, at first, its speech is less particular and informal than it is general – 'Behold, the Messiah! – but it is also because such representations of the mass as a single, unified body are at first glimpse credible within the parameters of generic verisimilitude: a verisimilitude, the sequence goes on to suggest, that conceals a highly problematic ideological value.

Such comic strategies indicate then what is really exposed as 'silly' in the Pythons' best film work: the capacity of popular genre cinema to obviate its own artifice, and more pertinently, its ability to sublimate violence and ideology to spectacle. The re-release of *Life of Brian* in 2004, with Mel Gibson's

The Passion of the Christ still very fresh in the memory, may well have been an attempt to cash in on the latter film's unprecedented success. But *Life of Brian*'s all-singing, almost-dancing mass crucifixion finale – with its famous chorus of 'Always Look on the Bright Side of Life' – does not exactly turn the 'straight' Christ film on its head. Much of the publicity around Gibson's R-rated film focused on its extreme representations of violence and suffering on the part of its titular protagonist, suffering that, nevertheless, drew in huge audiences (the film grossed over $600m worldwide), making it 2004's least likely blockbuster. What, after all, is more potentially strange than the idea of tortuous, ritualised death as a key part of mainstream cinema: a wide-screen, Technicolor tool to elicit pity, wonder and spiritual succour in equal measure?[60] From this viewpoint, *Life of Brian*'s 'silly' ending merely makes explicit what, though admittedly in a very complex way, is already to an extent present in the biblical epic, both in the distant and more recent past.

Conclusion: Where Does Parody Begin?

Consistent throughout the Pythons' film work, then, is this exploration of the absurdities and paradoxes already latent but concealed within popular cinematic genres. Despite their apparent 'silliness', the films are a corrective to the idea that parody texts take what is natural and normal and simply overturn that for comic purposes. This type of view overlooks the way parody can work to expose the constructedness of such 'natural' forms. Let's return then to the point of departure, and the sequence from *The Meaning of Life*. Happy as we might be to smile at the incongruity of impoverished urchins careering in full-throated song down Victorian streets, singing about the joys of conception, how was it that the all-singing-and-dancing spectacle of mass poverty and child malnutrition – what we see, in fact, in a film like *Oliver!* – became so much part of our 'normal' cinematic mind-set that it required parodying at all?

3

History and Hysteria: *The Charge of the Light Brigade*, *Royal Flash* and *Ripping Yarns*

'The past', as L.P. Hartley famously wrote in *The Go-Between* (1953), 'is a foreign country. They do things differently there'. When Hartley began in this way his classic novel of innocence and experience, set during the summer of 1900, he might not have anticipated just how this idea would take root in the decades that followed. Nor would he have been in a position to determine the various ways this eloquent sentence could be re-interpreted and re-packaged. What I think Hartley meant was that the late Victorian past, reachable mostly through distant memory and imprecise images, was so indistinct as to be another place altogether: an alternate England of increasingly indecipherable rituals, actions and motivations. At the same time – and as much British film and television from the 1970s and onwards would indicate – an idea of the past not just as different, but exotically, even *reassuringly* different from our present, would exert a considerable force on audiences.

The focus of this chapter will be the ways in which certain texts, mainly from the end of the 1960s to the late 1970s, explore this question of the past's difference. Focusing mainly on two films – *The Charge of the Light Brigade* (1968) and *Royal Flash* (1975) – and one series of short films for television, *Ripping Yarns* (BBC, 1976–79), and looking at these works alongside other films and television shows from the period, I will consider the way such texts explore the cultural and political significance of the national past in the contexts of their times. As we will see, this period in question, in terms at least of British history and identity, is notable for the complex ways in which the past signifies: at once a source of fascination and anxiety, of pride and shame, of celebration and critical retrospection. Given its ability to evoke the form and feeling of the past and its art works, and in the same gesture call them into question, parody is well placed as a mode for representing the ambivalence of the age. Indeed, one of my main points will be that these films, far from offering a straightforward and unilateral critique of the past, are in fact themselves frequently ambivalent and complex.

I have chosen to look at these particular texts because of the series of associations linking them. These associations are partly inter-textual, sharing as they sometimes do prior texts as points of reference. In this specific context, though, the network of allusion and association across the films is mainly as a form of cultural resonance. The two films are linked predominantly by their reference to a shared past; in this instance, the early Victorian era. Notably, in the end of the 1960s and the decade that followed, the heyday of Imperialism is revisited as the sun, finally, sets on it. The British Empire is less explicitly, though also unavoidably, the main backdrop for *Ripping Yarns*, written by the *Monty Python* partnership of Michael Palin and Terry Jones, and starring Palin in all nine episodes. Given its illustrious origins, *Ripping Yarns* has received surprisingly little academic attention, beyond fairly journalistic accounts of its development and reception.[1] My main contention here is that *Ripping Yarns*, like the other films discussed in this chapter, is highly revealing of the complex ways that imperial history figures in it. In addition, it – like the other films that preceded it – proves illuminating with regard to the content and themes of English film and television in the ensuing decades, and the projection of Englishness as a cultural product both domestically and globally.

Re-viewing the National: 1970s cinema

The volume of recent criticism concerning British cinema of the 1970s has been invaluable in its efforts to rethink, if not necessarily the quality, then at least the cultural pertinence of the films in question. The question of national identity is central to these discussions: this was a time when the country's position on the world stage and the influence of its cinematic industry was severely undermined, but also a period that saw a significant questioning of dominant ideologies. As Sue Harper, in one recent collection of essays on 1970s film, puts it:

> An attractive way of thinking about the 1970s is that it was a period when the innovations [in personal life] of the 1960s – experienced by a few – were assimilated by the many [...] On the economic side, it's important to recognize that the 1970s was a period of extreme economic uncertainty in Britain [...] What is certain is that the older, stable definitions of class ascription were transformed in the 1970s. The culture of deference was in terminal decline [and] the older sexual order was transformed too [...] These, combined with acute economic instability, produced a society where little could be taken for granted.[2]

The decline of Empire may not always be at the foreground of this cultural change, but what comes through in a number of films of the period is the extent to which the social and ideological underpinnings of Empire – religion, the private education system, the military, attitudes to race and gender, the idea of 'Britishness', or more accurately, given the regional and cultural specificity of most of its representations, Englishness – are the intrinsically related targets of critique. The British Empire in this sense becomes a wider symbol for a network of associations all very much pertinent to the contemporary climate.

The process of decolonisation that had begun after World War II, principally with the partition and independence of India in 1947, had continued throughout the 1950s and 1960s, with the majority of Britain's former colonies, mainly in Africa, achieving independence. Needless to say, the traces of decolonisation were still present into the 1970s. As Dominic Sandbrook observes, this decade was characterised by an extensive revisiting of the Imperial past in works of social history and historical fiction. But just as significantly, this past was visible by its absence; the ways in which, in espionage novels such as John le Carré's *Tinker Tailor Soldier Spy* (1974), the headquarters of British intelligence, a symbolic axis point for Britain's global reach (and as late as the 1960s, in the first James Bond movies, still a polished and confident site of British power), were shown as run-down and badly organised: 'a shabby, peeling relic, steadily slipping into dereliction'.[3] This was a period when, as one character from le Carré's novel put it, 'Englishmen […] trained to rule the waves' had found it all 'taken away',[4] the once mighty Empire now consisting of tiny islands such as the Seychelles and the Falklands.

Just as significantly, the mid-point of the 1970s, which saw the production of *Royal Flash* and the first series of *Ripping Yarns*, was marked by an acute economic crisis whose wider effects had already been felt by the British film industry. Part of the reason why many 1960s British films seem so buoyant and popular is not so much because England was really 'swinging', but because it was being bankrolled by American movie producers keen to be part of a scene the American media had helped define.[5] By the early 1970s, though, as Robert Shail puts it, 'the American majors had seemingly fallen out of love' with Britain.[6] British production consequently saw a significant decrease in American investment, its corollary being a drop off in British films exported to the lucrative US market.[7] Britain's most significant contribution to international cinema was from this point (and to an extent, the Warner Bros. *Harry Potter* franchise [2001–11] being a case in point, still is) its status as a cost-effective site for Hollywood production, making use of British technical personnel and studio space. So it was that a film like *Star Wars*, the most commercially successful and most culturally impacting film of the 1970s, came to be made in England – at the same time as the UK's Labour government requested a bail-out loan from the International Monetary Fund.

Working out exactly what this means for the production of film is, though, not a straightforward task. As Harper rightly adds there is no natural or necessary correlation between 'the cycles of cultural production' and 'economic and political' ones,[8] and we should be wary of assuming that cultural products always reflect their contexts, either directly or obliquely. From the viewpoint of this book, we also need to be attentive to the complex and often limiting ways that nationality, and questions of national identity and culture, can be mapped onto something as multi-faceted as a big-budget feature film, shaped as it is by numerous economic forces and designed for varied constituencies of viewers. For example, 1976 saw the release of *The Eagle Has Landed*, produced by the English media mogul Lew Grade's ITC, based on the novel by Jack Higgins. A very strange film to watch now, *The Eagle Has Landed* reminds us how unwieldy the 'British' feature film can be in this decade. Stiffly directed by veteran American director John Sturges, who alternates between inert dialogue scenes and clunky helicopter shots of landscape, *The Eagle Has Landed* blends forms of documentary authenticity (the film begins with a strident narration, over actual black and white footage, recounting Hitler's efforts to rescue Mussolini in 1943) and a procession of British and American stars (Michael Caine, Robert Duvall, Donald Pleasence) dressed as Nazis. The film reworks the Ealing wartime film *Went the Day Well* (1942) in its story of German paratroopers infiltrating a Norfolk village, with the aim of kidnapping Winston Churchill. As Ruth Barton has discussed, behind this rather awkward façade (the paratroopers led by Michael Caine's intense Kurt Steiner manage, of all things, to wear German uniform underneath their disguises) is a complex mesh of cultural and historical contexts. The film's casting of Caine as both romantic and sympathetic suggests, Barton argues, a shift in historical attitude towards Germany and those who served the country during the war,[9] while the film's reference to British concentration camps in South Africa during the Second Boer War serves as a revisionist reminder 'that such institutions were not invented by the Germans'.[10] Consequently, Barton sees the film within the terms of other war thrillers of the decade, all of which worked to 'explore the cracks in the social fabric occasioned by the end of imperialism [...] and the shifting definitions of national identity that accompany social and historical change'.[11]

While it is legitimate to trace social and historical change via tendencies in a range of contemporary movies, such arguments nevertheless may occlude such films' status and function as popular *entertainment*. The impeccably-tailored, almost dandyish Nazi has in recent decades become such an emblem either of comic derision or of postmodern pastiche (witness Christoph Waltz's Oscar-winning turn in 2009's *Inglourious Basterds*) that it is almost impossible to look at Duvall's eye-patched, Russian-cigarette smoking officer without smiling; but this ironic modern viewpoint cannot account for the responses of contemporary audiences, nor the film's actual intention. Nor does Donald Sutherland's casting as a mostly drunk and apparently mercenary IRA member, hoping to unite Ireland at the expense of the 'bloody British Empire' (though only at the bequest of the highest bidder), suggest a drastic revision of Imperial ideology during a decade of renewed IRA activity on the British mainland. But it is above all the specifically material context and nature of *The Eagle Has Landed* that is most significant here; the fact that such a film, and such a story, should represent the global ambitions of an English cinema producer in the 1970s: a strangely unbalanced amalgam of history and pulp, of England and Hollywood.

If *The Eagle Has Landed* is not intentionally a parody, it inevitably lends itself to parody as a result of its excesses and incongruities (and as I shall discuss below, *Ripping Yarns* parodies a similar story to critical effect). As outlined above, though, there is an elusive element to the film that places it within the uneasy, questioning terms several critics have identified in the cinema of the 1970s. This chapter will identify certain 'structures of feeling' or ideological concerns across a range of texts, that encourage us to see them not simply as reflecting, but actively negotiating conceptions of cultural identity via particular aesthetic strategies. If Harper initially suggests that this 'is a cinema which [...] is easy to parody',[12] she goes on to point out the extent to which films of this period are already positioned tentatively between confident assertion and self-mockery:

> 1970s British cinema seems to be one which displays a mix of irony and deliberate awkwardness at the level of script, *mise-en-scène* and acting style [in films such as] *Monty Python and the Holy Grail*, *Zardoz*, *Royal Flash* and many others [...T]heir makers seem to want the films to function as a form of social play. Or to put it another way, it is a ludic cinema which foregrounds irony – that state of mind which evinces both belief and denial, and which simultaneously yearns and mocks.[13]

It should already be obvious that this idea of a text that simultaneously, and with an evident tension, both 'yearns and mocks', may draw on parodic modes. As I discussed in my introduction, parody frequently affords its viewers the pleasure of enjoying certain forms in the same gesture as (notionally) distancing us from them, or holding them up to critique. The key question here, though, is why, and to what ends? As I will suggest, texts such as *Ripping Yarns* and *Royal Flash* perform this double function, encouraging their viewers 'to imagine two contradictory things at once'.[14] What makes these particular texts so intriguing – and why, on the same score, they cannot be reduced instrumentally to simple reflections of contemporary cultural circumstances – is that they play this game with the same thing that, as apparently derisive comic fictions, they are presumed to be targeting: the character, narratives and ideology of the British Empire.

Boy's Own

As James Chapman notes, the national tradition of adventure stories, largely celebrating the endeavours of heroes within Imperial settings and contexts, is oddly positioned within British film studies. While consistently among the most commercially popular types of film between the 1930s and the 1960s (also the high point of classical Hollywood cinema), what Chapman calls the adventure or 'Boy's Own' film has rarely been the focus of critical attention. As Chapman argues, the main reason for this may be that such films do not fit into either of the critically dominant criteria of 'realism and quality'; added to which, the politically conservative tendencies of these films seem to prohibit their potential for 'transgressive pleasures'.[15] From this point of view, and paradoxically, the Boy's Own film has a kind of occult quality within British cinema. It is a popular genre and one which, because of its subject matter, perennially focuses on 'stories of heroism, patriotism and duty',[16] and is therefore amongst the most national and mythical of genres; at the same time, it is disavowed, repressed or ignored by the critical forces shaping ideas of 'national cinema'.

Ripping Yarns, a televisual-filmic reflection on the cultural memory of such 'Boy's Own' culture, emphasises the importance of this 'repressed' genre. The first film, 'Tomkinson's Schooldays', is a public school tale set just before World War I. Other shows from series one include a World War I prison-escape tale, 'Escape from Stalag Luft 112B', and 'Across the Andes by Frog', a story of intrepid Edwardian exploration in South America. The shorter second series (1979) includes 'Whinfrey's Last Case': a spy story set in 1913 that nods clearly to John Buchan's Richard Hannay novels, as well as *The Eagle Has Landed*; and 'Roger of the Raj', about a young Englishman torn between duty and radicalism within the privileged society of British India. My focus with regard to this series will be its precise relationship to this 'Boy's Own' genre, one that is at once disavowed *and* central to the popular imaginary of the pre- and post-war years.

The relationship of *Ripping Yarns* to the popular representations, and in turn ideologies, of Imperialism are perhaps more complex than we might assume. An online blurb for a recent BBC television show exploring what it called the 'real *Ripping Yarns*', for instance, described the original series as a 'loving parody of the Boy's Own books and magazines of [Palin and Jones'] childhood', going on to describe the present show as 'celebrat[ing] a long-lost slice of Britishness' in the form of such literature.[17] The familiar and, as we have seen, problematic associations of 'loving parody' suggest here a much less stringent representation of the colonial imaginary than, I think, *Ripping Yarns* actually offers, yet the uncertainty inherent to the oxymoronic term is once again shared by the text in question. This is because the essentially *nostalgic* quality hinted at in the above description is one that is at some level shared by the series itself: especially, as we will see – and in a similar way to *The Holy Grail* and *Life of Brian* – through its attention to close visual and verbal detail, its nuances of performance, and overall approach to design and mise-en-scène. Yet the simultaneous emphasis on parody requires us to accommodate and negotiate these uses of nostalgia. From one point of view the antagonistic terms of 'loving parody' might collapse into the possibility of pastiche, and its apparently neutral recycling of genre and form; but this is inconsistent with the very marked nature, as we will see, of *Ripping Yarns*' engagement with Imperial ideologies.

It is important to come to terms with these complexities if we are to make proper sense of *Ripping Yarns*, and especially if we are to avoid the historical trap of seeing the show as vaguely representing the contemporaneous contexts of British post-imperialism. Reflectionist interpretation of this nature would hardly account for the specific nature of *Ripping Yarns* or any other text. Even within the terms of the more revisionist attitudes of decolonisation, we can still question the value and significance of this particular mode with regard to the subject, especially if – as may be the case in this instance – such modes treat this subject with ambivalence.

English Cinema: Global Audience

Equally, we need to be aware of the industrial circumstances and motivations underpinning these texts. Though, as a BBC television series of the 1970s, *Ripping Yarns* is institutionally set up in formal distinction from its big-screen counterpart, the BBC considered these filmed plays a 'prestigious' enterprise that ultimately had to be cancelled on the grounds of cost.[18] The series therefore aimed at the highest possible audience and eventually, like *Monty Python's Flying Circus*, would also be syndicated on US television. Taking the feature films out of their particular contexts to make a point about their representational strategies, meanwhile, would situate them misleadingly outside the broader trends and economic imperatives that determine them. This is especially significant in the case of *Royal Flash*. The film was directed by Richard Lester, the American filmmaker whose honorary 'Brit' status owes mainly to his association with The Beatles (as the director of *A Hard Day's Night* [1964] and *Help!* [1965]), but also through his work on films such as *The Knack* (1965), *How I Won the War* (1967) and *The Bed Sitting Room* (1969): all of which, in part because of their main actors (including John Lennon, Rita Tushingham, Peter Cook and Michael Crawford), are now synonymous with 1960s English cinema. Lester filmed *Royal Flash* from a screenplay by George MacDonald Fraser, author of the *Flashman* series of novels (1969–2005), of which *Royal Flash* was the second.[19] Fraser's novels, collectively entitled *The Flashman Papers*, fictionally chronicle the career of the Rugby School bully who tormented the eponymous hero of Thomas Hughes' *Tom Brown's Schooldays* (1857). *Royal Flash* narrates how Harry Flashman – played in the film by Malcolm McDowell, a prickly English screen icon from his earlier work with director Lindsay Anderson (*If...* [1968] and *Oh, Lucky Man!* [1973]), as well as his starring role as Alex in *A Clockwork Orange* (1971) – is captured by the young Otto von Bismarck and made to stand in as a double for a Danish Prince suffering from 'a social [that is, venereal] disease'.

In these respects, *Royal Flash* appears to be as English as Harry Flashman himself. However, though placed by Harper within the contexts of British cinema, from many perspectives *Royal Flash* hardly constitutes a 'British' film (let alone an English one) at all. To a significant extent, the film's 'Englishness' is merely as a commodity for domestic and export value. Big productions such as *Royal Flash* suggest the assumed currency of an English theme and identifiably English, or more widely British, personnel on board (the film also starred Alan Bates and Oliver Reed); as indicated, also, by productions from the same year such as *The Man Who Would Be King*, based on Rudyard Kipling's story of the same name, set in British-governed India and starring Michael Caine and Sean Connery. Notably, from a production point of view, both films, albeit in the 'post-classical' sense of the word, are *Hollywood* movies: *Royal Flash* was produced by Twentieth Century Fox, and *The Man Who Would Be King* by Columbia Pictures. Even the earlier *Charge of the Light Brigade*, though more clearly identifiable as an English film through its subject matter, its director (Tony Richardson), and stars from English theatre and screen (Vanessa Redgrave, Trevor Howard, David Hemmings, John Gielgud), was a co-production between the English company Woodfall and its Hollywood distributing partner United Artists.[20] Given that 'culturally English' cinema mostly operates through systems of co-production and distribution deals, nit-picking over the finer points of film funding and naming is slightly beside the point: more important is to identify the kinds of global aims and expectations underpinning these financial and production strategies.

As an extremely expensive production, aided by United Artists' input of $6.5m, *The Charge of the Light Brigade* carried with it hopes of big commercial success, based partly on its premise as an epic war film, but also as a piece of historical Victoriana. As an interesting precursor of the type of cinema (and television) product that would, in international terms, largely define British productions in subsequent decades – and which I discuss later in this chapter –financers were beginning towards the end of the 1960s to invest in classic literary adaptations and costume dramas. *Far from the Madding Crowd* (1968), based on the Thomas Hardy novel and starring Julie Christie and Terence Stamp, two English actors who in some respects epitomised the 1960s English 'scene', was viewed by its backers MGM as a 'roadshow film',[21] essentially a precursor of the 'event movie' or 'blockbuster' production strategy that was becoming preeminent in Hollywood.[22] The significant and similar investment on the part of United Artists clearly suggests they hoped *The Charge of the Light Brigade* would be their 'blockbuster' in 1968, but this also implied that a specific type of English literary-cinematic product was in mind. The eventual film has as its central focus the disastrous, mismanaged assault on Russian forces by the titular Light Brigade in 1854, during the Crimean War. The film's title alludes both to the earlier Warner Bros. film, directed by Michael Curtiz in 1936, and Alfred Tennyson's 1854 poem commemorating the event. The actual charge in Richardson's version, however, only takes up a small amount of the film, with the rest given over to a detailed and fiercely satirical study of British Victorian military life. As Mark Connelly has documented, it was the seeming hesitation in the film between the epic and the satirical that led partly to the film's mixed critical reception and – crucially for its makers and producers – lack of commercial success in America, whose interest in British historical themes had seemed to make the film a strong proposition.[23] As the recent film-historical work on the 1970s has identified, nostalgic period films, and the production values associated with costume drama and literary adaptation, had assumed an important (or desperate) role for a beleaguered British cinema industry trying to court American audiences.[24]

By the end of the decade, thanks largely to the impact of *Star Wars*, the big-budget blockbuster had come both to dominate international markets and consolidate a model for future Hollywood production. Yet the 1970s was for the most part also a period of economic hardship and risk for the transforming and indebted Hollywood major studios.[25] While this partly explains the withdrawal of wider economic investment, with its consequent impact on English film production, it also accounts for the varied and in some cases short-lived efforts on the part of these major studios to exploit different types of product, including, in this instance, the English historical movie. Identifying these films in purely 'critical' or 'revisionist' terms, then, would belie their status as transnational products aimed at international audiences, for whom historical themes and settings are in theory an *attraction* as much as a subject for historical interrogation. That Lester and MacDonald came to be making *Royal Flash* at all, in fact, may owe something to their previous collaboration on the lavish, starrily-cast and highly successful period adventures *The Three Musketeers* (1973) and *The Four Musketeers* (1974).

English Film and Television and the Aesthetics of Heritage

An important historical framework both for these films, then, and also for *Ripping Yarns*, is the wider film and television traditions of period and costume drama. The aesthetic but also ideological appeal of the past, as a country that is both exotically different from our present and at the same time contained, manageable and reassuring, underpins what Andrew Higson has described as a 'heritage' aesthetic in British cinema and television. This is mostly synonymous with a tendency in production during the 1980s, especially in terms of those films produced and directed, respectively, by Ishmael Merchant and James Ivory, including *A Room with a View* (1985) and *Maurice* (1987), and could also include other E. M. Forster adaptations such as the David Lean-directed *A Passage to India* (1984), as well as television literary adaptations such as *Brideshead Revisited* (ITV, 1981) or *The Jewel in the Crown* (ITV, 1983). As Higson argues, 'heritage' cinema 'may be seen as a relatively conservative and nostalgic attempt to turn away from contemporary realities and seek an image of national stability in some golden age of the past'.[26] This is achieved partly by the way these films tend not to offer any apparent alternatives to the world represented or the mode of representation. This structural endorsement of the 'reality' of the films' screen world is supported by a largely pictorial aesthetic that displays the traditions and properties of the dominant (upper) class of these texts, in a way so as to enhance their aesthetic splendour: these films, then, despite often representing 'golden ages... that were already crumbling' (as, for example, in *The Jewel in the Crown*, based on Paul Scott's novel) obviated these historical contexts by 'display[ing] the attractions of the heritage, including the heritage of cinema, with its own conventions of artistry and glamour'.[27] Such cinematic 'heritage' and 'conventions' would include the privileging of star actors, and/or those associated with the classical theatre, together with a strong emphasis on period art design and costume, authentic country-house settings and lush cinematography.

Higson is keen to point out that the heritage aesthetic was not invented in the 1980s, only 'exploited on a massive commercial scale' at that point in time.[28] Received understanding of the heritage cycle and, more broadly, what Robert Hewison called the 'heritage industry',[29] locates the nostalgic turn with 1980s Thatcherite politics. Led as it largely was by politically left-leaning cultural critics responding unfavourably to these popular films, the notion of an actual 'heritage film' as mode of practice has been criticised, viewed in this regard as a retroactive concept imposed on a more disparate and less ideologically-loaded set of texts.[30] That the heritage aesthetic could be inferred from a series of prior texts nevertheless indicates some form of commonality; and more intriguingly, one less obviously associated with conservative ideologies or Conservative politics. As Sandbrook argues, the interest in aspects of English past and nostalgia emerged most evidently in the previous decade, indicated partly by television shows such as *All Creatures Great and Small* (BBC, 1978–90), *The Onedin Line* (BBC, 1971–80) and *Upstairs Downstairs* (ITV, 1971–75), but also by the backward-looking tendencies of much film production of the time, as in *The Eagle Has Landed*, *Murder on the Orient Express* (1974) and *The Thirty Nine Steps* (1978), the third (and in this instance, de-hyphenated) film adaptation of John Buchan's book.[31] Sandbrook's historicist desire to read his culture in question via a handful of texts is somewhat self-serving, but as we have seen, the fact that at a famously low point in the British film industry producers should turn to 'nostalgic escapism' and 'patriotic derring-do'[32] suggests a lot about what such producers assumed to be the contemporary national inclination.[33] The assumption that the appeal of heritage was unilaterally tied to the front guard of political reaction, furthermore, underestimates the way that the return to the values of the past, and especially to ideas of 'the land', bridged political inclinations during the 1970s. The nascent ecological movements of the decade, for example, may have both informed and been informed by the fascination for Arthurian and Tolkeinian mythology, though as Sandbrook pointedly notes, the eco-politics of *Lord of the Rings*, with its Edenic rural opening in The Shire, and even the pre-technological rabbit-world of Richard Adams' hugely successful *Watership Down* (1974), 'came with more than a hint of old-fashioned conservatism';[34] or in critic Alexander Walker's words, such works offered 'a cosy idealisation of England's past [...] where everyone had their place in the warren and kept to it'.[35]

Such contexts for a series like *Ripping Yarns* suggest to me that it is much more ambiguous and complex than it might instinctively appear – or at least, than we might *assume* it to be, based on the anecdotal assumption that it shares affinities with *Monty Python's Flying Circus*. If we assume that the show is at an oppositional pole to the later heritage film, purely on the basis that it pokes fun at Victorian and Edwardian class structure and moral codes, the Raj, and cultures and institutions of privilege, such as sports and boarding schools, we overlook the fact that *Ripping Yarns* is also *about* them, and encapsulates their fascination and often counter-intuitive hold over our imagination – a point reflected in the aforementioned tendency to see the series as ambivalently poised between mockery and affection. It is also important to work out some of the ways *Ripping Yarns* actually anticipates some of the aesthetic characteristics of 'heritage' film and television, or more precisely sits within a longer tendency of film and television depictions of the past.

Indeed, the most obvious textual framework for viewing and understanding *Ripping Yarns* is its opening title sequence, which turns out to be entirely free of parodic inversions, misdirections or exaggerations, and is therefore readable within the more neutral terms of pastiche. Here, a series of close, animated panning shots move over the various pages of a picture book, replete with images of adventure and 'derring-do': a man in a pith helmet punching an unspecified African native, armed with spear and shield; two men, possibly spies, hiding behind a hillock; a boy in cricket whites plucking a ball from the air. Finally the image moves out to reveal the cover of a book on a wooden school desk, the book's title, *Ripping Yarns*, becoming at the same time that of the show. Any questioning of these images and their apparent endorsement through the framework of this 'Boys' Own'-style book-within-the-show must logically come from a viewer's particular competences and viewing position; in other words, the perspective of someone 'knowing' or assuming this is a parody text, or who knows, from a position of political correctness, that such unquestioned images of adventure and play are shaped by the expectations and structures of class, privilege and Empire. But these are not attitudes *within* the opening sequence itself, to the extent that there is little – if anything – to distinguish here between a 'straight' representation of these nostalgic tales and a parodic take on them.

This brings back clearly into play the unspoken question raised by *Ripping Yarns*: to what extent is its pleasure predicated not so much on the *rejection* of its 'targeted' forms and values, but rather on the *complicity* with these same forms and values? Speaking from personal experience as a viewer of such films and television series in the 1980s and now, the heritage aesthetic may provide a variety of pleasures even for the viewer fully aware of its possible ideological connotations. My own very youthful response to these texts under discussion here, was, I recall, one of fascination and uncertainty: aware as I was of their being about the past, I could not so easily cut them off from this same past as I might do now. While clearly

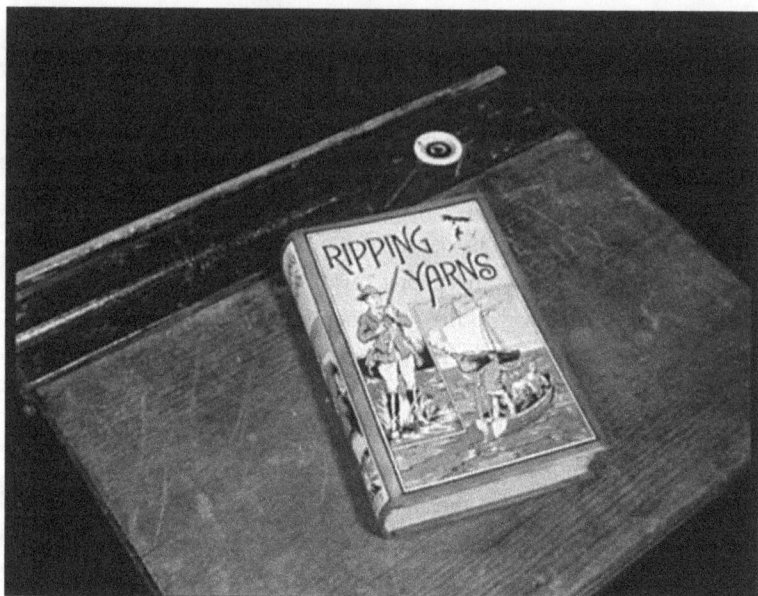

3.1 'Straight' parody? The title image for *Ripping Yarns* (1976–79)

seeing as an adult what strategies these works adopt with regard to their fictional world, my childhood ability to discern parodic distance from the closeness of historical representation was less well formed: what I now take for parody, in other words, I once saw as the 'real'. This suggests to me that we cannot dismiss the effects of such films out of hand, nor forego such effects even within the terms of parody. A significant way of approaching *Ripping Yarns* will therefore be to identify the way it often works through and within paradigms of 'heritage' viewing pleasure, in ways that encourage us to think more carefully about the nature of its parodic performances.

Post-Imperialism and the 'Parodic Turn'

Adopting a detailed analytical approach is also important if we are to distinguish a show like *Ripping Yarns* from other texts of the period, with which the series might find itself aligned. *Ripping Yarns* can be located, for example, alongside the notional 'turn' in the James Bond series of films, away from confident fantasies of classless consumerism (embodied by Sean Connery's performance as 007), and towards a more self-effacing tone (via Roger Moore's more camp Bond), highlighting the incongruity of the Bond persona in the more economically and politically troubled contexts of the mid-1970s.[36] It has become something of a received idea that the Roger Moore Bond movies offer purely 'escapist' rather than 'aspirational' images of identification,[37] and tongue-in-cheek takes on British imperial dominance; epitomised by the pre-credit climax to *The Spy Who Loved Me*, which sees Bond effecting a high-altitude escape using a Union Jack parachute. As Robert Shail has argued, the tendency for such sequences to highlight 'ingenuity and wit', rather than exploit the mechanics of 'tense excitement', has the effect of 'push[ing] the audience out from identification and involvement in the narrative'.[38]

As Shail suggests, what stops this constituting an actual self-parody of the Bond series is that there is no specific 'real world' target here, meaning that even the jokey extremes of the 1970s films are entirely contained within their own cinematic system. Shail may equate parody too closely with satire here, and overlook the point that parody of cinematic genre is itself a type of engagement with the 'real world', given genre films' ideological power. The more obvious point is that such moments, their display of 'ingenuity and wit' notwithstanding, are still sufficiently integrated into the narrative not to seem to comment disparagingly *on* those same narratives; indeed, ingenuity and wit in acts of daring escape or pursuit are precisely hallmarks of the 007 screen brand.

A similar issue relates to *Raiders of the Lost Ark* (1981) and its more immediate sequels (*Indiana Jones and the Temple of Doom* [1984], *Indiana Jones and the Last Crusade* [1989]), which in their historical pastiche style are in many respects close relations of both *Royal Flash* and (especially) *Ripping Yarns*. As James Chapman and Nicholas Cull note, *Raiders of the Lost Ark* was at the time of its release widely celebrated as a 'homage' to an older and often forgotten Hollywood, in its allusions to Rider Haggard's 1885 novel (and more specifically, film adaptations [1937, 1950] of) *King Solomon's Mines*, as well as 'B' movie colonial-era adventures and weekly serial productions.[39] Notably, and like the 1970s Bonds, *Raiders of the Lost Ark* integrates its elements of inter-textuality within a storytelling structure that often demonises, disregards or generates humour out of the foreign 'other', in a way that potentially, for all its pastiche style, reiterates an Imperial mythology. The exploits of the American archaeologist-adventurer therefore risk playing out not so much a nostalgic fantasy as 'a narrative of US intervention...[that] effectively endorses the plundering of religious artefacts and cultural treasures of the Third World to support the geopolitical interests of the United States'.[40] In other words, at few if any points does the series call into question or undermine the authority of its American, white male hero.

If this highlights the problem of making overly-simplistic comparisons between texts, the example of the *Carry On* series would also indicate the problem of making comparative assumptions through context. As Chapman and Cull note, the popular British series also reflected issues of decolonisation in the late 1960s and 1970s, in films such as *Follow That Camel* (1967) and *Carry on Up the Jungle* (1970), parodic takes on the *Beau Geste* and *Tarzan* films respectively. As already noted, the Python team were keen in their film of *The Holy Grail* that they did not simply make 'Carry on King Arthur', but this is arguably more than just a reflection of stylistic concerns. It is a neglected aspect of the *Carry On* series that its interest in historical or semi-mythical figures made them at some level a source of 'knowledge' for the young viewers who grew up watching them (I again include myself here, acknowledging films like *Don't Lose Your Head* [1966] as my first contact with the history of the French Revolution). But the ideological implications of this knowledge remain questionable if, as is the case in these films, the focus is as much on the exaggerated and often uncomfortable comic mileage derived from the representation of foreigners, especially the knowing jokes around names and religious or cultural traditions, via characters such as Mustapha Leak and Khasi,[41] both of whom appear in *Carry on...Up the Khyber* (1968). More significantly, viewer identification in these films is in theory oriented around the anachronistic 'everyday' personas of actors like Sid James and Jim Dale,[42] whose presence roots the experience of the films from a contemporary perspective of cultural difference. Engagement with the foreign or the Imperial past is consequently placed firmly on the other side of what Chapman and Cull call an 'imagined community of humour' that relied on 'nationally specific slang'.[43]

Given that *Ripping Yarns* explores a similar fictional terrain as these films, and even draws on comparative points of reference, it begs the question what this particular series does differently; and indeed, to what extent it avoids the ideologically problematic bind the *Carry On* films place themselves in. Because it plays so overtly with archetypes, and indeed stereotypes, of the Imperial past, *Ripping Yarns* inevitably flirts with reiterating its ideologies, in similar ways to the *Carry On* series. Episodes like 'Across the Andes by Frog' and 'The Curse of the Claw', for example, both play up representations of ethnicity (dozy Andean villagers and a priapic Burmese tribe, respectively) that, while not intrinsically plumbed for comic mileage in the *Carry On* vein, at least make rather uncomfortable viewing by contemporary standards. This may partly have to do with the fact that these characters are often played by various non-ethnic actors in a way now embarrassingly familiar to us from other television comedy of the 1970s, in series such as *Mind Your Language* (ITV, 1977–79) and *It Ain't Half Hot Mum* (BBC, 1974–81).[44] While it is impossible to 'correct' an essentially institutional characteristic of 1970s British comedy, we need to consider how (if at all) *Ripping Yarns* manages to get around its potentially problematic representation of the foreign 'other'.

Royal Flash is certainly in appearance very close to *Ripping Yarns*, and it is notable that these contemporaneous works both engage, implicitly or very explicitly, with one particular text. As already noted, the eponymous (anti-)hero of the *Flashman* novels is the older manifestation of Harry Flashman, the infamous bully of Rugby School's fifth form in *Tom Brown's Schooldays*. Hughes' book, as its title suggests, is an obvious influence on 'Tomkinson's Schooldays', which features its own chronicling of public school ritual and routine, as well as its own self-designated School Bully. In its subject matter and casting, *Royal Flash* also indicates its affinity with both *The Charge of the Light Brigade* and *If...*. Set in an expensive contemporary boarding school, *If...* aims to make clear rhetorical points about the anachronistic nature of the public school system in its emphasis on traditional, repressive modes of educational and disciplinary regimes. As such, it looks in many respects like a period film (and 'Tomkinson's Schooldays', if not actually referencing *If...*, inevitably shares much of its iconography); a point further reinforced by the allusion to Rudyard Kipling's famous poem 'If –' in the film's title.

Revisiting History

The Charge of the Light Brigade, Royal Flash and much of *Ripping Yarns* all exemplify then a type of post-Imperial text through their efforts to revisit aspects of British history over which, in principle, recent events had drawn a line. But they also establish a critical dialogue with other filmic representations of this past which, while already removed from that past in time, found themselves by the 1960s further removed in light of contemporary critical discussion. The previous film version of *The Charge of the Light Brigade* is distinguished from its successor not just by the ideological and narrative demands of classical Hollywood and the star system (the film, one of several period-adventure collaborations between Curtiz and his star Errol Flynn, represents the Charge as having a justified and heroic moral purpose), but by later developments in historical criticism. Cecil Woodham-Smith's *The Reason Why* (1953), her reading of the Charge as a tragedy of chronic mismanagement and the idiocies of the class system, was a main source of inspiration for the later film. In the same way, as Derek Paget has shown, the disposition toward historical revisionism in 1960s culture was determined partly by the 'new histories' emerging in the academy during this time. Paget refers specifically to three key works on the history of World War I – Leon Wolff's *In Flanders Fields* (1959), Alan Clark's *The Donkeys* (1961), and Barbara Tuchman's *August 1914* (1962) – which were all used as research material for Joan Littlewood's 1963 Theatre Workshop collaboration *Oh! What a Lovely War*: the satirical musical about Britain's entry into World War I, which was subsequently filmed by Richard Attenborough in 1969. As Paget suggests, the longer-term impact of these popular histories (along with the screening of television documentary series such as BBC's *The Great War* [1964]), and also an increasingly post-modern sensibility towards historical representation, is 'a *knowingness* about history'[45] that finds its more recent flourishing in equally revisionist series like *Blackadder Goes Forth* (BBC, 1989). For Paget, the latter series, possibly because it was the only *Blackadder* to have a photographically documented context for its fiction, best exemplifies what he calls the 'veritable force-fields of intertextuality' such shows set up 'through their spoofs on superseded ideas and ideologies'.[46] Paget draws attention here to the way *Blackadder*, and I would suggest also the films and television series under discussion in this chapter, are constantly alive and attentive to the work of prior representations and their ideological value; to the point, in fact, where ideology becomes the subject itself.

The main focus of *The Charge of the Light Brigade* (scripted by Charles Wood, who also wrote the screenplay for Lester's *How I Won the War*) is the culture and politics of the 11th Hussars, Lord Cardigan's impeccably tailored cavalry regiment, who would play a central role in the ill-fated charge. The Cardigan of the 1968 film, played by a suitably red-faced Trevor Howard as a splenetic and perennially randy boar, excruciatingly and violently obsessed by etiquette and fastidiousness, finds a similarly caustic depiction in the first of the Flashman novels, when Flashman has his first military posting in the Hussars. Cardigan would in fact return in the fourth Flashman novel, *Flashman at the Charge* (1973), with his lordship upholding the reputation established for him in Richardson's film: in this case, by being found in bed with Flashman's wife. Appropriately for a character who, in the introduction to his memoirs, refers to himself as 'a scoundrel, a liar, a thief, a cheat, [and] a coward',[47] Flashman's most notable act of the Charge, besides being in the minority that survive it, is to surrender the moment he crosses Russian lines.

As Andrew Sanders reflects in his introduction to *Tom Brown's Schooldays*, 'it is perhaps significant that [Tom's] story should have stimulated such antipathy in the twentieth century and that the one participant in his destiny who has been vigorously resurrected should be Harry Flashman'.[48] That a novel like *Tom Brown's Schooldays* should be a target for counter-cultural ire may, as Sanders notes, be a rather unfortunate fate for a novel whose main interest – through the depiction of Thomas Arnold, the real-life headmaster of Rugby, and father of Matthew Arnold – is that of political reform and the role of education in moral and spiritual development. The 1940 Hollywood adaptation of the novel, effectively a biopic of Arnold, actually begins with the novel's conclusion, as an older Tom visits Arnold's tomb in the school chapel. The problem is that the 'public' legacy of the so-called public school had lost much if not all of its more liberal connotations by the 1960s, partly explaining why, in a film like *If...*, it comes to function as a microcosm of class hierarchies, and the protection of tradition and national insularity; very much in line, in fact, with Arnold's vision of public schools as models of a ' "miniature England" [...] on which future patterns of justice and social order could be based'.[49] It is interesting to note, in fact, how the ideologies of a book like *Tom Brown's Schooldays* find their echo not just in more direct parodies such as 'Tomkinson's Schooldays' but also in the other films under discussion. As Connelly observes, the idea of old school connections and dynasties, of 'inheritance of service and dedication' to that same service, are depicted in an entirely straight fashion within the more heroic terms of the 1936 *Charge of the Light Brigade*.[50] If the later version explores the debilitating and catastrophic consequences of such inheritance and dedication, *Royal Flash*'s superannuated school bully represents the slightly different but equally grotesque consequences of deferring to this system reluctantly, in this case through cowardice and toadying.

If... sees a violent and distinctly non-conformist type of action, embodied by McDowell's Mick Travis, as the natural response to such models of the nation during the period of decolonisation. It is in turn keen to identify militarism as the natural corollary of the public school mentality (and hence Travis's fateful dismissal of a prefect's military service colours as 'that bit of wool on your tit'). One of the things that makes *Tom Brown's Schooldays* such an interesting text for parodic revision is the way it frames its disquisition into moral being and the future generation of the English ruling classes through a focus on 'play', most prominently in the game of rugby football to which Tom is so forcibly introduced on his first day at school. Hughes in fact on two occasions describes the game through visual allusions to war: first, to a battle fought between Wellington's English and the French,[51] then to an attack by Napoleon's Old Guard at Waterloo.[52] What is most striking, though, is the way such apparently sublimated military movement is underpinned by the promise of reward, and its romanticism seen as an analogy for youthful development, all in a tone whose ripe sense of enjoyment characterises the tension between affection and ridicule we see throughout *The Charge of the Light Brigade*, *Royal Flash* and *Ripping Yarns*:

> Meet them like Englishmen, you School-house boys, and charge them home. Now is the time to show what mettle is in you – and there shall be a warm seat by the hall fire, and honour, and lots of bottled beer to-night, for him who does his duty [...] This is

worth living for; the whole sum of school-boy existence gathered up into one straining, struggling half-hour, a half-hour worth a year of common life.[53]

Two Opening Sequences: *The Charge of the Light Brigade* and *Royal Flash*

As I have said, the historical revisionism at work in these texts also needs to be seen in light of prevailing fashions, and above all, the potential attractions of period, theme and style to the films' global audience. *The Charge of the Light Brigade* is consequently a work strangely in tune with the often paradoxical cultural tendencies of the time. As Connelly notes, the late 1960s in England was a period infused as much with a sense of conservatism and nostalgia as it was with the counter-cultural and left-wing agenda that is its more common (though rather stereotypical and metropolitan) association; a combination Connelly summarises as a conjunction of 'patriotism and modernity' that 'merged to create the original Cool Britannia.'[54] More specifically, the 'look' of *The Charge of the Light Brigade* was as much representative of 'Swinging London' style as it was an attempt to recreate a lost period of the past: how different, Connelly asks, was the film's fascination with the Hussar's regalia from the Beatles' experiments with bygone military fashions in their *Sgt Pepper* phase of 1967?[55]

As Neil Sinyard observes, discussing Lester's second Beatles movie *Help!*, the film's script, co-written by Wood, is suffused with motifs of the British Imperial past (mock-Oriental and Germanic villains, references to Captain Scott and James Bond), creating a satirical vision of the ephemeral nature both of Empire and pop culture, to the point where they become blurred: 'Britain's contemporary cultural phenomenon keeps coming into collision with an evocative array of allusions to Britain's national heritage. The ghosts of Britain past, present and future flicker through the fabric of the film.'[56] For Lester, *Help!* was apparently a pop-art take on Wilkie Collins' novel *The Moonstone* (1868), a detective story about a mysterious South-Asian jewel and the efforts of three Indian devotees to retrieve it. Watching *Help!* today, which opens with the English actors Eleanor Bron and Leo McKern made up and talking in the guise of Indian cult worshippers, is a somewhat awkward experience, though its largely parodic take on *The Moonstone* invites us to

3.2 An appropriate level of parody? Eleanor Bron and Leo McKern, and their human sacrifice to the goddess Kaili, in *Help!* (1965)

reflect on whether a more realistic take on Collins' novel – fully immersed as it is in the orientalist imagery and ideologies of the British Empire – would be a more suitable, indeed 'realistic', treatment of the subject. *Help!*, in other words, asks whether parodying the historical, Imperial representation of the past and the foreign is the most decent thing to do. Yet *Help!* reveals a deeply ambivalent relationship to its Imperial past. Alexander Walker describes the way both Lester and Wood 'shared an *affectionate mockery* of Britain's imperial past':[57] such a movement between affection and mockery, as already suggested, lies at the heart of these various films' complex efforts to integrate historical revisionism with popular appeal. Following his work with Lester and The Beatles, Wood went on to bring this same ambivalence to his script for *The Charge of the Light Brigade*.

This ambiguity, however, contributed to the mixed critical and commercial reception of the finished film. Many critics at the time responded positively to the film's gorgeous production values, especially its attention to 'the sense of period style';[58] though often the same critics felt confused by its focus and coherence, split as the film apparently was between its qualities as 'adventure epic' and its 'bitterly ironic comment'.[59] The focus on period detail in the costumes and art design (the film had its own

'Colour and Period Consultant', Lila de Nobili), brought out through David
Watkin's impressionistic cinematography, as well as a narrative interest in
the practice and adventure of war (through the character of the idealist and
romantic Captain Nolan, played by Hemmings), gives the film an earnestness and lush sense of the past that is often difficult to reconcile with its
more caricatural aspects. The most prominent of the latter are a series of
animations by Richard Williams that run throughout the film, and which,
drawing on the stylistic iconography of nineteenth-century magazines
such as *Punch*, provide images that are powerfully evocative of the idea of
Victorian energy and endeavour (the raising of the Crystal Palace), while
also, to more contemporary eyes at least, embodying fiercely xenophobic
and disproportionately violent attitudes (A pack of British Bulldogs, for
example, tearing apart the Russian Bear).[60]

The Charge of the Light Brigade moves, therefore, between virulent
critique and nostalgic celebration, and is indicative of the complex ways
parody can function both as a form of historical representation as well as a
productive and morally engaged criticism. As already seen with *The Holy
Grail*, this fascination with the past, or more specifically, with representations of this past, needs to be recognised in our reading and understanding
of this same past. From an ethical perspective, this process is important
precisely because it admits the possibility of the past's attraction to the
present; but recognising this attraction is part of the way we understand
the ideologies of the past, and why such structures of feeling and belief
'worked' in the first place – and in turn, why they now need analysing and
critiquing.

This explains why so many of the texts in question skirt so close to the
edge of pure pastiche, flirting with the very ideologies they are in principle critiquing. The illustrations that give *The Charge of the Light Brigade*
its emphatic start have a clear stylistic precedent in the cartoons of the
nineteenth-century journal. What gives them their force is largely the
effect of transcontextualisation (to use Hutcheon's term), in which the aesthetic and ideological norms of another historical context are as it were
foisted into another: the incongruity produces the jolt that often produces
laughter, and/or the recognition of difference on the part of the contemporary reader or viewer. The film's initial animated sequence has the apparently helpless nations of continental Europe – represented by the French

3.3 England's sleeping lion rises at the beginning of *The Charge of the Light Brigade* (1968)

cockerel and the Austro-Hungarian Empire's double-headed eagle – witness the Russian Bear's ravaging of (a) Turkey, before turning imploringly across the channel in appeal to England's sleeping lion. As the first, slow phase of the musical introduction reaches a crescendo, the lion awakes, now filling the whole frame. As the key changes from minor to major, a triumphal refrain heralds the woken lion as it puts on – somewhat absurdly, given its characteristic shape – a policeman's helmet.

Following this, we have a symmetrical image with the various machineries of war: cannons and cannonballs on either flank, with lances, flags and swords helping to produce a wing-like composition. At once the title of the film is imposed on the image, while a couplet, 'The trump of fame in clarion strong / Their dauntless deeds shall vibrate long', is displayed along the bottom. Such images have a literal, performative function here: the music and image combine to form an audio-visual 'clarion' whose emotive effect is the 'vibration' of heroic endeavour. As if to demonstrate this, the image shifts to another symmetrical composition of the female embodiment of Britannia (we note that the images in the sequence indiscriminately conflate England and Britain), flanked this time by steam locomotives and symbols of trade and industry (a merchant ship on the left; the recently-finished Crystal Palace on the right), this time with the unfurled inscription 'Britannia encourages the industry of the globe'. The specific political target of these illustrations is subtly embedded in the progression from one image to the next. A chorus of female voices (who would have had no vote in the contexts of the 1850s) takes up the refrain. We now see a line of belching chimneys, followed by a cross-section of a mine: here, in a rhythmic, repetitive illustration of manual labour, we see women (their appearance a visual echo of the voices), and also children, bent by the tunnel, repeatedly filling their carts with coal to power the previously-seen smokestacks. What is unsettling here is that this shot does not disrupt the narrative flow of the images in their depiction of Britain's industry and, as here also implied, appointed role as generator of international trade and global policeman. Exploited labour is here aestheticised to form a harmonious piece of the overall vision, a vision that becomes structurally and hence emotionally transparent to us; but also one that, through its relocation within contemporary contexts and judgments, is also targeted and condemned. This rhetorical approach in the opening sequence prescribes the tone for the film as a whole.

The *Flashman* novels are an interesting comparison here for the way they also articulate a type of obvious-yet-unspoken Victorian ideology. On one side, the narrator of *Royal Flash* can inform us that his status as a war hero, having 'taken a distinguished part in the fiasco known as the First Afghan War', was achieved despite the fact 'that [he] had gone through the campaign in a state of abject terror – lying, deceiving, bluffing and running for dear life wherever possible'.[61] At the same time, Flashman's self-deprecating assessment of his own valour is consistently offset by his self-satisfaction in reaping the benefits of his unwarranted reputation ('They were the golden days [...] The ideal time to be a hero is when the battle is over and the other fellows are dead, God rest 'em, and you take the credit'[62]). Moreover, any idea that the narrator's scepticism towards British institutions is an indication of progressive thought is frequently undercut by a brash political ignorance and casually xenophobic jingoism:

> I grant you things are a bit slack, here and there, and my wife
> has remarked that good servants are getting damned hard to
> find. But if you think England's in for revolution, you're well
> off the mark. We leave that sort of thing to Frogs and niggers.[63]

We cannot discount the possibility here that part of Flashman's appeal is an essentially infantile pleasure in saying what can't be spoken, to the troubling extent that he echoes an only partly-repressed Imperial cultural memory.

What in my view stops it from being offensive is its consistency with the narrator's voice in general, and with this, a sense of excess and plain idiocy. Flashman's views are stated in such an obviously unacceptable and unreasoned way that it is hard to take them seriously, even if we recognise that *he* probably does. What emerges through this mode of double address is a type of historical, critical text. We read through the eyes of a character expressing what we may now recognise as the ideologies and beliefs of his time, in a way that would not be so evident during these previous times, when such ideologies were couched in the narratives of popular myth.

Fraser understands the palimpsestic and dialogical nature of this parodic approach, identifying as he does in an appendix to *Royal Flash* an alternative narrative for Flashman's adventures, in the form of Anthony Hope's 1894 'Ruritanian' novel *The Prisoner of Zenda* (twice adapted into Hollywood films, in 1937 and 1952). This is not just a nod to a literary borrowing (though *Royal Flash* does openly make use of *Zenda*'s very similar plot), but rather a playful indication of the limitations and omissions of earlier, fictional texts, and their ideological construction within their own cultural and historical contexts. As I've already touched upon, the 'remake' of *The Charge of the Light Brigade* has a similar purpose, not just in its dialogue with the ethos of Tennyson's famous poem, but also with the 1936 film, which – as one made within the ideological currents of the 1930s and the Production Code – could not have entertained the same level of frankness and criticism. The 'forcefields of intertextuality' described above in relation to *Blackadder Goes Forth* are already emerging here in what is the formative period of postmodern cinema, where the weight of our wider cinematic knowledge and film-historical consciousness is brought to bear on our efforts to represent the past; to represent it, that is, both through and beyond the density of textual allusion via which we attempt to read the past in the first place.

Like *The Charge of the Light Brigade*, the opening of the film of *Royal Flash* shows its awareness of the Victorian context, but also the work of cinematic representation in constructing an impression of the past. The film opens with a close up on McDowell's face, as he tells firstly us (a direct look to camera), and then, as the camera tracks back, to an off-screen audience, to 'play up and play the game', 'say your prayers' and 'take a cold bath every day', in order that we might 'look the world in the eye like an

English gentleman'. At this point, a reverse-shot reveals the listening hall of schoolboys, while a subsequent low-angle shot from the side reveals the white light softly illuminating the hall through great arched windows, a similar use of architecture and chiaroscuro to that which begins the 1940 film of *Tom Brown's Schooldays*, with its divine associations of holy light and the grave of Thomas Arnold. There is possibly a direct allusion to this in Fraser's script, in the way Flashman, reaching the climax of his speech, interweaves God and school, faith, patriotism and warfare, in a hyperbolic mix of metaphors: 'When the last roll call comes, you'll be able to go up to the Great Headmaster with a clean British conscience and say, "Well, Sir, I tried to do my duty!"'

Such hyperbole charges metaphor in a way that becomes too over-loaded to be workable; a stylistic choice here that is further reiterated by the use of a huge British flag behind the stage (one which echoes the simi-lar, and to an extent similarly ironic, use of the Stars-and-Stripes in a scene from the biopic *Patton* [1970], about the famously uncompromising and profane American general), as well as the sound of the 'Land of Hope and Glory' refrain from Elgar's 'Pomp and Circumstance': once more, we see that Britain and its diverse qualities are subsumed in the film within a very particular idea of *Englishness*. This tone is not sustained for long, however. Just as he did in the *Musketeers* movies, Lester exploits the ways sound and image in film can be combined for incongruous comic effect. As Michael Hordern's headmaster intones the legacy of Flashman's military achieve-ments (a summary of the first novel), a flashback sequence shows the actual events, with Flashman panicking before the Afghan attack on Piper's Fort and banging at the door to get back inside, his high-pitched squeals of 'Let me in!' undercutting the headmaster's praise. This more obviously parodic use of juxtaposition establishes much of the tone for *Royal Flash*, with its comic swipe at British military self-perception.

Such nuance is not always sustained throughout the film, though. Following Flashman's various narrow escapes from the insidious efforts of his Prussian captors, for example, *Royal Flash* insists on the narrative trope of good fortune, but it also implicitly affirms the idea of a particu-lar British genius for escape, pursuit and seduction – all of which bring it much closer to the contemporary Bond films than we might ordinar-ily suppose.[64] If *Royal Flash* really is a film defined by its post-Imperial contexts, it begs significant questions about the particular nature of response to these contexts: in other words, to respond to them by mimicking the same fictions, myths and motifs that shaped the Imperial narrative in the first place. Notably, the grey area between parody and a more neutral pastiche is underscored here by the film's meticulous production design, use of striking European settings, and a visually gorgeous use of suffused light in the cinematography: *Royal Flash* was photographed by Geoffrey Unsworth, who in films as varied as *Cabaret* (1972) and *Superman* (1978) showed a capacity to evoke fabled cities (pre-war Berlin) or mythical ones (Metropolis) through a subtle use of light and colour combined with opulent set and costume design. The effect in *Royal Flash* is to connote a painterly rendering of a European golden age, criss-crossed by carriages and galloping steeds (a very similar look, in fact, to that created by cinematographer Ghislain Cloquet and director Woody Allen in *Love and Death*, Allen's parodic take on the Great Russian Novel, also made in 1975).

As discussed in the previous chapter, a possible way of reading this fascination with look, with the details of art and costume design, with the particular textures of photography or the peculiarities of language, is that the film is not so much interested in historical reconstruction and the pursuit of period authenticity, but is a stylistic exercise around the idea of verisimilitude and 'authenticity' itself. As I argued with reference to *The Holy Grail*, the effort to find a suitable photographic register for the film, as much as it allowed the film to engage meaningfully with the geographical and social realities of its depicted period, also indicated an inevitably limited set of parameters marking the (im)possibilities of recording the medieval past. Similarly, the effort to find a visual register to evoke the mid-nineteenth century in both *The Charge of the Light Brigade* and *Royal Flash* is inevitably an effort to represent this period through existing visualisations: images, such as portraiture, painting and the stilted forms of early photography, that are themselves already inscribed semiotically with the very values – patriotism, propriety, the celebration of masculine courage and virtue, homosocial space – that the films are also critically exploring. Such images and modes of representation are also by necessity received in a transcontextual form, requiring us to see them from the perspective of contemporary attitudes and values.

This is an optimistic reading, though, and it is difficult to establish within the ideological work of the narrative fiction film at what point cinematic aesthetics actually subsume dialogue and mediation, becoming in effect the context themselves: this, in fact, is Jameson's issue with the pastiche sensibility, in terms of the way such 'blank' imitation of past forms erodes the historicity of the art work. Sinyard ultimately sees the ambivalent aesthetic of *Royal Flash* as a problem, as 'in dealing with a superficial hero and a superficial society, the film runs the risk of seeming superficial itself'.[65] Indeed, *Royal Flash* relies on a certain knowingness that may or may not be shared by its viewers, but more problematically – not unlike the contemporary James Bond films or the *Carry On* movies from which *Royal Flash* is only superficially distinct – the film's often 'blank' parody borders on a reiteration of the same values it notionally critiques. Arguably this absence of didacticism and unsettling ambiguity make the film, like the novels it is derived from, a very potent indicator of the complex period of decolonisation. As Sinyard remarks, though, it remains, possibly for these reasons, a film stuck in its time: 'In its international perspective, it reflects a crisis in national confidence. In its rather desperate and uncomfortable sense of what constitutes popular appeal, it reflects a crisis within escapist entertainment'.[66] This may explain why, though the film remains something of a cultish enigma of the 1970s, it was a significant box-office flop.

Ripping Yarns: Ambivalence as Critique

As suggested by its opening titles, which distil the world into the pictures of a Boy's Own adventure story, *Ripping Yarns* is a representation not of 'reality', but of representations themselves. It is about the past, and hence to some extent about a memory of, even nostalgia for, that past; though a past shaped and constructed through representations, and above all, cinematic ones. How it avoids the more problematic connotations of, for example, the *Carry On* films or *Raiders of the Lost Ark* is through its insistence on a very precise formal and stylistic representational system that in many respects – semantically and syntactically – tries to stay within clearly marked generic boundaries. The main difference between *Ripping Yarns*, then, and these other texts is its commitment to a type of generic verisimilitude. The complexity of the show is in the way it moves deftly both within and outside this representational system; firstly, by working within clear stylistic, structural and thematic parameters, and secondly, by the way these parameters and conventions are inscribed as past, as distant, via numerous markers of discontinuity. The series in this sense operates through the 'repetition with distance' Hutcheon identifies in parody.[67]

This idea of complicity *and* distance is important here because it underlines the way *Ripping Yarns* works: in this case, by communicating a sense of pleasurable engagement with its generic points of reference. The uses of parody in the show typically work through subtle inversions of an implied textual source or convention, but as with much parody the pleasure in these inversions cannot be separated from our own familiarity with, and possible enjoyment of, these same parodied motifs and structures. Put simply, if the parody of *Ripping Yarns* works, it is to some extent because we recognise what it is parodying; but part of its pleasure, consequently, involves acknowledging the form of these motifs or structures, and enjoying the new form in which they find themselves being shaped.

'Tomkinson's Schooldays', for example, frequently employs the pictorial style of obvious generic precedents, in particular the British adaptations of *Tom Brown's Schooldays* made for the cinema in 1951 and BBC television in 1971, and to a certain extent the Hollywood version of 1940. Like these, 'Tomkinson's Schooldays' affords its location shooting a significant amount of coverage: it is a distinguishing feature of *Ripping Yarns* that it commits to being shot on film with single cameras, rather than in the television studio (the exception being this opening film, originally a stand-alone show from 1976, which combined location with some studio filming). The series was therefore emphasising not just the types of national myths from which it drew inspiration, but also the heritage of cinema itself, making these aesthetic conventions a central part of the series' meaning. This privileging is especially apparent in the opening shots of the school buildings: shots which, as Higson identifies in the 1980s–90s heritage cycle of films, 'display ostentatiously the[ir] seductive mise-en-scène',[68] besides their narrative function as establishing shots.

Given the generic links both to *Tom Brown's Schooldays* and to Boy's Own serial fictions, we should also acknowledge the ways 'Tomkinson's Schooldays' shows its awareness of structure, even within the constraints of a 30-minute film. The capacity for serial and school narratives, both in prose and on screen, to provide a reflection of the school-age readers' own regulated and progressive experience is testified to by its pertinence up to and beyond the *Harry Potter* series, with its close association of the rhythms and progressions of school life with the heroes' broader life experience and challenges. In 'Tomkinson's Schooldays', for example, much mileage is had from the nuanced parodying of certain tropes, primarily those concerning repetition, ritual and discipline. The show starts with a series of inversions, as we are introduced to particular routines of school life. The opening voiceover describing the 'dour, forbidding place' of Graybridge School is accompanied by the sound of cane strikes, followed by the image of a row of boys (with Palin at the end) outside a closed door. Palin's voiceover as Tomkinson then reveals that the boys are waiting to beat the headmaster. (In a similar inversion, we later hear the assembled schoolboys being reprimanded for 'helping masters to escape'.) Following this, Palin's voiceover describes the ritual of Saint Tadger's Day, in which 'boys who had been at the school for less than two years were allowed to be nailed to the wall by senior pupils': subsequently, this outrageous premise is literalised, with the image of boys in crucified poses high above the school yard. As Palin pointed out in the recent BBC4 programme on the show, there is a subtle touch here insofar as this is not a punishment but a privilege ('were allowed to be'); a detail which, along with the inversion of the caning trope that begins the show, highlights the barely repressed masochism that we might say is inherent to 'Boy's Own' ideals of self-control and physical and mental endurance (indeed, the subsequent glimpse of the headmaster's morning prayers has him extolling 'Thy gift of discipline', explaining that it is 'only through the constraints of others that we come to know ourselves' and that 'only through true misery can we find true contentment').

'Roger of the Raj', meanwhile, while it has been discussed within the terms of the same 'spoof imperial adventure' as the earlier *Carry On* films,[69] is markedly different in its formal approach. A sustained five-minute central scene, in which an after-dinner table of regimental officers each commit individual breaches of social etiquette, incrementally from the ridiculous (passing the port from left to right) to the sublime (the desire to found a socialist republic), is a virtuoso piece of slow-burn absurdity, as the transgressors are politely asked by the host to do the decent thing: in this case, to go out into the next room and shoot themselves. Yet the derision

3.4 'Heritage' art design and mise-en-scène in 'Roger of the Raj', one of the BBC's *Ripping Yarns* (1979)

of outmoded norms of etiquette, here emphasised by the reiterative and disproportionate response, is most effectively conveyed through its formal restraint and, to a large extent, the realist conviction of its playing, all of which works to make the men's response seem justified within the terms of the fiction. This is enhanced by the lighting, subtly constructed around candles in the centre of the scene, and mostly by the framing of the sequence, which intermittently returns to a symmetrical long shot of the whole table – a shot that, in its detailing of costume, the accoutrements of the table and the dark wooden furnishings and walls, offers the kind of display of finery we would later associate with Raj-era drama such as *The Jewel in the Crown*. Such commitment to verisimilitude at the level of design and mise-en-scène is matched by the largely contained performance style, which plays as if each suicide were no more than an unfortunate but unavoidable outcome of circumstances; as well as the dialogue, that has one officer responding to the port-passing misdemeanour with the earnest injunction, 'Think of your wife, your children... Think of the regiment!'

It is this commitment to a consistent framework of representation, then, that enables the series to work, through the sense of 'complicity and distance' previously discussed. But it is also through this mode that the more problematic connotations of ethnic representation are offset, insofar as the protagonists are themselves part of the same representational system. In the aforementioned *Carry On* films, the idiomatic and frequently lewd reactions of actors like Sid James assumes a point of identification for English audiences, in turn normalising attitudes and responses from a contemporary perspective. In 'The Curse of the Claw', on the other hand, the Burmese tribe's sexualised gyrations before the titular claw are met only with fearful recognition on the part of Palin's elderly Sir Kevin, who consequently recounts his youthful encounter with the accursed limb. The claw's erotic power is in fact offset by the episode's undercurrent of Victorian sexual repression and innocence. Young Kevin grows up with a mother who knits herself a black stocking that covers her entire body; later, on board a transatlantic ship, Kevin experiences undefined urges towards the ship's Chief Petty Officer, whose revelation to Kevin as a highly sexual woman, though entirely obvious to the audience, appears a surprise to both parties.

'Whinfrey's Last Case' is also notable for the way it inverts generic motifs for parodic effect, while maintaining a consistent sense of style and atmosphere. Starting with a montage of sepia-tinted photographs, featuring the titular hero Gerald Whinfrey (Palin) in a variety of Empire-era scenes (piloting an early aeroplane; capturing big game, and so on), the episode goes on to depict Whinfrey's unwitting involvement in foiling a German bid to start World War I. Deciding he is tired of saving the country, Whinfrey takes a holiday in a Cornish cottage, only to find that it and the neighbouring village are in the hands of German agents, posing as house staff and bearded fishermen, the first step in their intended slow colonisation of Britain. 'Whinfrey's Last Case' at once acknowledges and inverts the same tropes of narrative improbability and unerring British heroism that are hallmarks of novels like *The Thirty-Nine Steps*. Here, the eponymous hero literally ambles into a ready-made espionage plot from which he actually fails to escape: only in this case, stereotypes of English courage and innate German cowardice are played up and parodied, as the entire German cohort surrenders en masse to the solitary, admired English agent.

111

As this suggests, the serious aspect of 'Whinfrey's Last Case' is to parody the assumptions of British military and intelligence supremacy on a global scale – in a decade, significantly, when such assumptions were the focus of keen debate. The episode in fact conflates the opening part of Michael Powell and Emeric Pressburger's satirical *The Life and Death of Colonel Blimp* (1943), a film very much focused on the tension between traditional 'sporting' attitudes to warfare and its modern realities, and the previously-discussed *The Charge of the Light Brigade*, much of which deals with the portioning and preparation of war as both a form of national-industrial enterprise and upper-class pastime. 'Whinfrey's Last Case' opens with a Whitehall-office discussion about the respective armed forces' readiness for war, focusing largely on the availability of suitable crockery and cutlery, and complaints to the effect that the Germans are planning to start the war 'too early'.[70] The same combined generals return at the conclusion to reveal that the Germans have finally specified an agreed and convenient date: 4 August 1914, the actual day Britain declared war on Germany. This forms a neat parallel with the ending of the earlier 'Escape from Stalag Luft 112B', about a legendary war escapee whose multiple efforts to flee the titular prison are 'tragically ended' (in the words of the film's narrative voiceover) not by his death, but by the armistice being signed.

In both this episode and in 'Whinfrey's Last Case', though, it is not just the idea of war as a game that is the subject of parody, but also the practices of a film-entertainment industry that, in an era of relative peacetime, continues to mine the mythology of British and Allied wartime endeavour to ideological and economic effect. As already discussed, *The Eagle Has Landed* was one of several British films from the period to draw on this wartime context, and its story of German infiltration of English village life is arguably an influence on the *Ripping Yarns* film. And as previously noted, the third film adaptation of *The Thirty-Nine Steps*, produced by Rank, came out at the end of 1978 (a year before the BBC screening of 'Whinfrey's Last Case'), and may also have been an influence.[71] Whether it was or not, significantly, this was the first of the film adaptations of Buchan's novel to depict the story in its original 1913 setting, making it at once the most loyal adaptation as far as the novel is concerned, but also the most overtly focused on the aesthetics of late-Imperial heritage.

Of course, as I have emphasised throughout this chapter, *Ripping Yarns* is itself not exempt from these associations. From one point of view, *Ripping Yarns* is not entirely 'parody' at all, inasmuch as its specific 'targets' frequently remain diffuse. But the more pertinent question concerns style. Even in more obviously targeted episodes such as 'Escape from Stalag Luft 112B" and 'Whinfrey's Last Case', the commitment to generic verisimilitude means that the referential and the reverential are difficult to segregate. A potential criticism of the series (or at least, a counter to its identification as parody) is that it often remains more within the terms of pastiche, which as we know – within Jameson's terms at least – would undermine its critical value. In the end, the significance of this distinction depends largely on whether or not we see pastiche in such 'blank' terms as Jameson, or recognise, as Dyer does, that our viewing of pastiche always involves some negotiation between the ideologies of past representations and our contemporary worldview. Whatever the case, any hesitation with regard to *Ripping Yarns* partly resides in the fact that its target 'sources' are more composite than specific, relating more to a type of broader textual and cultural imaginary than any one or even collection of texts. This raises a significant methodological point about how we should make sense of a series such as *Ripping Yarns*.

Conclusion: Parody as Re-Construction

Some might suggest that this approach encourages a 'misreading' of the 'intended' parody, or the failure to recognise it at all. But this would, on the one hand, refuse the legitimately varied viewing positions and different contexts in which the text can be read. Moreover, it would assume that the absence of appropriate knowledge could in effect neutralise parodic intent: a problematic argument implying that *Ripping Yarns* might be read as 'straight' period drama. This would overlook the fact that most viewers familiar, if not with *Tom Brown's Schooldays* or its associated fictional genre, but with the forms of television drama, not to mention any experience of school life, would recognise the inherent inversions and incongruities punctuating 'Tomkinson's Schooldays'. Or at least, the whole of *Ripping Yarns* 'generates a modality' of parodic expectation,[72] partly by its willingness to misdirect the viewer, but also by its contexts; in this case, a series by and starring Michael Palin, whose own frequently incongruous position in the form of multiple parts contributes to the way we receive the show.

The 'competent reader' view of parody is, as already suggested, no more than a projection of the critic whose aims go little further than ticking inter-textual boxes. Such an approach fails to acknowledge the possible ways parody can go beyond the overly-comfortable framework of parody production and reception – what Harries calls the 'snug' framework of ' "matching" competencies' between producer and reader[73] – where recognising the sources of a parody text establishes the sole horizon of meaning and expectation. Harries, for example, agrees with most theorists that some competence in the parody/parodied text's 'logonomic system' (the rules of genre, say) is vital to the appreciation of parody.[74] Yet *exactly* what readers get out of a parody text, Harries argues, is impossible to prescribe, just as it is equally difficult to place strictures on the range of authorial intention behind the parody. To apply this to *Ripping Yarns*, there can be no 'correct' reading, but in this particular instance the historical and cognitive distance from the 'sources' of parody make the possibility for any kind of 'preferred' reading even more unlikely.

One implication of this is that the *Ripping Yarns* films are not so obviously bound within a binary dialogue with a prior text or even texts, one(s) to which all readings must defer: a corollary of this is that the films also work self-sufficiently, promoting and constructing their own field and range of signification. Consequently, if I laugh at the incongruities, inversions or comic exaggerations of 'Across the Andes by Frog' or 'Roger of the Raj' – in my particular case, as someone who saw these films before seeing and identifying any obvious inter-texts – these films are also *constructing* the very mythology or historical narrative that they are notionally attacking. Through the same practices by which these texts exploit and make humour from the structures of Boy's Own-style narratives, they are also implicitly acknowledging the potency and charm of such narratives; possibly because these stories of containment and discipline find their fictional form in tales that are themselves neat, unambiguous and therefore – at some level – reassuring. And as we have established, it is precisely the reassuring nature of these bygone fictions, their nostalgia for the orderly world of the past, that makes them worthy of criticism, *because these fictions work.*

Like the other texts considered in this chapter, *Ripping Yarns* works through a form of doubled representation. It allows us to take pleasure in the narrative structures and iconography of its nostalgic representation, but at the same time, the practices of exaggeration and inversion point to its constructed and ideologically distant nature. It is in this process of marking distance from the parodied subject via its most potentially seductive elements (public school ritual, Victorian exploration, the decorum of gentlemanly conduct) that it effectively narrates a history of such traditions while also critiquing it. From this perspective *Ripping Yarns* may be construed as having its cake and eating it too, conveniently separating the formal content from the ideological context. Against this, I would say that it is precisely its closeness to its notional targets, its near fetishistic investment in the textures and worldviews of its subject matter, that gives the series its almost hysterical comic quality, hysterical in the sense that, like much of the most interesting comedy, *Ripping Yarns* makes humour from our own ambivalence to the world it depicts.

4

'The Shit Just Got Real': Negotiating Hollywood in *The Strike, Spaced, Shaun of the Dead* and *Hot Fuzz*

I began this book with two sequences from television comedy at the turn of the millennium, both of which drew on iconic images and scenes from the Hollywood blockbuster. The use of Hollywood to parodic effect is the subject of this chapter, though as we will see, exactly what we mean by the *parody* of Hollywood is not always so clear cut. As we saw in the introduction, referencing the narratives and motifs of the Hollywood blockbuster within the contexts of a Channel 4 sitcom might seem to assume a negative attitude towards this parodic subject; as I suggested, though, this is far from the case. In the case of both *Father Ted* and *Spaced*, there is an ambivalence that leaves the real target of parody, and the shows' relationship to Hollywood, uncertain.

If these two examples tell us anything, they indicate that the Hollywood blockbuster shapes our cinematic imaginary within the late twentieth and twenty-first centuries. As we will see in this chapter, the influence of Hollywood informs and structures some of the more successful English comedy film of the last two decades. What becomes more notable, though, is how this engagement with Hollywood assumes the role of a *global* exhibition strategy, as these English parodies circulate as international film products. This, I will suggest, is significant not merely for our understanding of popular 'English' film, but for our understanding of what parody actually does and means in contemporary cinema terms.

When, for example, *Hot Fuzz* was first screened in the UK in 2007, one of its publicity images showed the film's stars, Simon Pegg and Nick Frost, in a swaggering mock action-movie pose. Pegg, wearing the Aviator shades he puts on towards the end of the film, is carrying a shotgun and a pistol. Yet this is offset by the presence of Frost behind him in a British policeman's helmet, grounding the image in a specifically local context; one that it further inscribed by the tagline at the top: 'Big Cops. Small Town. Moderate Violence'. A similar image was used for the US release, but with significant differences. Here, Frost is also wearing sunglasses and has lost his hat, but gained a shotgun, and toothpicks have been placed dangling from both actors' lips. The UK poster's cloudy sky is replaced by a huge fireball, creating an overall image very similar to the poster for *Bad Boys II* (2003), an important reference point for *Hot Fuzz*. Underlining this connection, the tagline establishes very clearly the contexts through which the film is to be read: 'They're Bad Boys; They're Die Hards; They're Lethal Weapons; They are… *Hot Fuzz*'. The interesting point here is the way the Hollywood subjects of *Hot Fuzz*'s parody are used in the US context to sell the film to American viewers: the same American viewers, if we follow Harries' assessment of contemporary Hollywood parody,[1] who would also be watching 'straight' action movies.

This apparently counter-intuitive idea of Hollywood genre parody as a *way into* the global market of Hollywood films represents a significant shift in our idea of English parody film. *Hot Fuzz* is hardly unique in its uses of Hollywood tropes, and English film comedy in the light of the contemporary blockbuster's global dominance – particularly, since the beginning of the 1980s – has not turned a blind eye. But it has often been an inward-looking one, with little horizon beyond its domestic confines. The quality of films like *Morons from Outer Space* (1985), in which comedians Mel Smith and Griff Rhys Jones flipped the alien-visitor logic of *Close Encounters of the Third Kind* (1977) and *E.T.: The Extra-Terrestrial* (1982), or of *Lesbian Vampire Killers* (2009) – a horror comedy with James Corden and Matthew Horne (stars of the hit BBC show *Gavin and Stacey* [2007–10]) – might be an issue for debate. That hardly anyone outside Great Britain bothered about them, however, is beyond discussion; indeed, box-office figures suggest hardly anyone *in* Great Britain was bothered about them either. Why a film like *Hot Fuzz* avoided the same fate owes to a variety of factors, some of them to do with changes in the structures and attitudes of the British film industry. But as I will argue here, it also owes a lot to the specific relationship with Hollywood cinema – and, conversely, the English cinema that is its notional other – that the film constructs through its parodic techniques.

As we have seen, the often prevailing assumption that parody 'mocks' its targets has helped establish a largely divisive and critical view of parody's use. This is especially so when the parody is coming from the peripheries of global cinema production ('world' or 'national' cinemas), and when its apparent target is the dominant centre: in other words, Hollywood. This binary view underestimates parody's frequently ambivalent relationship to the same supposed object of derision. But just as importantly, it also overlooks the often complex negotiations contemporary non-Hollywood cinemas find themselves making with Hollywood itself, or the impact of the latter on our very ideas of the 'national'. If, as I will suggest here, 'Hollywood' is not so easily positioned to the side of contemporary 'non-Hollywood' cinemas, how do we understand the role of parody as participating in a construction of national cultural identity?

As I will discuss here, then, parody, within the contexts of 'culturally English' film production, acts as a locus for the various issues shaping 'national' cinemas within globalisation. In the examples discussed here, parody is used to highlight and explore a series of tensions: the tension between the imperatives of economic sustainability, and the maintenance of national or local specificities; between the pursuit of globally-exportable aesthetic models and the preservation of culturally distinct filmmaking practices. At its most reduced, then, this tension brings into focus the efforts to reconcile industrial and cultural frameworks for national cinemas within an increasingly globalised economy.

I have chosen to look at four texts made over a 20-year period and in different contexts of British film production. *The Strike* is a 1988 film co-written and directed by Peter Richardson as part of Channel 4's first *The Comic Strip Presents* series (1982–90). *The Strike* tells the story of a writer from a Welsh former mining town whose screenplay about the 1984–85 miners' strike is picked up by a British production team, bankrolled by an American studio. The film derives comic mileage both from its pointed jokes about British filmmaking tendencies of the 1980s, and the ideological and aesthetic characteristics of Hollywood cinema – exploited here through recourse to the film-within-the-film, here called simply *Strike! Spaced*, written by and starring Simon Pegg and Jessica Stevenson, and directed by Edgar Wright, was as we know screened on Channel 4 in 1999 and 2001. Pegg and Wright subsequently teamed up as co-writers, and as actor and director, on *Shaun of the Dead* (2004) and *Hot Fuzz*, with both films produced by Working Title. While I will look at the ways both *Spaced* and *Shaun of the Dead* make use of their various cinematic inter-texts, my main focus will be on *Hot Fuzz*, about a former Metropolitan police officer striving to restore law and order to a murderous middle-England village. In particular, I will consider the ways *Hot Fuzz*, in a slightly different way to *The Strike*, incorporates Hollywood genre cinema into its story, here in the form of the DVDs watched, and eventually imitated, by the films' two main protagonists: Police Sergeant Nicholas Angel (Pegg), and Police Constable Danny Butterman (Frost), both of whom are part of the police force in the (fictional) village of Sandford.

Two similar sequences from *The Strike* and *Hot Fuzz* give a useful indication of the points of continuity and difference between them, especially in terms of their engagement with Hollywood. Towards the end of *The Strike*, the writer, Paul (Alexei Sayle), drinks heavily from a whisky bottle while watching a trailer for the forthcoming film produced from his script. On the television, we see a tousle-haired, tanned actor, backlit by a low sun, calling out to an off-screen figure: 'You'll never get away with this McGregor!' In a reverse shot, his interlocutor, pointing a gun at the head of a man in a miner's helmet, responds: 'Take one day off work, Scargill, and this miner gets it'. When the miner calls out 'Strike, Arthur, Strike!' we hear a bullet fired, at which point Scargill falls on his knees, imploring the heavens in a similar gesture to that of the dying, bullet-riddled Willem Dafoe in *Platoon* (1986). Paul's horrified reaction to what he is seeing – a hysterically excessive fiction of the dispute between Arthur Scargill, leader of the National Union of Mineworkers, and Ian McGregor, the head of the National Coal Board – which sees him cover his eyes and turn with increased fervour to the whisky, would seem to position him synonymously with our own viewing position.

Halfway through *Hot Fuzz*, meanwhile, after an evening's drinking at the local pub, Angel and Butterman go to the latter's house and watch a double-bill of action movies, starting with *Point Break* (1991), followed by *Bad Boys II*.

As the pair drunkenly doze off, the film's editing nods toward the mixed and allusion-driven style that characterises the second half of film. In this instance, shots from *Bad Boys II*, with arcing cameras looping around actors Will Smith and Martin Lawrence, are intercut with parallel events elsewhere in Sandford, in the palatial house of a local kitchen-goods magnate. When the house subsequently ignites in a gas explosion, the words of Lawrence's character, responding to a narrative turn of events in his own film, voice those of *Hot Fuzz*'s ironically slumbering protagonists, if not ourselves: 'The shit just got real'.

Both these examples indicate the significance of American genre cinema to their narratives and comic imagination. But they also indicate very distinct viewpoints towards this subject. *The Strike* appears to place its audience in a specifically derisive and critical position towards the viewed film, while *Hot Fuzz* is more clearly ambivalent. *The Strike*'s internal film builds towards a face off, respectively, between Scargill and the militant miners aiming to blow up the Sellafield nuclear power plant, and then with the assembled MPs of the British House of Commons. *Hot Fuzz* moves towards a similar climax, in which Angel takes on Sandford's conspiratorial cluster of doctors, supermarket owners and pub landlords, who have secretly been killing off undesirable members of their community in order to preserve their 'Village of the Year' status. While it derives humour from mapping the Hollywood action response onto *Hot Fuzz*'s sleepy world, the editing in the above sequence integrates the action from *Bad Boys II* into the action of the film whose narrative we are following. The juxtaposition might amuse, but there is nothing inherently in the composition of the film at this point to suggest a critical standpoint on the part of *Hot Fuzz*: in narrative terms, the 'shit' really has 'got real' at this moment. As I will discuss in this chapter, then, these two diegetic viewing positions embody two different and very specific relationships to Hollywood cinema across the 20-year timeframe.

Realism, Parody, and the Binary Discourse of English Cinema

Studies of English and more broadly British national cinema in the contexts of the late twentieth and early twenty-first centuries are inevitably rendered complicated by the complexities of film production, both in terms of its origins (where is it from?) and its intentions (who is it for?). As a production of Working Title, the company that has successfully realised a globally exportable type of culturally English cinema, *Hot Fuzz* brings these key questions firmly into play. Recognising Working Title's achievement through films such as *Notting Hill* (1999), *Bridget Jones's Diary* (2001) and *Love Actually* (2003) is as much a recognition of commercial success as an artistic one. Any discussion of Working Title in the contexts of 'British' or 'English' cinema must also acknowledge the impact of major studio distribution deals – in this case, with Universal Pictures – on their global impact. Both factors raise the question of how the cultural and the economic interrelate within a national cinema culture.

Recent studies trying to answer this question have focused on the work of parody, and ironic, incongruous uses of genre, to establish a discourse of the national vis-à-vis Hollywood's dominant model. As James Leggott, for example, argues regarding the uses of genre in millennial British productions:

> [A] question relating to the deployment of genre concerns British cinema's oft-discussed commitment to realism, in terms of both a stylistic naturalism and a dedication to certain types of subject matter. This may well be the reason, coupled with budgetary confinements, why more fanciful types of filmmaking, like musicals and action films, have never taken root, other than in mocking (*Hot Fuzz*) or disguised form (*The Full Monty*).[2]

Leggott is, I think quite rightly, referring here to an acknowledged discourse of realism rather than prescribing it as the default mode for British cinema. It may in fact be legitimate to suggest that a realist agenda underpins much British cinema production and reception. But to emphasise in the same motion that this is in part a consequence of 'budgetary confinements' actually sidesteps the question of realism as an aesthetic commitment, and positions it as an aesthetic *consequence* determined by the economics of film production. Parody may be a stylistic approach to budgetary limitations, though in the case of *The Strike*, viewing its tendencies toward genre parody in this way would overlook its more pointedly political aspects of satire. Indeed, accounting for parody on the grounds of economic shortcomings problematically implies that such filmmaking practices would happily embrace the aesthetic models they affect to mock, given the resources.

Given this possibility, then, it is interesting that the quite generously budgeted *Hot Fuzz*, though making use of its greater resources in the construction of action sequences, is still operating in a mode of parody at all, given its potential to work in a more obviously 'straight' generic mode. The potentially judgmental terms of mockery also imply, again, an alternative and correct mode that disavows the more complex relationship of parody to its subject matter. We need to take a more considered view of the way parodic texts such as *Hot Fuzz* integrate and dialogue with their various inter-texts. But I would like to go further here, arguing that parody to a large extent undermines the binary relationship, the implications of 'our' cinema and 'theirs', that apparently sustains this discourse in the national context.

I will use as a model the conceptions of national cinema outlined, in several evolving contexts, by Andrew Higson.[3] Higson's work on the subject is characterised by its rigour with respect to the varied conceptions of 'the national' and what its persistence as a term means in the contexts – economic, cultural, political – of recent cinema production. As mentioned above, the problem in our efforts to pin down a working definition for a national cinema is that of reconciling often antagonistic conditions and demands. Higson identifies a range of potential interpretations of 'national cinema', seen respectively in terms of economics, exhibition and consumption, evaluation, and finally representation.[4] That Higson chooses to separate these readings as concepts 'mobilized in different ways, by different commentators',[5] indicates how difficult they are to cohere. As I will discuss, parody offers a way in which the competing demands and varied constituencies of national cinema may be reconciled, though not at the cost of delimiting the idea of the national or the aesthetics of national cinema.

If I argue for a commercially sustainable type of cinema (in this case, one with significant global appeal) it is not because I am privileging that model over any other. It is, however, a significant line of enquiry, given the extent to which the possible contradiction between a viable national cinema and the demands of a free-market economy have informed much work on the recent history and direction of national cinema. John Hill's work on British films of the 1980s, for instance,[6] dwells at some

length on the inherent tension between Thatcherite economic liberal-
ism and a cinema 'capable of registering the lived complexities of British
"national" life'.[7] This tension is made central to *The Strike*. Underpinning
this film's parodic strategies is an anxiety regarding the possibility of
Hill's model for British cinema – in the 1980s, if not beyond – within a
culture of shrinking state investment and growing privatisation, as well
as wider transnational factors. However, as I will also suggest, the highly
successful format of *The Strike*, its elements of parody especially, also
make it (perhaps unwittingly) a blueprint for commercial and exportable films such as *Hot Fuzz*.

Besides bringing the often conflicting interests of culture and commerce into play, considering films that draw on the vernacular of Hollywood also raises significant issues regarding representation and aesthetic
value. One of Higson's main concerns is the way evaluation and representation tend to dominate national cinema discourses at a critical, or
what he calls 'high cultural', level.[8] Within these terms popular or genre
forms are often opposed to that type of representation believed to ade-
quately represent the 'lived complexities of national life'. The problem
for Higson here (who specifically critiques Hill's model) is that this type
of demand is circular and prescriptive. Such a national cinema, in effect,
would only represent that which it already deemed suitable for representation, allowing only those films 'that seem amenable to [its] interpretation' of the national.[9] In this case, because of the over-determined
idea of British national life as 'lived complexity', far from being as inclu-
sive and diverse as the nation it evokes, this would really only imply 'a
very specific type of film: social dramas [...] attending to the specificities of multiculturalism and employing a more or less realist mode of
representation'.[10]

From Transcontextual to Transnational Parody

These earlier arguments are intriguing in the way they evoke the thorny
question of what actually constitutes Englishness in the early twenty-first
century, but they also raise the issue of why we need to invoke the idea of
'English cinema' *at all*. Trying to pin down and even advocate a national
cinema within an era of increasingly transnational consumption, but also

production, may be outdated. To merely adopt a *laissez-faire* or neoliberal position in this respect would, however, allow the possibility of hegemonic forms such as Hollywood cinema to assume cultural centrality under the benign guise of consumer choice. But this is the point where parody, especially in its global contexts, assumes a considerable force, because parody, in its practice, negotiates difference in response to the potential problem of sameness, while still exploiting these global forms.

Linda Hutcheon's model of transcontextual parody[11] has significant implications within a transnational context of film production and reception. *The Strike*, by foregrounding so specifically the incongruity of the Hollywood model in a 'realist' milieu, takes a more obviously demarcated approach to the two contexts across which textual components – in this instance, Hollywood genre – are transposed. Like *Hot Fuzz*, the parodic aims of *The Strike* work mainly through the incongruous juxtaposing of syntactic and semantic generic elements; or as Dan Harries defines it, 'recontextualizing a target or source text through the transformation of its textual (and contextual) elements' so as to create 'a level of ironic incongruity'.[12] In *The Strike*, both in the film and the finished production shown within it, comic effects are produced by situating the machinery of Hollywood production and stars (Al Pacino [Richardson] and Meryl Streep [Jennifer Saunders]) within Welsh and English rural working-class contexts. The concluding act of *Hot Fuzz*, meanwhile, offers us a fully tooled-up shoot-out, in the directorial style of John Woo and Michael Bay *inter alia*, in a village square, local supermarket and miniature model village.

As Geoff King has argued, parody and satire are closely inter-related and often confused. Satire has traditionally been seen as having 'real world' targets, such as 'social or political… institutions'; whereas parody's target is typically 'formal or aesthetic'.[13] King nevertheless notes that, because of the mythical and ideological focus of Hollywood cinema, film genres are themselves forms of 'institution' that may be the subject of criticism through parody: parody can therefore 'be seen as a form of attack, debunking and undermining familiar conventions in a manner that has potential social or political implications'.[14] *The Strike* makes this overlap very clear in its movement between more obvious aspects of satire (pointed references, as we shall see below, to contemporary film industries), and *Strike!*, the produced film that is seen to reflect the dominant ideological character of

Hollywood genre film. The implicit criticism within this internal text lies in its marked distance from the 'real world' circumstances of the events and community it depicts.

Quoting Robert Stam, João Luis Viera and Ismail Xavier, King subsequently identifies the way that parody, especially when produced outside Hollywood, can be 'well suited to the needs of oppositional culture [...] because it deploys the force of the dominant discourse against itself'.[15] This view recognises the productive impact of using the formal and narrative properties of 'mainstream' cinema as a means of articulating national and national-cinematic identities. In itself, though, this argument is imprecise in its schematic separation of 'dominant' and 'oppositional'. More specifically, with reference to *Hot Fuzz*, what do such terms mean within the context of English cultural identity in the twenty-first century? Influential as Hutcheon's model of 'transcontextualisation' has been, 30 years on it is now possibly too neat in its implication that contexts and texts can be so clearly identified and separated, in order for such transcontextual work to take place. The emphasis on movement in the transcontextual model does not quite cater for the more hybrid modes of transnational production.

More recent study in the area of globalisation theory, moreover, has alerted us to the ways conceptions of space and place, in an increasingly mediated and globalised culture, are already shaped by media such as film itself; the transition, to use Arjun Appadurai's term, from the traditional 'landscape' of a given place to forms of 'mediascape'.[16] To some extent Appadurai reiterates the oppositional-dominant paradigm in the way he identifies the appropriation and absorption of homogenised and homogenising cultural products by 'local political and cultural economies'.[17] Nevertheless, an important implication here is that 'dominant culture' is no longer strictly positioned *to the side of* 'local' culture, their interrelationship stressed over their opposition.

Hot Fuzz is effective in terms of identifying spaces and structures of identification and experience which do not fit neatly across the two sides of a putative national border. To some extent this emerges out of parody techniques, but it also embeds them more concretely within verisimilar representational spaces. If the idea of setting a sustained Michael Bay-style action sequence in a Gloucestershire village is an obviously incongruous one, we should note that incongruity is already structured into *Hot Fuzz*'s setting, in a way that provides a basis for its narrative and form. An emphasis on the various motifs of preserved middle-England life (the film was actually shot in the cathedral city of Wells, in Somerset) should not obscure the fact that much of the film's action takes place within what Marc Augé has called the 'non-places' of contemporary urban and suburban experience.[18] The local supermarket in which several sequences take place, including some of the climactic shoot-out, is effective in this film because of its place down the pecking order of British supermarket chains, connoting as it does a more distinctively provincial identity than would, say, a Sainsbury's or a Tesco. Yet the pristine, blank sterility of this supermarket, and its tacit identification as a normal part of provincial life, indicate the degree to which essentially 'place-less' spaces like this are already connoted within the terms of a 'national' geography within globalisation.

Hot Fuzz also identifies that, within certain demographic terms, our wider sense of the 'national cinema' culture operates within and through the supermarket, in the form of 'bargain bin' DVDs that Frost's PC Butterman sifts through while on the beat (we see him at one point poring over a copy of Jackie Chan's 1992 film *Super Cop*). The film even allows a momentary glimpse, in the same wire bin, of a copy of *Shaun of the Dead* (labelled here as *Zombies Party*), essentially an in-joke but also a tacit acknowledgement by Hot Fuzz's filmmakers of the same potential market for their film (I for one am prone to DVD impulse-buys at my local Morrison's supermarket, where Hot Fuzz has been prominently placed in recent years). Indeed, significantly for a film so interested in its cinematic precedents, Hot Fuzz is unconcerned with representing 'the cinema' in any material or participatory sense, to the extent that it hardly exists at all here beyond this form of bottom-end DVD consumption – and of course, fleeting visual gags like the one described above mostly exist for DVD consumers able to freeze the frame. In a similar moment, later in the film, Angel is returning to London, believing to have failed in his efforts to solve the Sandford murders and bring those responsible to justice. Stopping at a fluorescently-lit service station with a zombie-like cashier, he comes across another rack of cut-price action DVDs. This, it appears, is the motivation for Angel's subsequent return to Sandford and the climactic shoot-out that ensues. Hollywood is figured here as the narrative impetus, wherein the traditional idea of a national cinema culture, either as product or as location, is apparently side-stepped. By contrast, the meaning and possibility of a national cinema is explicitly foregrounded in *The Strike*, both in its various allusions to the contemporary contexts of British production, but also in its specific representation of the cinema building as a location in cultural life.

Parody in Context: *The Strike*

As I will discuss, *Hot Fuzz*'s integrated modes of parody are largely pertinent to discourses and practices of British – and more specifically, Working Title's – film production in the 2000s. Equally, though in a different way, *The Strike* sits at the nexus of a series of debates and tensions around the identity and future of British film in the 1980s. Central to these discussions was, as already noted, the significance of Thatcherite economic policies for the production and development of British cinema. As Hill outlines, the impact of neoliberal economics on the film industry included the suspension of a British film quota system; the effective privatisation of the National Film Finance Corporation, replacing it with the British Screen Finance Consortium; and the abolishment of capital allowances for film production.[19] These factors are seen to have contributed to a climate of decline in the 1980s, exacerbated by the lack of confidence on the part of investors, and the falling box-office figures resulting, in part at least, from the emergence of home video as a viewing platform. As Hill remarks, the British film industry was in these circumstances increasingly challenged in its efforts to compete with Hollywood, which, while also enduring a period of decline, was best placed globally to 'spread the financial risks of production in such a way as to make [their films] consistently profitable'.[20]

The Strike forges connections between domains of cultural and material production, consistent with its targeting of Thatcherism. The initial shots of the one-street former mining-village in *The Strike* feature a run-down, traditional four-wall cinema, with the title of the (made-up) film *Bludgeon III* (tagline: *The Carnage Continues*) displayed above the entrance. This opening shot suggests the incongruous dominance of the Hollywood imaginary in depressed British life, but also – in its implicit allusion to the 'video nasty' furore during the early 1980s – the type of low-end product that, in the burgeoning era of VHS, represented a threat to traditional paradigms of film production and consumption. Bernard, the left-wing (though, in a pointed reference to one negative image of metropolitan socialism at the time, champagne-drinking) film director appointed to take on the script, shares Paul's vision of a film depicting 'the biggest blow to the Labour movement in years', describing the story as 'a socialist epic'. But the opening deal is overseen by an unnamed English film producer, whose thick crop of greying hair and beard are clearly supposed to allude to David Puttnam. An explicit reference to the contexts of British production in the mid-1980s, this allusion connects the producers of Paul's script with the tendency toward American style and scale of production, hallmarks of Puttnam's work with the company Goldcrest, in films such as *Chariots of Fire* (1981), *The Killing Fields* (1984) and *The Mission* (1986). The producer discusses his wish to 'revitalise the British film industry from an American perspective', adding that a film 'about the miners' strike' is 'just the film to do it'. At which incongruous point, he turns to the cigar-smoking and up to now silent figure across the table – as it turns out, the American producer of *Bludgeon III* who bankrolls the project – asking whether Al Pacino could play Scargill. Far from an arbitrary joke, this specifically references the casting of Pacino in *Revolution* (1985): the commercially disastrous Goldcrest-produced film about the American Revolutionary War, filmed in England by *Chariots of Fire* director Hugh Hudson.

In a parallel to *Revolution*, the star casting and large budget of which underlined its pretensions toward global exhibition,[21] the film *Strike!* becomes essentially a Hollywood production. Commitment to the miners' strike's historical realities are consequently subordinated to the demands of Hollywood narrative structure, with its own ideological commitment to clear character goals and trajectories, and the development of love interest as a corollary of the individual's social quest. The 1980s setting is reworked to create a pastiche of a mining village from the 1930s: a satirical nod perhaps to the then current tendencies toward 'heritage' location and design, especially in the 'Merchant-Ivory' productions discussed in the previous chapter. When the British director criticises the script's change of direction, he is fired, while Paul is persuaded – thanks to a hefty advance – to rewrite his script, and Pacino and Streep are brought in to play Scargill and his wife. Consequently, the planned film, to use Richard Maltby's phrase, will 'succumb [...] to the industrial logic of the star system'[22] by having

4.1 Arthur Scargill, as played by Al Pacino, as played by Peter Richardson: *The Strike* (1988)

Scargill more-or-less singlehandedly win the strike and re-write British history.

It is one of the ironies of *The Strike*, though, that its long-term interest lies perhaps less in its contemporary references to the British film industry, and more in its juxtaposition of the Hollywood epic or action film with a regional story and milieu. The film also raises significant questions about the ideological work of such satirical comedy. The clear critical aims of satire, especially when its target is the dominant representational institution of Hollywood, imply that there is a preferred alternative representation alluded to via the satire itself. In other words, the actual story of the striking miners is the implied real of *The Strike/Strike!*. However, we do not see this alternative, and instead are left with a series of potent – if no less parodic – scenes borrowed from the Hollywood image-bank and invested in a very distinct locale: Scargill on his motorbike tearing through a village graveyard, or running desperately down The Mall in London; Scargill making an impassioned plea to the House of Commons, with cutaways to his listening wife, weeping MPs and the blubbing miners listening on the radio. *The Strike* demonstrates how, in such parody, the latent power of the targeted genre remains at once its subject and structuring force. The film is most effective when it highlights the emotive manipulations and structures of Hollywood drama: for example, the point after Scargill's speech, when the assorted MPs vote to give in to the miners' demands, and Scargill's crippled daughter (her legs having previously been crushed in a mine explosion) walks through the doors of the House into her father's arms. But this begs a pressing question: if *The Strike* has a critical intent, why is parody the preferred option here, and not the 'lost' film-within-the-film that does not get made, but is the implied 'good' object within the satire? *The Strike* is in this sense illustrative of the double-bind in which parody can find itself: at once transgressive in its potential for 'humorous [...] and subversive play' with dominant cultural discourses,[23] such as the Hollywood genre film; but also conservative in its 'possible regeneration and continuation of [the] tradition' it notionally undermines.[24] Here, then, a critical practice frequently reiterates, indeed confirms, the cultural dominance of the targeted mode and our own familiarity with it.

Parody in Context: *Spaced, Shaun of the Dead* and *Hot Fuzz*

The pertinent point here is that the borders separating supposedly dominant and minor cultural practices – between, say, Hollywood and English cinema or television – have within the 'postmodern' turn become much less clearly defined. *Spaced* is a useful case in point here because of the way it integrates so many cultural inter-texts, many of them from Hollywood, into the contextual spaces of a British sit-com setting and format. Watching the show involves negotiating a range of reference points constantly bursting into the action. Looking at their prospective new flat during the first episode, Daisy and Tim (Stevenson and Pegg) find two twin girl scouts in a wardrobe, in a marked visual allusion to *The Shining* (1980) ('Beginnings'); a game of paintballing involving Tim, his friend Mike, and Dwayne, the City boy who moved in with Tim's old girlfriend, borrows the weapon-loading crash-zooms from *Evil Dead 2* (1987) and the make-up and dialogue from *Predator* (1987) ('Battles'), while Tim's recent sense of betrayal by *The Phantom Menace* (1999) sees him lighting a funeral pyre of his collected *Star Wars* merchandise, in a formally exact reference to the scene in *Return of the Jedi* when Luke Skywalker cremates Darth Vader's body ('Back').

In the context of a British television comedy, such references and their relocation within an identifiably non-Hollywood context situates them in line with other appropriations of the Hollywood imaginary, in many comedy series from (as we have seen) *The Morecambe and Wise Show* to *French and Saunders* (BBC, 1987–2007). There are key differences here, though, relating both to *Spaced*'s narrative form and the style with which its moments of parody are represented. Fleeting allusions here to other texts through quotation are rarely reducible to comic interruption; rather, they become a means through which the traditional narrative values of plot promotion and character development are actually conveyed. The allusion to *Return of the Jedi*'s funeral pyre in 'Back' is coherent in the context of the show, highlighting Tim's mournful obsession with the *Star Wars* saga's dismaying return, one which resurfaces at various instances during the second series. But in using the very object of criticism to represent this response, such parodic references also mark Tim's ambivalence and failure to leave *Star Wars* behind. Also in 'Back', the use of two Agents clearly designed to evoke those in *The Matrix* (1999), replete with earpieces and sunglasses, is never entirely gratuitous or incongruous in the context of the episode. Here, they are two Customs and Excise officers on the trail of illicit material Daisy has unwittingly brought into the country from her backpacking holiday in Thailand. Their uniformity and stiff manner make them both objects of paranoia and bewilderment from Tim and Daisy's point of view, but also affords a final joke, paraphrasing *The Matrix*'s dialogue, about the thankless and less-than thrilling nature of such work ('I *hate* this job...').

The show is exemplary of the ways we experience contemporary media culture, marked as it is as a reflection on the various cultural texts that litter the world of *Spaced*'s protagonists. *Spaced* is not the first sit-com to be centered significantly around a television (the sit-com, as a domestic or familial type of show, is largely defined by the presence of a television set), though it does reflect the more recent tendency to turn the television (or increasingly, the computer terminal, in shows such as *The IT Crowd* [Channel 4, 2006–13]) into its subject matter; not simply in terms of what the characters talk about, but as a contributing influence to the show's form and look, its very depiction of the 'real world'. *Spaced* takes its

4.2 Quotation/reiteration as narration: Tim reacts to Daisy's dog impression in series one of *Spaced* (1999)

cue here from *The Simpsons*, which has made television its own source of comic and critical reflection in a proliferating and ironic *mise-en-abyme*. If we spend our lives watching television, *The Simpsons*' logic suggests, our lives become reflections of television itself: this explains why so much of *The Simpsons* works around parodies of the things we see on television, whether these be advertisements, news programming, reality shows, soap operas or dramas.[25]

As Jonathan Gray has noted, the fact that *The Simpsons* is an animation means it automatically, to some degree, parodies what it represents. This is because everything we see in *The Simpsons* that has its anchor in live-action is inherently made incongruous, or 'defamiliarised', when rendered in cartoon form. 'Bizarre camera angles; traditional ways of shooting a given scene or genre; devices such as fast editing, panning, close-ups and montage; and even how people move or make facial expressions':[26] all these things that live-action film or television make seem natural are made to look highly constructed and artificial when shown through the medium of *The Simpsons*' world. *Spaced* is a live-action television series, but what made it seem so novel in the context of British sitcoms was that it didn't really feel like one. This wasn't so much because the characters talked about

The X-Files or the game *Resident Evil* or *Return of the Jedi*, or even because they watched the film or played the game. Rather, it was because the series was carefully designed to look like them, at least within the remit of a British television show. *Spaced* was unusual for incorporating within the sitcom format a broad range of both televisual, but more prominently cinematic, stylistic techniques, most if not all of the ones Gray identifies in *The Simpsons*. By eschewing the traditional sitcom aesthetic, characterised by a theatrical mise-en-scène with a (laughing) audience as a form of 'fourth wall',[27] the series in fact confounds many of the cultural and media-specific connotations of the television sitcom form, effacing some of the distinctions between its supposed status as 'television' and the films it draws on. This is partly because, eschewing the traditional three-camera production mode of the studio sitcom, it is shot in cinematic style using single cameras; but it is also because many of the techniques Wright employs in *Spaced* – crazily titled angles, weird tracking shots, crash zooms, quick, unpredictable transitions from one scene to the next – exemplify animation's ability to 'resist notions of the real world',[28] and consequently make *Spaced* as much a cartoon as a traditional 'live-action' show.

Just as *The Simpsons* is (more or less) anchored in a real-world context from which its fantasies and parodies depart, *Spaced* balances its animated flights of fancy within the very mundane contexts of its location. But because point of view and in turn our own sense of the show's reality are always blurred and mixed-up (there are, for example, no marked 'dream sequences' in *Spaced*), we have no choice but to read the show as representing a world experienced through the consumption and imagination of the films, other TV series and videogames it references. Much of the humour of *Spaced* comes from the way its protagonists enact such rich appropriations of their favourite pop-cultural texts in such ordinary surroundings. It is the frequent contrast between 'big' frames of reference (*Star Wars*, *Predator*, *The Matrix*) and 'little' settings (a flat, paintballing, the local pub) that makes *Spaced* feel so 'local', even if – as we also saw in the *Wallace and Gromit* series – this is a result of introducing so many 'global' cultural references into its mix. Significantly, though, none of the references in *Spaced* seem intended for mockery: their use in the show does not signal their failure to mean anything in the 'local' world that is its context; rather, it changes how we understand the local itself.

Like *Spaced*, *Hot Fuzz* integrates its reference points in a way that suggests 'mockery' is not quite the point. There is a moment during the film's supermarket showdown when Nicholas and Danny take a break to discuss suitable fight-ending lines. The action around them takes a convenient break as the two men share the following exchange:

DANNY: Where's the trolley boy?

NICHOLAS: In the freezer.

DANNY: Did you say 'cool off?'

NICHOLAS: No I didn't say anything...

DANNY: Shame.

NICHOLAS: Well, there was the bit that you missed where I distracted him with the cuddly monkey, then I said 'play time's over' and I hit him in the head with the peace lily.

DANNY: You're off the fucking chain!

The humour derives here from the clearly displayed analysis of genre convention, but also because this unlikely pause in proceedings reiterates the same, equally unlikely way that action sequences can pause for the delivery of pay-off dialogue. But this sequence in itself acknowledges a familiarity with these same cinematic moments; moments that are hardly disguised, but rather an obvious source of expectation and pleasure for fans of such films. One implication here is that the filmmakers have, and ask us to share, an easy familiarity and delight with these conventions in spite of – or, I'd say, because of – their predictability, or indeed silliness. The other important implication is that 'Hollywood' no longer functions as the bad object of parody – on the other side of which, presumably, we find good English cinema. But it doesn't mean we buy into an illusion offered by Hollywood. Because it is marked as parody, 'Hollywood' becomes a style to play around with: just as in *Spaced*, everything gets mixed up in *Hot Fuzz* to the extent that the borders between Hollywood and Sandford become less clearly discernible.

In *Shaun of the Dead*, meanwhile, the mass media is implied as part of the film's narrative problem, but it is also the horizon of the film's point of view. *Shaun of the Dead*'s comic technique is to play off our omniscient narrative perspective against its protagonist's restricted point of view. Generic presupposition and expectation on our part – once again assuming an awareness of, and participation within, the rules and codes of genre – enable us to see signs of the encroaching zombie invasion (a shuffling man trying to grab and eat pigeons; a man feasting on a woman's neck outside the pub) where Shaun only sees reiterations of daily life (an elderly vagrant; a drunk couple making out). Elsewhere, Wright repeats an entire, elaborate sequence shot in which Shaun goes out to his local shop. In the second version, which occurs after the zombie infestation has gone into full swing, everyday instances from the earlier sequence (a man jogging, for example) are subtly reshaped to the new context (the same man running for his life). Again, the humour derives from Shaun's sleepy inability to distinguish one environment from the other. There is parodic play at work, specifically in the appropriation and acknowledgement of certain generic motifs not recognised by the film's hero. But as in *Spaced* and *Hot Fuzz*, the reference points are not obvious targets of comic derision in themselves: their comic value is produced through their insertion into the narrative and its context.

Television becomes central to this comic process as Shaun, 'zapping' between various channels, inadvertently creates a message of impending doom, editing between footage of The Smiths performing 'Panic', voice-overs from wildlife documentaries, and football commentary. *Shaun of the Dead* is of course astute in making its referential title as much an observation about its own narrative as it is a knowing reference to its own major influence, George Romero's *Dawn of the Dead* (1978), the second in an ongoing series of films that began in 1968 with *Night of the Living Dead*. Shaun is the centre of comic attention and criticism because he is literally 'of' the dead, even though he is never infected.[29] The film's main comic conceit is its depiction of a mass inertia that makes the zombie invasion barely distinguishable from any other day. And here, as with the fleeting allusion to *Shaun of the Dead* in *Hot Fuzz*, there is no obvious distinction between the domestic frameworks of film viewing and the same ones within which *Shaun of the Dead* would actually be watched. But in distinction from a film like *The Strike*, here there is no implied alternative model. On the contrary, Shaun's response, to fight the zombie hordes and win back the respect of his girlfriend, is entirely consistent with the generic demands of the genre it notionally parodies; in this sense, *Shaun of the Dead* locates itself entirely within the same mass media production that 'causes' the dead to come alive in the first place.

As this suggests, in a transnational context, parody enables films to exploit the form and content of genre films, while also functioning independently of them as 'national'. This is exactly the case in *Shaun of the Dead*, where the formal conventions and motifs of the genre are exploited in a way that privileges local specificity, while working entirely within a straight generic framework. In *Hot Fuzz*, by virtue of the fact that Sandford is not the place for an action sequence, and that Pegg and Frost are not obvious action heroes, we are able to enjoy what is essentially an undiluted action aesthetic within the guise of a comic film. Such films enable us to enjoy genre with 'impunity', as it were, inasmuch as the separation of semantics and syntax in them lets us appreciate and enjoy style in different contexts. *Hot Fuzz* appropriates the aesthetics of a film such as *Bad Boys II*, freeing it in the process from the more unpalatable ideological aspects of the latter film that can typically function through the cohesion of syntax and semantics within genre, promoting generic verisimilitude.

As suggested here, then, parody in *Hot Fuzz* is not intrinsically comic. Looking at aspects of the film's style suggests the consistent use of a similar aesthetic to other films of the same period. The film's opening sequence, for example, a montage outlining Angel's meteoric rise through the London Metropolitan Police force, exploits the range of aesthetic options commonly known (following David Bordwell) as 'intensified continuity':[30] arcing cameras, interrupted tracking shots, zooms and push-ins, fleeting increases in film speed ('ramping'), momentary freeze-frames and super-impositions across cuts, cutting through pulses of light or punctuating actions, and the frequent use of 'wipe-by' edits (where a passing foreground figure covers a reframed transition). Within the formalist practices of film parody identified by Harries, such techniques would be used in a way that would deviate from their typical grammatical use within narrative film: such acknowledgement of, and deviation from, grammatical conventions, would work through and against viewer expectations in order to highlight and disrupt genre's 'logonomic system'.[31] In such instances, the artifice, and the hyperbolic or arbitrary nature of such techniques (what Harries calls 'the relative instability of any filmic convention'[32]), are identified through parodic subversion. It is not hard, for example, to imagine a parodic version of the wipe-by cut where, cartoon-like, the formal aspect of 'wiping' the screen interfered with the diegetic action on either side of the wipe.[33] In *Hot Fuzz*, though, deviation from convention is entirely due to context, not film language. The incongruity of the aesthetic techniques in the opening sequence, for instance, relates solely to aspects of the mise-en-scène, in terms of performance and setting. The dynamic edits in the opening sequence cut shots across ball-point pens being clicked, or chess time-clocks being pinged; while wipe-by cuts show Angel, in identical but relocated compositions, giving advice to elderly couples in different parts of London. Seeing Angel on a mountain bike skidding into the foreground of a shot, cutting to an extreme close-up of Pegg staring intensely in cycling goggles and helmet, is not humorous because of any deviation in style, but because the concept of 'advanced cycling', as Pegg's voiceover describes it, is incongruous within the expectations of the action aesthetic.

More obvious jokes about the form and expectations of the action genre, meanwhile, are similarly integrated within the genre's stylistic and structural norms. Toward the end of the film, Nicholas and Danny look out from a first-floor supermarket window to see their adversary, the supermarket owner Simon Skinner, making a getaway. Nicholas says to Danny: 'We need to get down there'. 'How?' asks Danny. Nicholas, looking down, replies 'Skip!' The next shot gives us a high-angle framing of Angel leaping down into a waiting skip full of black rubbish bags. This gag therefore uses both literalisation and misdirection, in its play with expectation and outcome.[34] Angel's initial injunction to 'skip' is already bizarre, out of keeping as it is with the very masculine connotations of the Hollywood action hero – not to mention the fact that it is a very ineffective way of chasing anyone. The revelation that this 'skip' is actually the object below makes Angel's sudden shift off-genre 'normal' again, but at the same time it highlights the ways action films can provide such ludicrously fortuitous get-outs for their protagonists – the softly padded skip simply waiting, it seems, for the heroes to dive into, satisfying the spectacular demands of the action movie. Consequently, this parodic sequence disrupts the action genre's system of representation, exposing its gendered and highly arbitrary construction. And yet, nothing here interrupts either the status of the filmed stunt as spectacle, nor its development within the narrative progression of the policemen's pursuit. It therefore keeps both sides of representation alive and in play, collapsing neither into unreflective imitation or

4.3 Beyond belief, beyond parody? Simon Pegg as the avenging Angel in *Hot Fuzz* (2007)

pastiche, nor into an overtly critical mode implying some putatively 'real' cinematic practice.

Parody as 'Global' National Cinema

In his study of British television comedy at the turn of the millennium, Ben Thompson argues that this particular period was characterised by a change in the broader conception of culture, and above all, a re-evaluation of our understanding of 'low' or 'popular' culture. Quoted in the same book, Pegg makes the point that the political inflections of 1980s comedy (Pegg specifically refers to *The Young Ones* [1982–84], though *The Comic Strip Presents…*, which shared personnel with the former show, would be a better example) gave way in the 1990s to 'the *lack* of any kind of incendiary political situation [and] the death of opposition'.[35] Thompson may be correct in asserting that the 'carefree' atmosphere in the early years of the New Labour government, such as they existed, gave rise to more 'childlike' cultural manifestations,[36] such as the fascination with comics and sci-fi in *Spaced*, or indeed the uses of the action movie in *Hot Fuzz*. In the next chapter, I will consider in more detail the way recent parody brings into view transformed conceptions of taste and cultural value – indeed, the undermining of traditional conceptions of 'good' and 'bad' cinema, I have argued here, is one of the main points and productive aims of *Hot Fuzz*. It would nevertheless be reductive to ascribe this entirely to the variable contexts of British politics; rather, as I have suggested, they need to be seen in terms of the longer historical contexts and effects of globalisation, and the impact of the latter on conceptions of the nation and national identity.

The apparently non-judgemental appropriations of style at work in *Shaun of the Dead* and *Hot Fuzz* indicate the more fluid, less contextually-bound ways that film forms circulate and signify within a global film culture. Politically speaking, they also suggest that Hollywood images are not necessarily the dominant mode which we either accept or reject, but they are rather 'only one node of a complex transnational construction of imaginary landscapes'.[37] By contrast, what dates *The Strike* within its particular time and contexts is its inherent resistance to more nuanced conceptions of the national and its cinema. We might forgive its rather reductive depiction of Hollywood's ability to engage either politically or with cultural specificity, partly because its strategies are rhetorically excessive, but also because its main target is not Hollywood in its entirety, but the emerging tendencies of 'high-concept' filmmaking in the Don Simpson/Jerry Bruckheimer mode (in films such as *Beverly Hills Cop* [1984] and *Top Gun* [1986]).[38] But because its parodic targets are so crudely obvious, its satirical strategies brook no mediation between Hollywood and English cinematic identity. It appears to position its viewers clearly on one side of a representational equation: to quote Dyer's criticism of parody as a mode, *The Strike*'s positioning of the viewer 'implies a sure position outside of that to which it refers, one of secure judgement and knowledge'.[39] This limiting of viewer interpretation also ends up severely limiting the possibilities of what its implied national cinema might be like.

A film like *Hot Fuzz*, meanwhile, allows us to reconfigure the trajectories of globalisation, which the Hollywood-targeting model of parody (and Dyer's somewhat restricted view of parody generally) would otherwise imply to be one-way. As Higson argues, Englishness (or indeed Britishness) is now increasingly difficult to define beyond its own performance or construction. In other words, we can hardly assume an indexical bond between films representing England and England itself. From one perspective, this is simply down to the difficulty in pinning down the meaning of 'English' in a country traditionally characterised by class distinctions, and increasingly by multiculturalism. But Higson's discussion is subtle in that it mostly avoids the irresolvable issue of 'accurate' representation, and considers the hard economic determinism shaping representations of Englishness in the global cinematic market. As Higson demonstrates, the scale of the UK film market is too limited on its own to sustain anything but low-budget films, meaning that the bid for a more global reach requires filmmakers and producers to find 'appropriate means of exploiting a local brand on a transnational or global scale'.[40] Higson goes on to discuss the way 'Englishness' is consequently 'packaged'[41] both for the wider English audience, but more importantly the export market, for whom representations of the domestically 'ordinary' – Higson uses here the example of Hugh Grant in *Notting Hill* – are reconfigured in terms of 'exotic otherness'.[42]

It is of course easy to read the 'packaging of Englishness' described by Higson as little more than a compromise, a genuflection to the dominant cultural mode. Even the critical or oppositional view of parody is itself an indirect acknowledgement of Hollywood's global power. Beyond the question, though, of whether Hollywood style is in reality nationally and culturally specific, and the previous issue of whether national filmmaking styles can be prescribed at all, the assumption of compromise overlooks two things: firstly, the way in which the performance of Englishness through film works both to play up and also *play with* this idea, in ways that may appeal to both overseas *and* domestic audiences; and secondly, that the very forces and flows of globalisation have already reshaped what it means to be English in the first place. To quote Higson once more:

> The cross-border flow of cultural commodities, personnel, ideas and creative practices necessarily challenges the idea of discrete, distinctive and unique national economies, cultures, audiences and public spheres[; it] enables a cultural and representational practice that mixes elements from different sources [and] thus potentially challenges traditional ideas of the nation and national identity.[43]

Hot Fuzz offers an interesting model for this type of 'challenging' representational practice because of the way it mediates between representations, between the 'fantasy' and the 'real'. Neither side is allowed within this particular mode of parody to cohere within either term, as this would imply a stable and reductive concept of identity from which to speak. *Hot Fuzz*, by contrast, works through its playful resistance to making *any* representation feel natural.

The film is then quintessentially transnational in the way it bridges the economic imperatives, film aesthetics and genre semantics pertaining to both English and American contexts. In this sense it shares characteristics with other contemporary output, also produced by Working Title, which brings together the syntax and industrial logic of Hollywood with the semantics of English space and iconography. Films such as *Four Weddings and a Funeral, Notting Hill, Bridget Jones's Diary* and *Love Actually* all work through the manipulation of romantic comedy, transatlantic casting strategies, and the inter-textual reference points of heritage sites and English literature. Yet while these films show aspects of knowingness and in-jokes in terms of their representational approaches, they do not explicitly foreground incongruity. The incongruities of parody, on the other hand, encourage us to focus on specificities of place and identity, constructed or otherwise, in a way that the transnational rom-com frequently does not. Both *Notting Hill* and *Love Actually*, for instance, rather avoid the question of specificity by making the national (or at least London) feel already international. *Hot Fuzz*, in contrast, asks us to think about how film style and genre are linked to the representation of cultural identity, but it does not set fixed parameters on such representations or their implications. To follow Roland Robertson's terms,[44] the film indicates how the 'local' re-emerges as an intrinsic aspect of globalisation's tendency to homogenise and hybridise, to the extent to which a film like *Hot Fuzz* represents not so much the globalised nature of contemporary English popular film, but its frequently 'glocalised' character.

Parody's significance as a mode within the contexts of a national cinema is consequently that it enables the performance of varied cinematic identities without collapsing (formally, ideologically) into any one of them. It therefore gets round the 'problem' of national cinema as a prescriptive type of film, while retaining vestiges of national identity in the form of a dialogue with other cinematic practices. When Higson writes in the 1990s that 'for a cinema to be nationally popular, it must paradoxically also be international in scope', he adds that this typically implies 'work[ing] with Hollywood's international standards'.[45] While Higson himself indicates that this is not the only option, other theorists have offered nuance to this formula. Thomas Elsaesser's notion of 'impersoNation' is here a case in point. For Elsaesser, many European films within a globalised film economy are turning toward more ironic, even self-parodic representations of national place and character in order to 'reflect the image that (one assumes) the other has of oneself' (Elsaesser's main example is the 1996 adaptation of *Trainspotting*).[46] Such films enable both domestic and global audiences to enjoy a version, say, of 'Scottishness', or 'Englishness' in the case of the Working Title rom-coms, without necessarily buying into the accuracy of their representations.

Perhaps inadvertently, *The Strike*'s internal film is itself a fine example of an 'impersoNational' identity in cinema. The Hollywood action-aesthetic of *Strike!* is here embedded within diverse signifiers of cinematic, and indeed heritage, Englishness: the rural mining village, full of soot-smeared men and boys in cloth caps; bucolic villages through which Scargill tears on his way to Parliament; a House of Commons peopled with ageing men in hats, tails and bow ties, claiming to speak for internationally-recognisable constituencies such as 'Oxford and Cambridge', 'Stratford-upon-Avon' and 'The Cotswolds'. As already suggested, *The Strike*'s framing device and its obvious satirical targets position these representations within the terms of a Hollywood vision of England. But the assumption that this joke will be shared by its viewers indicates a tacit awareness of the ways Englishness can be reduced to such potent archetypes. Once again, *The Strike*'s satirical approach disavows the way such representations are recognised, and potentially enjoyed with an ironised view, by the predominantly British audience to whom the film (as a Channel 4 television production) is primarily directed.

Conclusion: a Positively English Parody

From a starting point which suggested that parody negatively signifies what national cinema 'cannot be', I have argued that it is in fact central to the construction of a national cinema within the circumstances of globalisation and globalised cinema practices. To return one last time to Higson's earlier 'idea of national cinema', we can see the ways that a film like *Hot Fuzz* reconciles many of the tensions and problems inherent to his competing models. Such films get round the opposition between commerce and representation by making the question of representation, through the dialogue of semantics and syntax, central to their commercial appeal. They work entirely within the formal aesthetic systems of popular genres while at the same time drawing attention to the cultural construction of those genres, in a way that also works to define the texts as 'English'. This itself becomes another marker of commercial appeal, but also a discursive marker of national film identity.

Spaced, Shaun of the Dead and *Hot Fuzz* are also especially effective in working to define the contemporary spaces and affiliations of a 'national cinema' culture – the 'place' where we 'come together' to watch 'our' films – as effectively without territory, or rather, that the territory of national film culture cannot be prescriptively defined within the boundaries of either particular sites of reception or films' origins of production. *Hot Fuzz* in particular is very successful in identifying both the dispersed, increasingly domesticated sites of reception, and the apparent incongruities of consumed product within these sites, and incorporating this into its form and narrative. It works to claim the cinematic 'other' (that is, Hollywood) within the terms of the domestic, though without capitulating to the idea of a Hollywood aesthetic and ideology posing as a 'global' or 'post-national' film style. Ultimately, in distinction to a film such as *The Strike*, its achievement is to nuance the terms and significance of parody film beyond the binary logic of satire. As I have also argued, though, the longer and possibly inadvertent legacy of *The Strike* may be to have devised a successful model for this type of national film comedy in the era of globalisation.

I do not think it is too big a claim to put forward these films not so much as a viable model for a national parody film but as a model for national cinema *in itself*. It is possibly the associations of *Shaun of the Dead* and (especially) *Hot Fuzz* with parody and with 'low' cultural reference points that has made them largely resistant to academic consideration, or the kind of critical legitimation afforded to more awards-friendly products, conforming more to the standards of the 'quality' film (literary adaptations, for example) or to the tenets of English 'realism', this despite (or maybe because of) the evident international success of these films in generating significant returns on their financial investments. In line with my arguments from earlier chapters, a sense of realism, of claims to represent the lived social and cultural experience of England, is very much in evidence in these films; especially as this experience is shown to be ceaselessly uncertain and ironic, subject to playful performances and other cultural borrowings. As we saw earlier, taking a light-hearted and sceptical view of national identity is, within recent political contexts, hardly a bad thing. And from the economic viewpoint of cinema production, if it can bring to the table domestic *and* international audiences on a substantial scale, it should be a cause for celebration.

5

From Distance to Difference: Parody, Participation and the Cultural Canon

One of the most significant developments in recent media output is the ubiquity of so-called 'DIY' or 'user-generated' content. Such productions, often limited- or no-budget remakes or re-workings of some of Hollywood's most potent franchises, have gathered an ever-increasing prominence online, particularly through the proliferating channels of social media networks and delivery platforms such as YouTube. Such appropriation and adaptation of content is not so new: first published in 1992, Henry Jenkins' *Textual Poachers* was one of the first major academic works to consider the impact of productions such as *Star Trek* fan fiction and artworks on our prior notions of authorship and intellectual property. What has changed mostly is the scale and accessibility of this production, generated by the internet. As Siobhan O'Flynn notes, the available digital technologies and collaborative impact of 'crowdsourcing' enabled one particular user, Casey Pugh, to orchestrate in 2009 a shot-by-shot remake of *Star Wars* in the form of 473 15-second clips:

> Fans from roughly 20 countries remade clips in a wide range
> of styles, including live action, multiple styles of animation
> and anime, puppets, LEGO, grindhouse, Yellow Submarine-
> style, stop motion – the list goes on [...] The result is a glori-
> ous, hilarious testimony to fan devotion and enthusiasm for

playing with the 'original' content, and to adaptation as an act of communal ownership [...] Pugh's crowdsourced adaptation, [in Robert Lloyd's words] 'an official, perfectly imperfect shadow of the original film' [...] was posted live online as *Star Wars Uncut* in August 2010, and then went on to receive an Emmy for 'outstanding creative achievement in interactive media'.[1]

As both O'Flynn and Jenkins (in his later *Convergence Culture*) describe, user-generated content such as the above and the earlier *Toy Wars* (2002), another *Star Wars* remake made entirely with action figures,[2] find themselves situated in the longstanding contestation over intellectual property rights with George Lucas, founder of Lucasfilm, the rights owner of the *Star Wars* property. Lucas's resistance to such adaptations reflects his apparent desire to maintain control over the *Star Wars* 'canon', implying as it does that the issue is not just ownership *per se*, but the use, and more specifically here the *misuse*, of the saga, its narratives and its protagonists.

In the broadest sense of parodic 'transcontextualisation', or in O'Flynn's words, 'transcoding', where the representational, institutional and generic 'codes' of one (dominant) media form find themselves relocated elsewhere, DIY films like *Toy Wars* and *Star Wars Uncut* represent 'spoofs' of the material they 'poach'. We have already seen this in *Spaced*, which through its sitcom framework revisions the *Star Wars* films, amongst others, bringing their epic connotations down to an everyday level. Occasional collaborators of Edgar Wright and Simon Pegg, Adam Buxton and Joe Cornish,[3] already did similar things to *Spaced* in their series *The Adam and Joe Show* (Channel 4, 1996–2001), which was ahead of the game in using toys to recreate contemporary movies such as *Trainspotting* and *Titanic*. Appearing as they did in the wake of Jenkins' *Textual Poachers*, and in a period which saw the gradual repositioning not only of fan culture but also of so-called 'geek' interests and associated screen entertainments (computers, videogames, and science-fiction film and television being the most obvious amongst these), both *Spaced* and *The Adam and Joe Show* seem to have been prescient in identifying and depicting the pleasures of fandom and textual re-creation – and a decade before a mainstream American TV show, *The Big Bang Theory* (CBS, 2007–) would do the same.

An important point here is that, if this kind of 'textual poaching' uses erstwhile methods of parody, its *function* cannot be so readily assumed: to the extent, inevitably, that the terms of 'spoof' and 'parody' are called into question. Looking at O'Flynn's comments regarding *Star Wars Uncut*, we can see to what extent such appropriating practices confuse simplistic distinctions not just between 'producer' and 'receiver', but also between fidelity and travesty, canonicity and resistance. At once a 'hilarious testimony' to fan production, it is also a testimony to the 'ownership', albeit communally, of the *Star Wars* brand and text. While its 473-clip premise suggests fragmentation and dispersal, the sections are designed to come together in a way that pays utmost respect to the original film's integrity. Not only this, but the film goes on to be recognised by the same institutions (the Emmy awards) that formally established clear parameters between legitimate and non-legitimate modes of production. Jenkins' analysis of the home-made *Star Wars* films is similarly revealing in its choice of terms. Jenkins refers specifically to 'the *Star Wars* parodies', citing *George Lucas in Love* (1999) as one of the best known,[4] and going on to say that such films offer 'spoofs' of Lucas's original film. Yet Jenkins' broader point is that these films embody the status of *Star Wars* as modern 'legend' for this generation of filmmakers, the 'catalyst' for their own creative ventures: indeed, Joseph Levy, the creator of *George Lucas in Love* and a graduate of Lucas's *alma mater* USC, goes so far as to describe the *Star Wars* director as 'the god'.[5]

As we saw earlier, Richard Dyer has insisted that parody not only signals its textual process of adaptation, but marks it evaluatively in negative terms. Dyer might reasonably suggest that what we see in *Spaced* or *Toy Wars* is in actual fact parody's evaluative opposite, namely homage. But this does not really hold with the marked shift of register in such works, especially in the way the change in location, production values and connotation inevitably reshape the affective impact, and hence the ideological register, of the Hollywood genre film. When Dyer discusses homage there is a notable parallel, or at least an intended one, between the work and that which it positively references; whether this be the composer Debussy referencing his predecessors Haydn and Rameau, Robbie Williams covering Frank Sinatra's songs, or, in Todd Haynes' *Far From Heaven* (2002), the stylistically precise evocation of Douglas Sirk's 1950s melodramas.[6] What instead characterises a show like *Spaced* or Adam and Joe's 'Toymovies', like the DIY *Star Wars* films, is the way they 'pull [the movies they reference] down to the same level as countless other amateur filmmakers, and in so doing, help blur the line between the fantastical…and the familiar realm of everyday life'.[7] Part of the appeal of *Spaced* was to make its protagonists, and any viewers who cared to share the points of reference, into performers and participants of 'big' movies within the 'little' environment of the domestic sitcom setting. And as this suggests, the emphasis is here more on the active *practices* of participation, and less on any critical targets in the sourced text.

Dyer's view of parody as 'hysterical'[8] remains, I think, very relevant for the way it sums up some of parody's inherent contradictions – the way, as we have just seen, it is split at once between its efforts to mark its difference from the parodied text and remain so implicitly loyal to it. Dyer's belief that this is because parody 'minds being inexorably implicated in that from which it seeks to distance itself',[9] however, seems slightly off the mark. What I would like to argue in this chapter is that we can continue to discuss the practices of parody without necessarily having recourse to loaded critical and oppositional terms such as 'distance'. As hinted above, the key motivation in these forms of non-oppositional parodies is not so much critical distance but *authorial difference*. Makeshift re-creations and low-budget techniques such as stop-motion and the use of action figures is here less a reflexive commentary on the 'parodied' text than it is, more practically, the available means for these 'prosumers'[10] to express themselves. Parodying through appropriation and re-configured media, then, can be seen as no more than a form of signature, a way of showing you have played a distinctive part (and, to borrow the simultaneously collective and individual rhetoric of YouTube, you have 'broadcasted yourself').

The End of Parody? Culture and Taste in the Twenty-First Century

A key implication here is that if we remove the evaluative element of parody, we also call into question the idea of *value* more broadly. In the shift from distance to difference, criteria of aesthetic judgment or ideological critique seem less important than the marking of creative endeavour on the part of the individual or collective consumer-producer. As we saw in the introduction, for some proponents of postmodern parody, the significance of the latter is to call into question the notion that there exists at all some meaningful idea of one kind of cultural production being 'better' than any other, or indeed, that 'culture', as some sort of ennobling and educative practice and product, has any meaning at all. The 'longstanding parodic energies' that Dentith sees erupting from popular culture more generally[11] are in this sense the pragmatic counter to Matthew Arnold's notion of Culture (as espoused in his 1869 book *Culture and Anarchy*) as 'the form of a transcendent ideal of [...] perfection'.[12] For Arnold, this Culture is 'the best that humankind can achieve'.[13] For postmodern parody, it is the best that you or I or we can achieve with the available means, against which overarching, idealist frameworks of a 'transcendent ideal' assume much less importance.

The misassumption is in thinking that this implies a systematic devaluation of culture in general; as in the lamentably over-used notion of 'dumbing down', a phrase which, ironically, tends to be used unthinkingly as a mere assertion of personal taste and cultural distinction. What such a view overlooks is the importance to postmodern production of a more democratic idea of who and what gets produced. But parody's inherent awareness of how forms like genre cinema are constructed, and its sense of the meanings produced by them, also underlines how so many of the critical contexts previously underpinning notions of 'good' culture have to some extent been rendered superfluous. Most prominent here is the traditional target of mass culture's 'ideological' content, allied to what Theodor Adorno, from a specifically Marxist perspective, would call the 'culture industry';[14] the idea that industrially-produced, popular and generic forms like Hollywood cinema contributed to the mass audience's false consciousness, their (self-)deceptive and imaginary relationship to the reality of their social and economic existence. The more pronounced turn in film and television studies toward questions of reception and fan responses has brought more clearly into view how movies and television shows, far from the unquestioned and ideologically subjecting vehicles earlier theory deemed them to be, are in fact texts of varied potential interpretations and multiple uses. Informed by Michel de Certeau's[15] and Stuart Hall's[16] notions of 'poaching' and 'decoding', and finding its legs in the later study of fans and fan-produced texts, this turn towards the audience as the primary marker of textual signification debunked the idea that either the meaning or the value of a given film or television show can be prescribed by some seemingly transcendent aesthetic criteria.

In mapping the move from the discourses of 'Culture' to that of 'cult' in British cinema, Justin Smith identifies the importance of the 'cultural studies' turn associated with Hall, and also Raymond Williams.[17] This turn had at its material base transformations in consumer habits, disposable income and viewing technologies in the post-war era, an accumulation of factors which, especially since the 1960s, has contributed to 'the hegemonic blurring of erstwhile class-based divisions between high and popular categories of art and consumption practice'.[18] Allied to this grounding is the way, for Smith, cult practices of consumption and performance are marked by their '"disproportionate" enthusiasm'[19] for particular films or television shows. This idea of a 'disproportionate' response to a text is of course, as indicated by Smith's use of quotation marks, relative to established parameters for consumption and response. From a user-oriented perspective, there cannot be a disproportionate response, as the correct response is determined by whatever level of enthusiasm is brought to the text in question. Or as Scott McCracken puts it in his study of 'pulp' literature, our contemporary concern is less with 'abstract categories of high and low, good and bad', and more with deciphering 'the kinds of values a particular audience has a vested interest in creating or sustaining'.[20] We have already seen in the previous chapter how a film like *Hot Fuzz* uses a genre like the Hollywood action film not to criticise it exactly, but rather to *make use of it* in a way that reworks whatever 'problematic' value it may be supposed to have. *Hot Fuzz* in this sense narrates what happens to mass-cultural products like the action movie as they are received across global contexts. The action movie hence becomes separated from its (notional) status as an ideologically-informed Hollywood product, and becomes a new, disseminated text amenable to all manner of potential readings and re-purposings, of which *Hot Fuzz* is just one possible example.

Horror Parody, or Parody as Horror?

Besides *Hot Fuzz*'s integration of action cinema aesthetics within the contexts of English heritage, there is also at work in the film a pronounced use of the conventions of horror cinema. It is possibly easy to overlook, within the wealth of textual allusion in the film, that Pegg's Sergeant Angel very nearly perishes at the hands of murderous, ostensibly satanic cabal of villagers: the members of the Neighbourhood Watch Association who meet in nocturnal graveyards to intone their commitment to 'The Greater Good'. As I will discuss in the rest of this chapter, the horror genre offers a revealing case study for thinking about the relationship of parody texts to their notional 'targets'; and in turn, how parody may shape or even encourage us to rethink our own relationship to forms such as horror.

The idea of horror parody as at the same time a kind of horror practice in itself inevitably begs some theoretical questions. As McCracken has observed, horror as a genre is in principle based on its ability to disturb the reader's (or viewer's) cognitive framework for interpretation: 'The very effectiveness of the horror story depends upon the reader's inability to rationalise the source of the terror.'[21] Speaking for himself as an academic coming to analyse such fictions, McCracken is consequently aware of the 'fundamental contradiction' between the work of critical analysis and 'the function of the horror narrative'.[22] Insofar as it works to foreground the mechanics of the genre, horror parody represents a similar kind of contradictory text. There are comparative implications here for parodies of science fiction (the focus of my final chapter), though as with both the latter genre and horror, which share a number of characteristics, there are also medium-specific defining issues concerning *cinematic* genres that need addressing.

In *Hot Fuzz*, the satanic N.W.A. (whose titular acknowledgement of Compton's most famous rap outfit was presumably not on the group's agenda) alludes more obliquely to a particular demonic strain of English horror cinema (those films, for example, based on Dennis Wheatley's occult novels, such as *The Devil Rides Out* [1968]). Its main reference point, though, is in its structural plot similarity to *The Wicker Man* (1973). In *Hot Fuzz*, an idealistic and morally incorruptible policeman from the capital is called to a rural village and winds up investigating a series of murders, ignorant of the more bizarre reality behind the crimes. In *The Wicker Man*, a religiously devout and morally incorruptible policeman from the Scottish mainland (played by Edward Woodward, the head of the N.W.A. in *Hot Fuzz*) goes to a Hebridean island to investigate the disappearance of a young girl. Once there he finds out that its all-singing-and-dancing island-ers are still calling upon pagan gods to bless their failing crops, though he is also ignorant as to the actual truth of the matter: that the missing girl was a ruse to capture him – as required, an authority figure who is also a virgin and a fool – and sacrifice him to the gods in the giant 'wicker man' of the title.

In a similar way to *Hot Fuzz*'s appropriation of the action movie, its use of *The Wicker Man* is once more indicative of the ambiguous way prior texts and generic conventions are worked into the film. *Hot Fuzz*'s manipu-lation both of a parallel plot structure and character organisation suggests a significant debt to the earlier movie. The difference is largely to do with tone and context. Within the comic schema of *Hot Fuzz*, the sinister coven is actually not in thrall to any demonic forces, unless the desire to retain Village of the Year status is part of Satan's work. But this is precisely the joke in the film's referential reworking of filmic quotation: the 'little England' logic of The Greater Good, doublespeak for the exclusion of all unwelcome elements, is a force of evil; but here, notably, it is connoted parodically within the terms of a heritage film and television aesthetic, and its associ-ated insularity.

In the contexts of this chapter's main argument, it is important to note here that the parodic use of *The Wicker Man* and a fannish appreciation of the film are not at all mutually exclusive terms. *The Wicker Man* had already surfaced in a British comedy context before *Hot Fuzz*, in the first series of *The League of Gentlemen* (BBC, 1999), as written and performed by Steve Pemberton, Reece Shearsmith and Mark Gatiss (Jeremy Dyson being the fourth, non-performing member of the group). Here, the self-proclaimed 'local shop for local people' run by the grotesque Edward and Tubbs is the first sight for visitors to Royston Vasey, a small Northern-England town through which a motorway by-pass is being planned. Edward and Tubbs, in order to preserve the town's local status, are keen to put a stop to this, permanently removing road planners, workers, and even random hikers. When a policeman comes to inquire about the recent disappearances, it is not long before he too is caught and made to perish, in a form of demonic ritual performed in the shop by its now half-naked owners. In a way that *Hot Fuzz* would later exploit, *The League of Gentlemen* here appropriates the structure and contexts of *The Wicker Man* as part of its own darkly comic landscape, with its shopkeepers themselves performing their own pagan rites in order to preserve and reaffirm their sense of local identity.

There is more going on here, though. Using *The Wicker Man* in this way to a specifically comic effect establishes a difference between its original function and its more parodic/satirical use in the later texts. As Smith has discussed in detail,[23] *The Wicker Man* has since its release assumed a cult following that, in the case of this film, owes something to its own links to the early 1970s counter-culture, its paganism, and its own performance of (oc)cult practice. The obsessions and participatory practices of the film's fans, many of whom travel to the film's setting in homage, have contributed to the film's status as cult text. As much as *The League of Gentlemen* and *Hot Fuzz*'s imitative appropriation of *The Wicker Man*'s plot shows its indebtedness to the earlier film, such use also changes the significance of the film, re-functioning whatever actual representational character or intent the film might have. As with every other referenced text in the film, ideological value is effectively flattened out: but to what extent does this forego or preserve the 'pleasures' of the films in question? If, as with *Hot Fuzz*'s use of the action movie, we can argue that the film maintains the films' fun but removes their less palatable associations, this inevitably impacts also upon the way we might view *The Wicker Man* from our contemporary perspective.

Parody without Parody: Horror as Comedy

As we have seen, the inherently reflexive nature of parody explicitly foregrounds the awareness of other texts and conventions. Parody from this point of view is not so much representation in the strict mimetic sense of the term – the imitative depiction, in other words, of real life – but what I will call the representation *of a response to representations*. As I suggested, the effect of this in the context of a film like *Hot Fuzz* is to represent not the illusion of reality in a coherent fictional world, but rather *the experience of watching films* in a transnational context.

Parody becomes a necessary part of this process, but importantly, does not necessarily imply a critical or derisive position with regard to the parodied text(s).

By the same token, we would be wrong to assume that the parodic use of *The Wicker Man* indicated a criticism or intended mockery. I suggest, rather, we see it as a form of recognition, an acknowledgement of its effect and persistence within *Hot Fuzz*'s cinematic imaginary. Neither parody nor homage are mere forms of neutral replication: they must be signaled and identified as such for them to make sense *as* either parody or homage.[24] Parody is one way in which these textual markers of re-presentation are constructed, though of course this still begs the question of how we understand the *comedic* within this practice. With horror as with the action film, comic transcontextualisations and inversions work to diffuse the 'reality effect' of such films' representations. To what *productive* end, though, remains to be seen.

As noted previously, Harries has explored what he sees as parody's 'resuscitation of genre', with a notable emphasis on the way semi-parodies like the *Scream* series (1996–) and *I Know What You Did Last Summer* (1997), and then parodies of these semi-parodies such as *Scary Movie* (2000), have in effect maintained the horror genre through their use, and hence perpetuation, of recognised generic motifs.[25] In *Spaced*, similarly, the very topicality of its reference points – recent films such as *The Matrix* and *The Phantom Menace*, TV shows like *The X-Files* (Fox, 1993–2002), contemporary videogames like *Tomb Raider* and *Resident Evil* – implicitly affirm the cultural centrality of such products, whatever their representation. The idea that genre is reaffirmed through its parody (and reiterating cycles of further parody) is a strong indicator of the way much of contemporary popular culture, as Harries puts it, works around 'varied routes of referential circularity'.[26] This would indicate however that parody has – as Harries puts it in the conclusion to his earlier book – 'long fled from the battle front'[27] in terms of its potential for generic or cultural *critique*, moving instead to the installing of a new 'canon' of parody films themselves.[28] The important point here, though, is that the practices of reception and reproduction so far outlined in this chapter already call into question the reality effects and ideological force of genre cinema, traditionally the target of parody's criticism. To say that parody has 'fled the battle front', in this sense, takes an effect as a cause, somewhat overlooking the fact that genres in their original sense are no longer what they once were.

There is a slightly different agenda in *Hot Fuzz*'s use of *The Wicker Man*, though, as a fairly low-budget British 'cult' film is very different in its cultural connotations from American genre cinema. Moreover, the traditions of British horror, unlike those of the American action movie, are frequently the subject of a type of academic protectionist discourse that laments its possible demise into the denigrations of parody. In terms of the adaptation of horror texts or their forms of remaking, the horror narrative is subject to a fair degree of interpretive policing. Looking, for example, at the 1931 Universal film *Frankenstein*, David Pirie identifies a number of 'blunders' made by the film, such as the monster's being accidentally given a criminal brain, and the wildly veering tone of actor Colin Clive in the title role. Pirie's attribution of 'blunder' refers here less to the coherence of these choices within the film's aesthetic whole, than to their deviation from the Mary Shelley novel on which the film is loosely based. Pirie's insistence that *Frankenstein*, 'in spite of these blunders [...] remains a magnificent example [...] of a particular baroque form of American expressionism'[29] shows a determination to make the film cohere within an acceptable (though not perfect) type of horror classification.

Assuming that parody 'mocks' or 'spoofs' the horror text's integrity, in fact, may overlook the way it is in fact part of the same genre's continuity. Pirie's landmark *A Heritage of Horror*, originally published in 1973, ends with a sustained lament for the declining force of what Pirie calls the English Gothic cinema. This is best exemplified for Pirie by Hammer's earlier horror efforts, such as *The Curse of Frankenstein* (1956) and *Dracula* (1957), a cinema whose possible maintenance or regeneration was at the time of writing negatively influenced by 'increasing public sophistication',[30] rendering it 'no longer possible to make naïve straightforward English horror films'.[31] In their introduction to the more recent *British Horror Cinema* (2002), Steve Chibnall and Julian Petley, starting from this passage from Pirie, expand upon what they and other historians of horror cinema saw as the absence of a meaningful post-Hammer English horror, and more particularly, the problems English film producers have in constructing an economically viable and (quoting Pirie once more) 'intrinsically *native*' type of horror film within the early twenty-first century cinema economy.[32]

Pirie argues that good horror filmmakers, especially those who 'under-stand the essential historical value of [the English] tradition',[33] are '[what] the British cinema needed (and still needs) so desperately badly'.[34] From one perspective this view seems over-stated: why do we 'need' a horror cinema, and why (a rather excessive touch) 'so desperately badly'? Such a view (reflective in part of its being written in the early 1970s) cannot real-istically countenance the rejection of historical continuity, cultural canons and hierarchies of taste that, as we have seen, are typical of postmodern production and thinking. But Pirie's conclusion also seems now resistant to the historical evolutions of genre in its prescriptive idea of the 'essential historical value' of English horror's 'tradition'; just as his intriguing desire to see 'naïve, straightforward English horror films', in its very terms, sug-gests a nostalgic blinkeredness to the realities of evolving film practices. By contrast, Chibnall and Petley's call for a native *but contemporary* horror cinema makes space for a different kind of film that can at least make use of such earlier representations.

Wallace and Gromit: The Curse of the Were-Rabbit, that I looked at briefly in Chapter 1, showed a particularly astute awareness of the ways this horror tradition could be repurposed, precisely in its resistance to 'straight-forward' representation and its willingness to use modes of classical horror as a source of parodic pleasure: as, for example, in the way Wallace's face and body are subjected to a variety of monstrous transformations, familiar both from Hollywood movies like *Hulk*, as well as English horrors such as *The Curse of the Werewolf*. Such 'old' effects and narratives find their contemporary 'native' place in Nick Park's unreal world of invention, a safe space for nostalgic enjoyment which is also, at the same time, modern in its self-reflexive sensibilities and technology. As I suggested previously, such parodic takes on specifically *English* horror motifs, while acknowledg-ing the debt to such past representations on the film's narrative, style and design, also draws a contemporary ideological line between earlier hor-ror's English Gothic contexts (establishing it, in turn, as something we can embrace *materially*, as something to be enjoyed, though without taking it *seriously*).

But *The Curse of the Were-Rabbit*, as we saw in an earlier chapter, also bridges both *The League of Gentlemen* and *Hot Fuzz* in making its 'local' village folk, assembled for the climactic vegetable show at Lady

Tottington's palatial manor house, the embodiment of monstrous sensibility, as – fusing the endings of *Frankenstein*, *King Kong* and *Hulk* – they
pick up their gardening tools to chase Wallace's unfortunate were-
creature to its (near-) death. Significantly for a film that, as we have seen,
offsets its 'local' qualities with technological savvy and global reference
points, the rural paganism so central to a film like *The Wicker Man* is the
excessive and incongruous source both of the film's narrative tension and
its comedy.

Shaun of the Dead's overt use of Romero's *Dawn of the Dead* (which
also includes borrowing some of its soundtrack) is similarly aware of
the persistence of older textual figures within contemporary film culture. Edgar Wright's film gets much of its comic mileage from the dis-
junctions between the prior movie and its reiteration in *Shaun of the
Dead*'s historical and geographical contexts. The main reason though
why *Shaun* can never simply rehash *Dawn* is that *Dawn* has already hap-
pened: *Shaun of the Dead*'s work is consequently to re-function *Dawn
of the Dead*'s narrative and motifs for a film audience and even film protagonists for whom the zombie invasion has already taken place. Thus
Shaun of the Dead enters and perpetuates the 'routes of referential circularity' discussed by Harries, and becomes symptomatic not only of early
twenty-first-century parody, but a type of early twenty-first-century
horror cinema. As previously noted, this does not mean in itself that the
film does not have any critical purchase, especially as the 'zombiefica-
tion' of consciousness *through* a mass-media culture underpins the film's
comedy. Yet here, the specifically ideological and economic targets of
Dawn of the Dead, with its biting allegory of mall-culture consumerism,
are largely voided through their re-location, in *Shaun of the Dead*, to the
solipsistic spaces of slacker culture, hermetically bordered from the real
world as such.

My suggestion here, similarly, is that *Hot Fuzz* pays suitable homage
to a film like *The Wicker Man*, while also acknowledging that it cannot
share the same contexts of production and reception. In the example given
in the previous chapter, and as reiterated at the beginning of this one, it
seems entirely coherent for *Spaced* to acknowledge its imaginative debt to
the earlier *Star Wars* movies without simply imitating those same films or
mocking them. But then, what would it mean to take the *Star Wars* films in

5.1 Our hero fails to notice the zombie apocalypse in *Shaun of the Dead* (2004)

a 'straight' way anyway? I think the same questions apply to horror. What would it mean to take a film like *The Wicker Man* 'seriously'? This is to some degree the question Smith answers in his study of the film, and the aim of this present chapter is not to debate those claims. How we understand the discursive value of such films, though, as they circulate through a range of texts balanced uncertainly between parody and homage, demands further interrogation, touching as it does on the uses and meanings of texts, 'cult' or otherwise, in our contemporary viewing contexts.

Cult Cinema: Parody Cinema

If we take Smith's view that cult texts can be born as such through the meeting of text and audience, and not, in Timothy Corrigan's words, only 'adopted',[35] we can see the points of contact between parody and cult cinema. As Corrigan argues, the cult audience 'is significant [for] its unusual disregard for textual authority and systemic coherence'; it is 'an instance of dominant viewing and semiotic practice that willfully refuses to play by the traditional rules of the game'.[36] Corrigan's prognosis for popular cinema at the turn of the millennium appears now very perceptive, insofar as much filmmaking and television production – Pegg and Wright's work being exemplary in this instance – have made such 'disregard' for 'systemic coherence' (if not necessarily 'textual authority' in its fullest sense) more usual than unusual, literally cult-ivating its audience through quotation and allusion.

What seems to concern a critic like Corrigan, whose work on cult cinema appears the same year as Fredric Jameson's book on postmodernism, is that such cult films are more concerned with recycling images than they are with attempting to accurately 'map' the contemporary time and place.[37] The implication is that such texts have a kind of 'anything goes' approach; but this would underestimate the way specific types of disproportionate response to other texts reflect specifically *historical* perspectives on these same texts. Smith's insistence on the 'camp' and 'kitsch' performances at work in *The Rocky Horror Picture Show* (1975),[38] the British-American production based on Richard O'Brien's hit London stage musical *The Rocky Horror Show*, may seem in line with Corrigan's take on the same film. Describing it as 'a low-budget, "hysterical" mish-mash of genres', Corrigan is constrained to view the film only in terms of its performance of wearable and discardable 'subjectivities'.[39] Smith's more nuanced take on the film only devolves to the same 'hysterical' take if we disregard camp's particular inflections and attitudes. The performances that Smith sees here as central to *The Rocky Horror Picture Show* are inseparable from its practices of parody, specifically of earlier science-fiction and horror film and television.[40] What makes them camp is less some vague quality of performance style, than it is a deliberately excessive use of generic motifs; excessive in the sense that their apparent signification is at odds with what is actually signified. The camp pleasures of *The Rocky Horror Picture Show* reside in the fact that its B-movie sci-fi tropes have lost whatever ideological or representational hold they might once have had. Now that they are 'cast off, floating free in a weightless semiotic space devoid of […] gravity and anchorage',[41] they are free to be appropriated and redeployed. As Smith adds, importantly, this reworking of genre in *The Rocky Horror Picture Show* has a poignancy in the way it retrieves generic motifs whose original significance has been lost to us. Such performance is therefore always in some sense nostalgic, but also historically conscious, because the use of such motifs is predicated on their past-ness: they only become camp because they were *once shocking*,[42] but no longer so.

In *The Rocky Horror Picture Show* parody is again transcontextual, the relocation of its generic elements emphasising their constructedness: their reduction to a specific time and place in which, to use Rick Altman's terms, 'the audience's ritual values coincide[d] with Hollywood's ideological ones'.[43]

159

The point, in other words, when genre 'made sense' to audiences in ways it no longer can (and as we will see in my final chapter, a similar approach is at work in *Flash Gordon* [1980], *Rocky Horror*'s not-too-distant sci-fi cousin). This retrospective paradigm for quotation and parody serves us well for understanding the use of *The Wicker Man* in both *Hot Fuzz* and *The League of Gentlemen*. The implication here is that we can no longer take *The Wicker Man* seriously, yet we can still enjoy its trappings, and the idea that it might have been shocking, or could be shocking in a wholly other context. Its use plays as comedy because it belongs to another time: in both *Hot Fuzz* and *The League of Gentlemen* this 'past-ness' or 'other world-ness' of *The Wicker Man* is used to specific effect, embodying as it does a comically exaggerated idea of the 'local' as both a site and object of pagan devotion.

Horror without Horror: *Garth Marenghi's Darkplace*

Garth Marenghi's Darkplace (henceforth *GMD*) (Channel 4, 2004) highlights the complexity of parody as a contemporary mode. This is because *GMD*, in a word, is bad. Or rather: the comic basis for the series involves a shared recognition between its makers and its audience of what constitutes 'bad television'. In this instance, the 'quality' of the show is paradoxically related to the skill and ingenuity with which 'bad' televisual aesthetics are identified, reworked and exaggerated.

The premise of *GMD* is developed along the lines of 'mockumentary' comedy such as that of the film *This is Spinal Tap*. 'Garth Marenghi's Darkplace' is the title of a show-within-the-show written by and starring bestselling horror novelist Garth Marenghi (played by the series' actual co-writer Matt Holness), made in the early days of Channel 4, but which was never broadcast (each internal episode nevertheless preserves Channel 4's multi-coloured logo from the 1980s). Darkplace is the name of the hospital, apparently near Romford in Essex, where the redundantly over-titled Dr Rick Dagless M.D. (played by Marenghi) is employed. As its name suggests, besides having to rise to the formidable challenge of being an English NHS hospital, Darkplace is also a portal for occult happenings, such as demonic possession, mutations and infestations of alien spores. As a self-professed former warlock, as well as a veteran of several wars, Dagless is called upon to fight the forces of evil, frequently ending up offering a ruminative voiceover as he gazes upon the fake Romford skyline.

Within the actual 2004 series, each 'rediscovered' episode of 'Garth Marenghi's Darkplace' is introduced by Marenghi, and intercut with comments by Marenghi and two other actors in the show: Dean Lerner (also Marenghi's agent and publisher, played by co-writer and director Richard Ayoade), and Todd Rivers (Matt Berry). This framing device provides another comic layer to the show, as the often earnest comments of the interviewees – self-aggrandising statements of aesthetic intent, laments for the state of current television drama, pot-shots at the cowardice of 1980s television programmers – are juxtaposed with a marked display of wooden acting style, terribly disjunctive film editing and thematic pretentiousness.

What is striking about GMD, though, is the level of *detail* in the narrative and production values, and the way that the whole package is designed in effect to 'be' the thing that is the notional subject of parody. In a similar way to the seminal show Police Squad, created by the makers of Airplane!, and which also ran for just one series before giving rise to the Naked Gun film franchise, GMD blurs the lines between parody and subject by functioning as six self-sufficient short dramas, linked by points of structural and semantic continuity (the reappearance of supporting characters; the consistent setting; the repeated credit sequences). Police Squad famously played with the conventions of American cop shows – though without specifically identifying any shows as such – through forms of inversion and misdirection: the 'special guest stars' who were introduced and killed off before the end of the opening titles; the closing freeze-frame in which random action continued around motionless, grinning actors. GMD equally exploits a range of genre tropes: the uses of now largely outmoded miniature and practical special effects, and obtrusive back projection; the obviously constructed sets and awkward staging of actors; the uncertain timing of dialogue and stilted performance styles. But especially as, like Police Squad, the precise 'targets' of parody in GMD are not identified, the show functions in a much less clear-cut way than is presumed in contemporary parody franchises, based as these frequently are around the shared recognition of specific reference points, by audiences highly aware of the particular texts and conventions being manipulated.

As Harries observes about recent Hollywood parody, the 'deconstructive display of a genre's components' is no more than 'a veil of critical distance'; to the effect that 'film parody ends up embodying the "master code" of a genre'.[44] As noted, this suggests that parody is more in collusion with the work of genre than its antithesis. Tim Bergfelder concurs with this in reference to the recent German cinematic context. A number of parody films, Bergfelder notes, frequently recycle recognisable motifs from earlier German movies, though without obvious commentary on these prior texts. Bergfelder argues that pastiche, dismissed by Jameson as 'blank parody',[45] has been more and more used as a way of reflecting on the values and representations of earlier film periods and genres; while contemporary parody, with its knowing, self-referential jokes, 'has itself become blank'.[46] But *GMD* is elusive in this respect. Its humour works largely around the particular parodied uses of film and television language and genre: its use of, for instance, accidental jump cuts and continuity errors; abrupt reframings of actors; the occasional excesses or slips in its synchronised dialogue track; also its imitation of 1980s television film stock. But its lack of an obvious target, as well as its more slippery generic connotations (that I will touch on below) make it less straightforward to read the show.

These initial reflections suggest that merely marking off *GMD* as a 'spoof' (of *what* exactly?) is inadequate to our understanding of it; and that, at some level, the show hardly mocks a particular generic type, but constructs one for itself. This is sustained at the paratextual level of reception, in the form of the Channel 4 DVD of the series, released in 2006. In much the same way that Marenghi offers an introduction to each episode, usually after a short reading from one of his bestselling 'chillers', the DVD's index screen is framed in the mode of occult horror cinema: a central television screen emits distorted snowy light and buzzes of white noise, similar to the demonic video in the Japanese film *Ring* (1999); the episode list, in a gothic font, is entitled 'The Visions', while 'Additionata' offers us a series of extras. Our knowledge of the show's constructed nature allows us to recognise the careful way that such paratextual framing replicates the language and iconography of horror texts: indeed, the show exemplifies one of the often overlooked aspects of parody: that it can actually inform us about a generic reference point by virtue of its detailed acts of parodic imitation. Significantly, then, the idea that this 'spoofs' horror can only be

5.2 Collapsing difference in the love of detail: the DVD menu for *Garth Marenghi's Darkplace* (2004)

an assumption based on the extent of our knowledge – in much the same way that our knowing enjoyment of Spinal Tap's hard-rock pomposity can only come from our recognition that the band is not real. The important implication here is that enjoyment of the texts in question may have a lot more to do with the supposedly 'parodied' subject matter than knowingly 'ironic' readings may acknowledge.

GMD operates less, then, through any supposed distance from its parodied subjects, but rather through *closeness*. While Marenghi sports a pair of large glasses in the style of Stephen King, very much the pre-eminent horror writer of the last century and even this one, the more baroque and obviously English trappings of *Darkplace*, and its often queasy subject matter, suggest a closer affinity to the slightly less best-selling James Herbert – the late author who made his name with books like *Rats* (1974) and *The Fog* (1975), both set, like much of Herbert's work, in the south of England. The DVD cover image for *GMD*, in fact, with Marenghi's face half in shadow, emulates the same author image

163

Herbert used for some of his books; while the cover art and typeface for these same books are echoed in the self-penned novels Marenghi reads from in the series.

Identifying a writer such as James Herbert as a prior reference point for *GMD*, we can see how much the show does not so much parody the aesthetic and narrative tendencies of a certain style of horror writing, as approximate it. We see this, for instance, by looking at the plot summaries of Herbert's novels, as selected here from my own copy of *Lair*:

> FLUKE […] Fluke was a dog – aptly named because it was obviously by a fluke that he was different from other dogs, or for that matter from other creatures in the animal world with whom he had mental communication.[47]

The needless repetitions in the prose style here, the grammatical awkwardness, the over-explanation, and the dramatic revelation that sounds no more than an incidental fact, find their echo in Garth's own tendencies toward long-winded reiterations and redundancies ('I decided I needed to go for a drive. That's why I'm in the car' ['The Creeping Moss from the Shores of Shuggoth']). This, like the dialogue in *GMD*, is 'bad' writing. But here, bad writing has its own kind of appeal and presumably unintended humour – which of course raises the issue of whether such writing is 'bad' at all. Similarly, in Herbert's authorial epilogues we see a forerunner of Marenghi's rather pompous hectoring, overstated shamanic power and moral righteousness, all (comically) counterpointed by climactic understatement; as, for example, from *Lair*:

> The locations used in this novel exist. The Conservation Centre, The Warren, the police training camp, the mobile home site, the little church at High Beach, are real places… *All* characters are figments of my own imagination, although their job titles are not.
>
> Because of the slight alarm caused by my first novel *The Rats* several years ago, I felt it might be wise to stress that while it is true that rats are becoming increasingly resistant to Warfarin, there are many other effective baits…constantly being introduced. So it will be some time before the ever-growing rat population in the United Kingdom reaches a critical level.[48]

Compare now the accompanying booklet for the DVD, written by Marenghi:

> Like Leonardo's 'copter, [*Darkplace*] was ahead of its time and, sadly, its lessons have not yet been learnt. War continues to rage in the Middle East, ecological disasters near tear our world in twain, and NHS staff are still denied access to firearms.

Again, our identification of this as parody owes most to our knowledge of what the show is doing. But even if this is the case, it still asks us to recognise the particular qualities inherent in Herbert's original work, as these are not so much reworked in *GMD* as reiterated.

The writing throughout *GMD* displays similar attributes of comic incongruities and bathetic punch-lines to dramatic assertions. Often this is seen in the excerpts from Marenghi's 'extensive canon of chillers' read by the author in the introductions to each episode:

> Something was pouring from his mouth. He examined his sleeve. Blood? *Blood*. Crimson, copper-smelling blood. His blood. Blood. Blood. *Blood*. And bits of sick ('Once Upon a Beginning').

> Who knew how long the place had stood there? 40 years? 50 years? *Tempus immemoria*, i.e. always? ('The Apes of Wrath')

To suggest once more that this offers a parody of bad writing is to miss somewhat the more subtle point that this offers us the *enjoyment* of bad writing in and of itself as style. 'Bad' is of course an evaluative concept, and from the point of view of a certain postmodern thinking, a meaningless one. 'Bad taste' or 'trash culture', in this respect, while it may persist to identify particular kinds of cultural production,[49] is a self-contradictory notion: bad taste within the terms of postmodern parody is simply one 'taste' amongst many.

This becomes an important aspect of *GMD*'s disruption of cultural hierarchies. When Marenghi claims in his introduction to the final episode, 'I've always loved the great tragedies. *King Lear. The Poseidon Adventure. Superman II*' ('The Creeping Moss from the Shores of Shuggoth'), he makes a significant if unintended point about the way contemporary canons of taste and value are less bound to strict notions of distinction or register. As much as we might wish to laugh at Marenghi's levelling of Shakespeare and Superman, this 'joke' reminds us of the indiscriminate ways we both consume and discuss texts in the contemporary era; to the extent, even, that inter-weaving superhero franchises can be discussed with the level of textual analysis and exegesis attributable formerly to Shakespearian scholarship – or that Shakespearian actors such as Ian McKellen and Kenneth Branagh can happily star in superhero movies (*X-Men* [2000]) or even direct them (*Thor* [2011]). Or indeed, that we might knowingly enjoy the notional incongruity between these cultural registers *and at the same time* happily engage as viewers, as I do, with both supermen and Shakespearean heroes, not to mention '*Garth Marenghi's Darkplace*' itself. But this canonical blurring is also part of what *GMD* is already doing formally, in its leaps between the sacred, the profane and the prosaic: this last episode, 'The Creeping Moss from the Shores of Shuggoth', manages in fact to incorporate allusions to *Romeo and Juliet* and quotes from Wordsworth, alongside MTV-style rock videos and advice for writing sex scenes.

It is perhaps more accurate to say then that *GMD* reflects an appreciation of its varied source materials as already 'bad', but with implications for understanding the way genres like horror are seen and discussed. While the evaluation of trash suggests a mode of 'camp' sensibility, many critics have noted the tendency already within British horror cinema traditions of the 1960s and 1970s towards what Steve Chibnall summarises as 'Gothic excess, self-satire and ironic quotation'.[50] Chibnall's reading of what we might call post-classical Hammer horror, noting its preference for 'sardonic genre parody', reflects a widely-received understanding of how genres develop through various stages of formation and reception. As Harries puts it, genres have often been seen to move through a 'classical' phase of 'conventional stabilization' before reaching a point of 'intellectualization' characterised by 'increased variation', until over-familiarity with generic conventions and possibilities brings about 'the self-reflexive stage in which parody typically arises'.[51] Peter Hutchings notes this self-reflexive dimension in many of the 'portmanteau' horror films produced by Amicus (Hammer's rival production company) during this period, such as *Dr Terror's House of Horrors* (1965), *Tales from the Crypt* (1972) and *Vault of Horror* (1973), primarily in the 'direct address to the camera/audience',[52] either through protagonists, 'dead narrators' or the 'horror hosts' (for example Doctor Schreck, played by Peter Cushing, in *Dr Terror's House of Horrors*). Such practices, along with breaking the conventions of classical film space, 'put the audience at a distance from the drama'.[53] With this in mind, especially as the whole series of *GMD* is a kind of portmanteau – each 'tale of terror' being introduced by the horror host, in suitably low-key lighting and gaudy colour schemes – the show is as much a perpetuation or reworking of this ironic English tradition as it is a parody of it. Much of the pleasure that *GMD* offers particular viewers, in fact, is precisely these barely inflected reworkings of horror- or sci-fi genre narratives and tropes: a dabbler in the occult who becomes a portal to another dimension ('Once Upon a Beginning'); a virus that makes humans devolve to apes ('The Apes of Wrath'); a spore infestation that turns a woman into broccoli ('The Creeping Moss from the Shores of Shuggoth').

At the visual level, similarly, *GMD* revels in a frequently 'gross' representation of horror special effects that also, by the comparative standards of today's CGI-led effects industries, look cheap as well as nasty. In episode one, 'Once Upon a Beginning', Dagless's former buddy, now a living gateway between Darkplace and Hell, explodes before Dagless's eyes: a shot that, in a nod to the prevailing aesthetics of the action special effect,[54] is also repeated from several angles and in slow motion, allowing in this instance the sticky mess of stage blood, model limbs, head and internal organs to bounce and splatter within the frame. The parodic dimension of the scene comes from the way its capacity to shock is undercut by incongruous elements: after his friend explodes, we hear Dagless's voice on the soundtrack asking rather vaguely 'are you all right'? He then proceeds to have a conversation with the remaining head, perched upon the mess of its own eviscerated body. But insofar as this shot is constructed and played out within the episode as a type of spectacle, and also one that is logically integrated into the narrative, it begs the question whether this is parody at all.

Looking at it historically, we can place such sequences referentially within the terms of the visual effects technologies of 'contemporary' (that is, early 1980s) horror cinema, in films such as *Zombie Flesh Eaters* (1979), *The Evil Dead* (1981) or *The Thing* (1981). All of these are linked by their predominant focus on extremely graphic practical effects, which in some instances came to be viewed as the films' main selling point, and led to the designers of such special effects assuming forms of auteur status amongst the horror fan community.[55] As theorists such as Steve Neale have discussed,[56] such special effects had a doubled spectacular significance, both for the protagonists within the diegesis, *and* for the viewer marvelling at the technical achievement; the implication being that the verisimilitude of these effects is always counterweighed by their status *as* special effect, and therefore as unreal. To this extent there is already a self-reflexive element structured into the horror special effect well before its appropriation in *GMD*.

The extra parodic layer added by *GMD* through the dialogue acknowledges the temporal distance between our viewing and its historical point of reference, while still enjoying the work of the effects in their capacity as pure surface and artifice. In this respect, the show conforms to Smith's view of the 'kitsch' horror text, celebrating the once-was-shocking from the perspective of the present. As McCracken notes (with reference to Dennis Wheatley's 1960 novel *The Satanist*), dated aspects of representation and style can convert terror to comedy,[57] yet the waning of impact does not mean such outdated texts somehow change genres; rather, their motifs and structures remain preserved in another time. Like the 'video nasty' that generated such a cultural stir in the 1980s (under which label films like *Zombie Flesh Eaters* and *The Evil Dead* were often discussed), films that no longer shock simply assume a different kind of value: old horror is still 'horror', but with the pathological elements removed. If they no longer have the power to terrify, they assume the unexpected role of aesthetic artefacts, audio-visual antiques, objects of delectation rather than disgust. Similarly, the appropriation of 'bad' pulp horror, in the form of Herbert's pastiched narrative style, suggests a nostalgic revisiting of something consumed avidly and unquestioningly in the context of another time – in my case, most definitely, as a pubescent male drawn to such novels' darkly lurid covers, and the illicit thrills and visceral narratives between them. As I have suggested in this chapter, whatever my adult critical awareness of such texts, I cannot disregard the way *GMD* draws on the residual memory of this early, pleasurable contact with the horror genre.

5.3 For the love of horror: the nostalgic spectacle of visual effects in *Garth Marenghi's Darkplace* (2004)

Conclusions: Beyond Good Taste

As with the uses of *The Wicker Man* in *Hot Fuzz* and *The League of Gentlemen*, then, the uses of horror in *GMD* work above all through a temporal framework. Framed as it is within the concept of a show from the early 1980s, it strikes me as less a 'mockery' of television and horror conventions (even a 'loving' one), and more of an affectionate take on the memory of such conventions. Parodic techniques mark the show as re-presentation, but the broader aim is more productive. This is because *GMD* is actually more various in its allusions than seems initially the case. The internal show's setting and structure, as well as its hero's over-lettered title, actually recall the American hospital-based series *Quincy M.E.* (Universal, 1976–83), starring Jack Klugman, which has aired perennially in the UK since its original production. Besides carrying out his official duties as a forensic pathologist, Quincy would frequently solve the crimes that brought bodies to the hospital; equally, like Dagless in *GMD*, events in the episodes would

169

give Quincy plentiful opportunity to rail against the injustices of society, and in the frequent confrontations with his long-suffering bosses, to lambast the deficiencies of his hospital and the wider health care system.

When put together, we start to see how limited the often negative or critical implications of parody or spoof are to a show like *GMD*, given its eclectic style, its attention to detail, and the total coherence of its diegetic world. Parody here marks an awareness of the show's status as re-creation: as a nostalgic revisiting, though not an ironic or derisive one, from the vantage point of the present. Its distinctiveness is in being at once ridiculous *and* entirely serious. It creates a consistent tone of 'horror' without, in fact, any actual horror to speak of. It at once signals the absurdity of a show like '*Garth Marenghi's Darkplace*', while, through the re-presentation of the show itself, bringing this unlikely creation to life.

A bit like the Frankenstein's monster to which this last image alludes, and not unlike the 1931 film that plays fast and loose with Shelley's novel, *GMD* is an unruly conglomeration of different elements. But this unruliness, this combination of 'excess and incongruity' Smith identifies at the heart of the cult text,[58] is potent in its capacity to disrupt the boundaries between genres, and between ideas of culture and taste. As I have suggested here, in its loyalty to the aesthetics of 'low' film, television and novel forms, *GMD*, allowing us to enjoy such things through the guise of laughing 'at' them, engineers an unexpected turnaround. Here, the knowing arbiters of good taste (both the show's creators and myself as a viewer) are revealed as fifth columnists, as our complicity with the pleasures of 'bad' taste is slowly made manifest. And in the process, the show upturns many of the suppositions that underpin conceptions about cultural value and hierarchies: suggesting, for example, that there is beauty in the sticky, plastic gore of the horror movie special effect; that there is a kind of poetry in what seems the crudely-wrought schlock of the best-selling paperback chiller.

This is where *GMD* proves itself very different to a series like *Spaced*, while superficially sharing many of its sensibilities. Emblematically, *Spaced*, though arguably capturing the peculiarities of political and social disconnection through the refraction of pop culture, inevitably affirms the centrality of this culture in its plethora of allusions (references to *King Lear* or Wordsworth, for example, would have no place in this show's schema). *Spaced* in this sense does not so much confuse cultural and canonical boundaries as merely replace them, investing a new set of pop icons as the horizon of its imagination (and leaving it to Pegg and Wright's later films, slightly more ranging in their influences, to change this paradigm somewhat).

The tone of *GMD*, by contrast, moves through a form of arcane lyricism bordering on, and slipping perennially into, a simultaneous parody of its own form, though without ever properly relinquishing the mode of horror in which it operates. The overall effect of this is a kind of horror text *that we cannot believe, but can love*. This parody without parody is the form for a horror without horror. Because of its parodic style, at no point does *GMD* allow us to take it seriously: parody's reflexive mode constantly establishes it as a form of pretending, of pure play. But this does not preclude the possibility that this playing is great fun; nor, in its attention to the specifics of language, image and sound, does it preclude the possibility of being serious about the enjoyment of horror, without 'taking it seriously'.

Briefly touching upon *GMD* at the end of his book on British television comedy, Ben Thompson writes:

> Some people might question what a TV series about a megalomaniac pulp-writer imagining himself as a heroic doctor trying to save a Romford hospital from the consequences of his having inadvertently opened the gates of hell could possibly have to say about life in twenty-first century Britain. But such sceptics obviously haven't seen it yet.[59]

Thompson points accurately here to the eclectic possibilities of comedy in what he calls England's 'determinedly non-ideological twenty-first century'.[60] We have seen this turn away from ideology, as argued in this chapter, largely in the shift from a cultural paradigm centred on producers and receivers, to one in which the viewer-creator is King or Queen. It is, in fact, the same shift we noted in the previous chapter, from the political and ideological parody of *The Comic Strip Presents...* to the apparently apolitical inflections of *Hot Fuzz*. 'Apolitical', that is, largely in the sense of not addressing – as *The Strike* is so keen to do –popular culture's role in generating the imaginary, ideological relationship we have to our economic structures.

As Thompson's remarks imply, and as *GMD* explores, whatever actual political circumstances still need to be addressed (and there are plenty of them), popular culture is no longer the designated object of this critique. The ideological genie is in this sense out of the bottle: having been told, either through university cultural studies courses, or the trickle-down of such learning in shows like *The Comic Strip Presents...*, what mass-cultural forms supposedly do, such forms no longer, if indeed they ever did, have the same force. The perhaps unexpected consequence here is that, once we've worked out what is really going on, there is no longer anything to worry about, and instead of consigning popular genres to the dustbin of cultural history, we are free to enjoy them as we always did; only with the added value that we don't need to be anxious or guilty about them any more.

In this move, the same processes of cultural-political critique, in the form of parody, that sought to do away with forms of cultural production end up – in a way I also argued in the previous chapter – reshaping and revitalising these same forms. When the evaluative and ideological associations of certain cultural products break down, there are consequences for the understanding and formation of cultural canons and hierarchies. But there are also repercussions for the way we view parody, once parody no longer feels compelled to take a stand.

6

Where No Joke Has Gone Before: Parody as Science Fiction in *The Hitchhiker's Guide to the Galaxy, Paul* and *Moon*

Whether in critical or more positive terms, many writers on film have identified the late 1970s as a watershed point, between the 'New Holly-wood' of director- and screenplay-led *auteur* cinema and the re-emergence of another type of new or 'post-classical' Hollywood, in the form of the blockbuster aesthetic and related industrial practices.[1] If *Jaws* (1975) pro-vided a model for this emerging dominant mode, the astonishing and unprecedented success in 1977 of *Star Wars* and *Close Encounters of the Third Kind* suggested that science fiction might be the best way to do it. We already saw in an earlier chapter the impacts of the prevailing block-buster aesthetic on national cinema and its comedic responses in film and television. This book would not be complete without considering the more specific impact of science fiction on English film and television comedy.

As is well known, films broadly associated with science fiction themes and content have dominated at the global box office in the last four dec-ades. Even adjusting for inflation, such films make up seven of the all-time 20 most commercially successful movies, while from 1977 onward, the number goes up to 11. But as this last point indicates, and as the largely unexpected success of *Star Wars* suggested, the apparent cultural inevi-tability of science fiction's dominance is contextually specific to a certain time and place. Nor can any consideration of science fiction's cultural dominance overlook the ways the genre's emphases on spectacle, enhanced by developments in special effects technologies, have helped make it central to Hollywood's spectacular remit.

As a dominant mode within the dominant cultural imaginary, science fiction is clearly a ripe target for parody. As the primary manifestation of the Hollywood blockbuster, science fiction cinema is underpinned by a logic of expenditure – through production, but also through marketing and distribution – with which non-Hollywood cinemas can rarely if ever compete. As I will discuss in this chapter, both the ideological character of science fiction, and its economic bases of production (which are to some extent already related), inform versions of science-fiction parody. But choosing to look at the parody of science fiction has a secondary value, in terms of the way it encourages us to think about what 'science fiction' is actually *about*. My deliberately imprecise reference above to films 'associated with science fiction themes' acknowledges both the slipperiness in trying to pin down the genre, but also the often vague or limited connotations of science fiction with respect to many so-called 'sci-fi' films, an uncertainty that in itself explains the slightly informal and sometimes pejorative abbreviation of 'sci-fi' itself (though for clarity's sake, I will henceforth use this term to refer specifically to filmed or televised science fiction). As I will discuss here, the particular engagement with Hollywood sci-fi encourages a closer consideration of the qualities and possibilities of science fiction on screen.

The first part of this chapter will focus mainly on two texts: the 1981 BBC television series *The Hitchhiker's Guide to the Galaxy* (henceforth *Hitchhiker's Guide*), written by Douglas Adams and directed by Alan J. Ball, and the film of the same name, made in 2005 from a script by Adams and Karey Kirkpatrick, and directed by the British filmmaker Garth Jennings. As I will discuss, both the series and film can be read in terms of Douglas Adams' parodic engagement with the narratives and tropes of science fiction. But the screen versions of Adams' comic space opera also allow us to reflect on the aesthetics and discourses of sci-fi (and specifically, with regard to the series, sci-fi film *as distinct from* television) in their specific contexts. The second section will look at two recent films, both technically British, even 'English', within the wider contexts of global distribution and transnational production: *Paul* (2011), written by and starring Simon Pegg and Nick Frost, and *Moon* (2009), the debut feature film of director

Duncan Jones. Both these films, I will suggest, engage with the imaginary of sci-fi, making this in fact the subject of their particular narratives. While they do this in very different ways – *Moon* is not obviously a parody at all, nor specifically comic, though as I argue, its inter-textuality and dialogue with other films justifies its discussion within these terms – both films offer pertinent reflections on the possibilities of science fiction and comedy, as well as the potential of non-Hollywood production to engage with sci-fi's cultural dominance.

Science Fiction and/as Parody

Most overviews of parody as a cinematic mode, and some of sci-fi as a film genre, provide some reference to sci-fi parody. Geoff King, for example, ends his survey of film parody with a reference to *Galaxy Quest* (1999) and *Spaceballs* (1987).[2] The latter film is described elsewhere by Wes Gehring, in terms of its status as both 'mild [...] social satire' and 'an affectionate spoof of George Lucas' films';[3] while in the same study Gehring discusses Woody Allen's *Sleeper* (1973) as a 'takeoff on science fiction'.[4] Elsewhere, Christine Cornea views John Carpenter's *Dark Star* (1974), about a crew of 'spaced-out' astronauts cruising the galaxies blowing up planets, as a 'low-budget parody';[5] while Vivian Sobchack, as well as referencing *Dark Star* and *Sleeper*, also cites the last section of Allen's earlier *Everything You Always Wanted to Know About Sex* (1972), which riffs on the theme of *Fantastic Voyage* (1966) and its miniaturised journey through the human body.[6] Much of the discourse around *Hitchhiker's Guide* (the BBC series especially), as we will see, adopts a similar line to these overviews, focusing on the parodic aspects of its low-budget approach, or its more general 'spoofing' of science fiction tropes.

From one point of view these various discussions avoid the question of whether 'science fiction parody' is science fiction at all. This is less of an issue when such films are considered primarily as works of parody, to the extent that they enact the 'debunking and undermining [of] familiar [formal or aesthetic] conventions',[7] and therefore have a critical function. While all these surveys of parody recognise that it is double-edged, at once 'affectionate' in its 'criticism',[8] or 'reaffirming' the subject of notional critique,[9] the emphasis is primarily on the way such parodies work through manipulation of the semantic, syntactic and stylistic characteristics of the target text. But this becomes problematic when such works are discussed more inclusively within the terms of sci-fi itself. This is because their parodic dimension potentially undermines their capacity to function *as* sci-fi in the first place. As a form of critique, it goes without saying that the 'debunking and undermining of conventions' is a problematic basis for parodies to function within their non-parodied generic terms: the act of undermining works through a deliberate and pointed exposure of the 'invisible' workings of genre films, the source of their verisimilitude;[10] and in turn their ideological value.[11]

But from another point of view, the discussion of 'parody science fiction' is especially significant, insofar as much academic discussion around 'science-fiction cinema' has focused on the latter's very possibility. Identifying what it is exactly that is parodied in so-called parody sci-fi may prove revealing as to what sci-fi is actually doing in the first place. Cornea's study, for example, picks up on the work of earlier theorists of science-fiction cinema such as Brooks Landon, in its suggestion that cinematic science fiction is based around the *image*, as distinct from the *idea*-driven nature of science fiction literature (frequently distinguished as 'SF').[12] For Landon, each medium is 'driven by very different concepts in pursuit of very different goals'.[13] Cornea stresses that the often economically overdetermined imperatives of cinema mean that sci-fi is mostly classified and marketed along consumer-driven lines, based on familiar motifs and references.[14] For critics such as Barry Keith Grant, however, economic aims are beside the point: the limitations of sci-fi are media specific. As he argues:

> Because film is primarily a visual medium, it tends to concentrate on the depiction of visual surfaces at the expense of contemplative depth [...] Unlike words [...] representational images are first and always objects in the material world, the things themselves before being symbolic of something else.[15]

This argument echoes a familiar and pejorative reduction of sci-fi special effects to 'mere' spectacle. Grant's literary-inflected target is the supposed incapacity of big-budget special effects to work through allusion and suggestion. As he puts it: 'If the reverential awe we accord science-fiction images is a debasement of science fiction's distinctive philosophical attitude, it is because the film medium work[s] to discourage this kind of speculative narrative'.[16] Grant is here drawing on Robert Scholes' work on science fiction as 'fabulation',[17] though overhanging all discussions of the specific qualities of science fiction is Darko Suvin's concepts of 'cognitive estrangement' and the representation of the *novum*: the "new thing" or 'cognitive innovation' that defines, for Suvin, the science fiction text: that which 'deviate[s] from the author's and implied reader's norm of reality'.[18]

Whether or not the predominantly visual spectacle of sci-fi precludes its potential *as* science fiction is a question to which I will return. But for the moment it is worth noting how frequently discussions around English science fiction film and television offer arguments that establish distinctions between their own practices and those of their Hollywood counterparts, focusing predominantly on the latter's recourse to spectacle. As we will see, such arguments construct a specific discourse concerning the character and value of English sci-fi. As I will suggest, though, these arguments are not always as consistent as they initially appear.

The Ambivalent Discourse of British Science Fiction

While the discussions above reflect the tension between screen sci-fi's notional lack of depth and, by contrast, the assumed value of literature, discussions within the English context are reconfigured around the contested and problematised terms of science fiction in itself, and especially its cultural connotations as *American*. As Derek Johnston has shown, the early era of BBC television production coincided with what some saw as 'a growing encroachment of American values onto British ones',[19] in part via the cultural invasion of 'pulp' US magazines such as *Amazing Stories*, first published in 1929 by Hugo Gernsback, to whom the term 'science fiction' is generally credited.[20] Because of these magazines' lurid and cheaply-printed appearance, and perhaps also because of their commercial status as serial publications, pulp science fiction would be held as inferior to the legitimate 'literature' of writers such as H. G. Wells, who preferred the term 'scientific romance' – notwithstanding the fact that Wells's work such as *The War of the Worlds* was itself serialised in *Amazing Stories*. Consequently, as

Johnston observes, the discussion of science fiction in Britain within this period became a cultural and political matter in face of the 'threat' of 'cheap and superficial American cultural imports [...] associated with infantilism and lack of intelligence'.[21]

This became especially pertinent within the BBC, whose stated public-service remit, at least within the contexts of the early 1950s, rejected the connotations of low culture. As Johnston puts it: 'To have admitted that the BBC was broadcasting "science fiction" [...] would have been to admit spreading this pernicious American cultural propaganda and undermining British culture'.[22] Around the 1953 BBC production of *The Quatermass Experiment*, whose historical identification as 'British science fiction television' is indicated by its coverage in books on this selfsame subject,[23] we see this cultural distinction at work. For its writer Nigel Kneale, *The Quatermass Experiment*, about an alien life form inadvertently brought back to Earth by an abortive rocket mission, 'was supposed to be something of a critique of science fiction of the time, those terrible American films that were full of flag-waving'.[24] It is not clear which films Kneale is referring to, though in the contexts of *Quatermass* he might be referring to Hollywood productions such as *Destination Moon* (1950) or *When Worlds Collide* (1951), neither of which are particularly 'flag-waving', but *are* predominantly American-centric in their emphasis on the US's technological power and the utopian possibilities of space travel. Kneale's comments, in any case, assert the critical, reflective virtues of an English sci-fi, affirming the hierarchical order of 'ideas' over 'image'.

What is certainly clear from the context of the 1950s is the centrality of an emerging sci-fi genre to Hollywood's popular and commercial aesthetic. As Cornea explains, the decline of the Hollywood studio system following the 1948 'Paramount Ruling' (that put an end to the major studios' practices of vertical integration) gave emphasis to the power of the 'new B film'. The science fiction movie was well-placed to take up this mantle, given the 'pre-existing fan base built up around the [science fiction] pulps and comics of the 1940s and early 1950s',[25] along with the increasing orientation of Hollywood product around the youthful suburban audience. The evolving use of Technicolor throughout the 1950s, meanwhile, lent itself to the spectacle of alien invasion or pan-terrestrial cataclysm in, respectively, *War of the Worlds* (1953) and the aforementioned *When Worlds Collide*, both produced for Paramount by George Pal. Further developments in special effects and the emergence of widescreen filming technologies such as Cinemascope, in films such as MGM's big-budget *Forbidden Planet* (1956), would help pave the way for the re-emergence, especially after the success of *Star Wars*, of what Tom Gunning describes as early film's 'cinema of attractions'.[26] Originally conceived in terms of cinema before the development of narrative continuity and the feature film, this new cinema of attractions is one that, for Cornea, 'frequently places emphasis upon the thrills and spills that film can evoke and upon the big-screen spectacle that effects can create'.[27]

From one perspective, the forsaking of narrative or even thematic concerns, and the 'emphasis on thrills and spills [and] big-screen spectacle', especially one driven by special effects technologies, fulfills sci-fi's supposed commitment to privileging the image over the idea. As James Chapman observes, *The Quatermass Experiment* pokes some fun at the contemporary vogue for sci-fi and related screening technologies – in this case, 3-D, which enjoyed its initial heyday in the early 1950s – by inserting a film within a film called *Planet of the Dragoons*, in which 'a space lieutenant and a space girl find true love whilst battling against (unseen) monsters on a distant planet';[28] an imagined Hollywood product which, Chapman suggests, 'seems deliberately parodic of the juvenile style of sf from which *Quatermass* sought to differentiate itself'.[29]

It is notable though that, within these same discursive contexts, both British sci-fi film and television are also the subject of some largely self-effacing commentary. Often within the same critical work, we encounter an uncertain shift between the confidence of British sci-fi's conceptual superiority and the awareness of its technological poverty, especially compared to American products of the same time. Tobias Hochscherf and James Leggott, for instance, in a recent book on the subject, stress that 'the British science fiction film remained for many a wretched thing, hamstrung at times by a reputation for being cheap'; adding that the wider lack of academic interest in British science fiction television can 'be explained by its perceived cheapness or inferiority to Hollywood equivalents'.[30] While these authors avoid this line of thinking, there seems in fact to be an inherent and self-defensive link made in much academic discussion between low production values and conceptual strength; a logic which, I will argue later in this chapter, is not always either coherent or consistent.

Largely because discourse around British or English sci-fi focuses so frequently on the opposition between a more impoverished national culture and its dominant American counterpart, the issue of parody within English science fiction is coloured and over-determined by expectations of parody as a critical mode. Appearing at a time when US science fiction cinema had quickly emerged as the commercially dominant genre, and also during which US television series, inspired by the science fiction cinema boom, were assuming primetime positions on UK screens, the television version of *Hitchhiker's Guide* might be read as a comic riposte to this cultural invasion from Planet Hollywood. Equally, the long gestation of the 2005 film (Adams, who had worked on the script, had died in 2001) had seen a variety of sci-fi and related end-of-the-world movies make an authentically big noise at box-offices: films such as *Independence Day* (1996), *Armageddon* (1998) and *Deep Impact* (1998); the imagery from which would, in fact, find its way into the *Hitchhiker's Guide* film.

As we will see, though, there are some limitations to this rather simplistic 'English parody complex', as I term it: the idea that English sci-fi can only mock what is bigger and more expensive. Not least of these limitations is the way such discourse places the culturally distinct national product in an inevitable binary relationship to the inferior-yet-dominant product from which is notionally distinguishes itself: one without which – to follow this logic *ad absurdum* – it would not actually exist at all. This encourages us to think carefully about what parody, such as it exists in texts such as *Hitchhiker's Guide*, is really doing, what its targets are, but also – and within the discursive framework of English sci-fi, a vital question – to what extent it is 'science fiction' at all. Looking at the film, especially, will also require us to take a nuanced view of the transnational production processes and aesthetics of contemporary cinema, of which the 2005 *Hitchhiker's Guide* is a key example.

Prevailing aesthetic and economic trends in television, along with the concurrent domestication of 'cinema' since the early 1980s, mean that we no longer worry so much about distinctions between the two viewing platforms. But the contexts of a BBC television show in the 1980s need to be weighed against the norms of dominant contemporary cinema, both English and American, as well as the norms of an equally dominant imported American television. Significantly for our comparative discussion of the 2005 film, though it was made by the British duo of Jennings and producer Nick Goldsmith, it was financed and distributed by Disney (in the respective form of Touchstone Pictures and Buena Vista), and called upon an array of American, as well as English, talent (including Martin Freeman as Arthur, Mos' Def as Ford and Sam Rockwell as Zaphod Beeblebrox). Such financial backing[31] brings with it expectations of global, rather than merely local, financial return, which inevitably determines – within global entertainment cinema's vicious circle – an aesthetic that at once justifies and demands that kind of expenditure. Looking conjunctly at the BBC series and the film is therefore a useful way to consider the impact of film aesthetics and economics on these two respective texts.

The Hitchhiker's Guide to the Galaxy on Television

'There is a popular perception that the television version of *The Hitchhiker's Guide to the Galaxy* is, frankly, not very good'.[32] So begins M. J. Simpson's essay on the production history of the oft-maligned BBC series. Speaking in the show's defence, one of Simpson's supporting arguments is that, contrary to its wide reputation as 'looking cheap', the series was in fact 'an extremely expensive programme to make for the time, to the extent that it sapped the entire special effects budget of the BBC Light Entertainment Department for 1980'.[33] Whatever this actually meant in real terms, it indicates the investment on the part of the BBC, as well as being a reminder that notions of 'looking cheap' are largely contextual and relative. We in turn run the risk of taking a condescending view of the BBC's *Hitchhiker's Guide* if we fail to consider the immediate circumstances of its production and reception.

Considering the production values of the television series from the vantage point of the twenty-first century lends itself to the idea that the show was intentionally flimsy, a joke about the prevailing 'naff' quality of television science fiction, and of British attempts at the form in particular. The creature technology, for one thing, looks clunky even compared to some contemporary BBC shows such as the original run of *Doctor Who* (1963–89), with the Vogons in particular – green semi-humanoids famous for their repulsive appearance and worse poetry – looking very much like actors smothered in coloured plastics and putty. Beyond its production values, much of the action is constrained by the demands of the television studio's immobility, with the result that the show frequently looks as static and unpolished as a filmed rehearsal; yet these are largely constraints of that particular period's technology and filming practices – not to mention, as Simpson reminds us, the constraints of BBC workers' union rules during that time.[34]

As introduced above, commentators on this period and key production personnel associated with it have emphasised the way economic and technological limitations chimed with specific national virtues. Graham Williams, producer of *Doctor Who* at the end of the 1970s – during which time Adams worked as script editor – echoes this line of thought in his assertion that the 'British' strengths of acting and writing were called upon in response to the US's 'money [and technological] expertise'.[35] Williams draws here on the earlier discursive distinction between narrative and spectacle. Indeed, as Chapman argues in his cultural history of the series, *Doctor Who* has throughout its various regenerations functioned as

> a site of cultural contestation for British critics [and fans] keen to protect its 'Britishness' against the encroaching effects of Americanisation. The terms of this opposition are familiar: 'British' equals small, quaint, eccentric and individual, whereas 'American' equals big, brash, conformist and corporate.[36]

Chapman is focusing specifically here on the 1996 *Doctor Who* television film, a co-production between the BBC, Universal and Fox. Chapman points out the way critical and fan attention of the ill-fated film (an intended follow-up series was cancelled due to the film's poor viewing figures) was frequently marked by a nostalgia for the television series' cheap and improvised 'Heath Robinson production values', and its resistance to the 'flashy' style associated with Hollywood. Williams' comments that *Doctor Who* opposed 'character' to 'hardware'[37] may have specifically been in light of the sci-fi films that changed the game as far as special effects were concerned, as well as imported American shows such as *Battlestar Galactica* (ABC, 1978–79) and *Buck Rogers in the 25th Century* (NBC, 1979–81), series which, in the recollection of this particular young viewer, competed very successfully for my attention over the likes of *Doctor Who*. But the challenge of, and relationship to, American film and television culture had actually shaped *Doctor Who* since the 1960s. This could be seen, Nicholas Cull argues, in the way Jon Pertwee-era *Doctor Who* (1970–74) responded to the competition of the UK screening of *Star Trek* (NBC, 1966–69) by assuming a more action-based approach,[38] or in the ill-received attempts of earlier *Doctor Who* (in 'The Chase' [1965] and 'The Gunslingers' [1966]) to make fun of American cultural archetypes such as silent-era Hollywood and the Western.[39]

While Cull suggests that *Star Trek* and *Doctor Who* respectively 'fitted the imagination of the culture that produced and embraced it',[40] we should be wary of being too prescriptive as to what this national 'culture' is. In part, this is because the tendency toward parody (in the Hartnell-era *Doctor Who*) is itself indicative of British culture's struggle 'to create a space for itself in America's world'.[41] But it is also because the threat – or let's face it, popularity – of a show like *Star Trek*, and its subsequent influence on British television production, suggests that the 'national culture' is always being reconfigured by the very thing that discourses of the 'national' construct themselves in opposition to. Ideologically, there is a chicken-and-egg situation here, in which the effects of Americanisation are used to justify an idea of Britishness or Englishness that is then made to *precede* Americanisation. Williams' defense of *Doctor Who*'s very British characteristics, in this light, seem somewhat self-serving: such claims retroactively construct a notion of essential national character which may disavow the historical, economic and technological factors shaping a national film and television aesthetics.

More importantly for our present concerns, this kind of 'parochial "Little Britain" discourse'[42] risks misrepresenting the texts themselves, as we see when we pay close attention to a show such as *Hitchhiker's Guide*. Given the contexts of British television at the beginning of the 1980s, and the link, via Douglas Adams, to the so-called 'parodic turn' of *Doctor Who*, such parochial discourses tend to accrue around the *Hitchhiker's Guide* series. John Cook and Peter Wright, for example, assert that in the economic recession of 1981, under a Thatcherite government, it was becoming increasingly hard to take science fiction on British TV seriously at all, as opposed to in the cinema where huge technical advances in special effects had made the physical representations of [...] visions of the future now highly believable. Faced with such circumstances, perhaps the only option left for British science fiction TV was to have a laugh at itself.[43]

Interestingly, British cinema's key contribution to sci-fi at this same time was the British-Italian co-production *Flash Gordon* (1980), which, while to some extent riding the wave of the sci-fi movie boom, was also happy to 'have a laugh at itself'; mainly through the gaudy excesses of its mise-en-scène, a knowingness in the dialogue about its generic narrative structure, and a 'pantomimic' performance style from its starry international cast.[44] As Mark Bould points out, though, this somewhat self-parodic approach is not directed towards the film itself in terms of any relative poverty; at $20m, the film was in fact very generously budgeted for the time. Self-parody is rather a means through which an 'ideologically problematic comic strip' from 50 years previously (with the brazenly Oriental 'Ming the Merciless' as its world-destroying villain) could be enjoyed 'ironically', allowing the audience to 'embrace [its] artifice' without needing to take it seriously.[45]

But even as a television show, with its comparatively lower production values, the self-mocking view of *Hitchhiker's Guide* does not in fact stand up to close analysis. This is mainly because, as we have seen, any assumption that the series made a joke out of its technical shortcomings is not consistent with facts about the show's expense and reception. But there is also a logical problem here: if British television sci-fi chose to 'laugh at itself' because it could not economically compete with its American counterpart, the implication is that, given the resources, it *would* imitate or compete with it. Indeed, Lincoln Geraghty goes so far as to suggest that the economic investment in *Hitchhiker's Guide* was 'a sign that [the BBC] were not only keen to produce series that looked like they were American but would also stand a chance of being exported back across the Atlantic'.[46] The discourse of parody through 'cheapness' consequently seems to seek moral validation and aesthetic compensation after the fact: there are, after all, much cheaper and less time-consuming ways to make television look rubbish. Like *Flash Gordon*, then, where a somewhat camp attitude to its narrative did not preclude the sumptuousness of its design, nor its appeal to American audiences, any parodic strategy on the part of *Hitchhiker's Guide* needs to be read not in terms of any perceived comparative poverty, but rather as a specifically ideological relationship to the material and its subject matter.

We can get a sense of the show's comic strategies, and how much the *Hitchhiker's Guide* series will pursue its own particular form of science fiction affect, by looking at the opening of Adams' novel. We see from this passage how *Hitchhiker's Guide* functions through modes of parody and, specifically, what Jerry Palmer calls comic *peripeteia* – originally, Aristotle's term from his *Poetics* to describe the moment of dramatic 'reversal' in Greek tragedy, though here referring to the abrupt shift in perspective that provokes laughter:[47]

> Far out in the uncharted backwaters of the unfashionable end of Western Spiral Arm of the Galaxy lies a small unregarded yellow sun.
>
> Orbiting this at a distance of roughly ninety-two million miles is an utterly insignificant little blue-green planet whose ape-descended life forms are so amazingly primitive they still think digital watches are a pretty neat idea.[48]

The parodic comedy proceeds then from the way its science fiction register, with its allusions to the scale of the cosmos, is inverted by the focus on Earth's insignificance; as well as its use of misdirection and incongruous juxtapositions, as the descriptive build-up leads to a revelation about human faith in digital watches.[49] As we have seen, such devices aim to undermine the internal coherence and verisimilitude of genre, its 'logonomic system'.[50] The important difference here is that science fiction, at least in its conception as 'cognitive estrangement', in part works *against* such coherence. Adams' inversions, though working through our recognition of genre convention, also have the aim of de-familiarisation; especially in their reduction of our species to 'ape-descended life forms'. It is precisely Adams' capacity to arrest the reader through such modes of inversion and incongruity that generate the 'cognitive estrangement' so central to the reading of science fiction. For example, when he writes about the Vogon demolition fleet that '[t]he ships hung in the sky in much the same way that bricks don't',[51] Adams is surprising in his use of the prosaic 'bricks' to evoke a space fleet; yet through the inversion in the simile, he imbues the unlovely craft both with unexpected mobility and an impending sense of violence.

A similar aesthetic is at work in the television series. The opening sequence has Arthur Dent attempting to stop the demolition of his house by the bureaucratic urban planner Mr Prosser, interrupted by the appearance of his friend (and unbeknownst to Arthur, inter-galactic hitchhiker) Ford Prefect; and ending in the actual destruction of the Earth by the Vogons to create an interstellar bypass. From one point of view, this play with size and relative perception is part of the wider intent to undermine, as Cook and Wright put it, 'the importance of human existence' and to parody 'the scale of human achievement'.[52] As a small-screen adaptation of a story that had already gone through several versions (on radio, stage and in the novel), a key question is where and how we situate the technological apparatus of television within this parodic intent to undermine 'the scale of human achievement', inasmuch as screen sci-fi is in itself a manifestation of this achievement. The spectacle of screen science fiction is rarely just *about* spectacle; it is also, as Garrett Stewart has remarked, about the marvels of screen technology, its display not just a representation of fictional wonders, but a wonder in itself: 'the fictional or fictive science *of* the cinema ...the future feats it may achieve scanned in line with the technical feat that conceives them right now'.[53]

If, as we have seen, the television series of *Hitchhiker's Guide* is not exactly cheap, there is evidence of its dialogue with the wider representations of recent science fiction *cinema*: a dialogue focused more on the specific contextual uses of special effects technologies and the ideological values they serve. The title credits for the series, for example, begin with a shiny-suited astronaut apparently free-floating in space, echoing the footage of the first space walks in the 1970s. But they also evoke the image of the stranded astronaut Frank Poole, cut adrift from his ship in *2001: A Space Odyssey* (1968). The sequence further exploits *2001*'s iconography of cosmic loneliness and estrangement, sending the floating figure through a rapidly moving tunnel of metallic light: a variation on the immersive type of 'tunnel vision' shot that, as Cornea observes, is a staple of science fiction imagery through films like *Forbidden Planet*, from the credit sequence

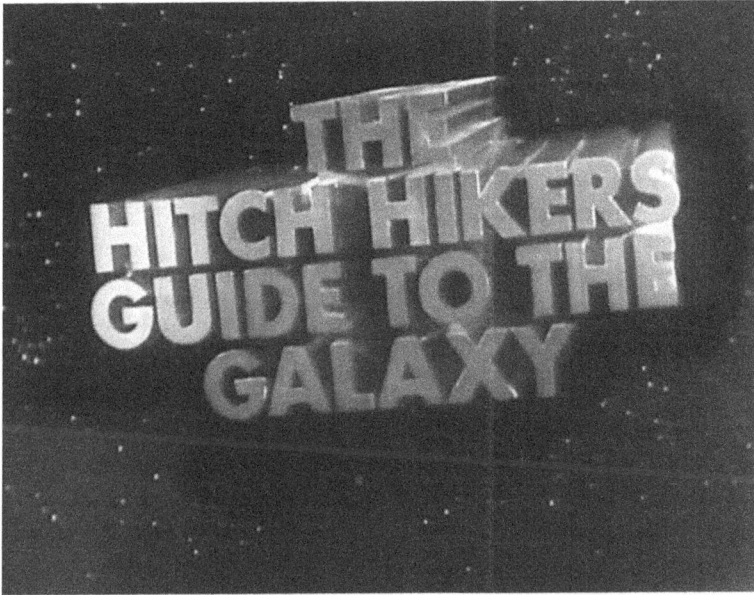

6.1 Inter-textuality across space and time: 'cinematic' opening titles for the BBC's
The Hitchhiker's Guide to the Galaxy (1981)

for *Doctor Who*, and in the 'Jupiter and Beyond the Infinite' sequence of
2001.[54] This tunnel, however, is not a cosmic gateway after the fashion of
Stanley Kubrick's film, but the 'O' in the title of the series, now floating
in huge three-dimensional letters. Another example of misdirection and
inversion, this unexpected reveal plays both with the syntax of the science-
fiction narrative and also the iconography of science fiction film, not just
2001, but also the title sequence of *Star Wars*, the latter's bold titular logo
graphically evoked in the composition here (and whose sequel, *The Empire
Strikes Back*, was released in the UK in May 1980, during the initial production stages of *Hitchhiker's Guide*).

This sequence works to establish a parodic tone for the show, but one
that is not undercut by technical poverty: the sequence in fact encourages
recognition of its technical achievement, inviting wonder, while also re-
routing this response through its inversions of generic motifs. While the
sequence aspires to a kind of 'cinematic' register in its reference points and
use of special effects, though, its parodic conclusion brings it firmly within

the parameters of a 1980s (English) television series. This dialogue between television and cinema plays a significant role in the rest of the first episode, which is generally very strategic in its uses of setting, mise-en-scène and effects. The opening recreation (skillfully done in miniature), of what will turn out to be the final sunrise over an English countryside, is effective in its careful construction of a 'local' space into which not so much global but cosmic forces will intervene, in the form of the Vogon demolition fleet. *Hitchhiker's Guide* is very specific in its use of place and its particular connotations: Arthur, for instance, lives in a rural cottage whose only obvious link to a wider community is the village pub. Such locales are in keeping with what Bould (though not referring to *Hitchhiker's Guide*) describes as 'a fantasy image of white "organic community"' in British science fiction,[55] part of an aesthetic disavowal of modern national circumstances in the contexts of post-imperial England (indeed, the near-absence of non-white faces in the television series dates the show significantly). Equally notable is the way the first episode, in the sequence where the Vogons bear down on London, draws on a now slightly antiquated image-bank of bowler-hatted City gents, and men with sandwich boards prophesying that 'The End is Nigh'.

And yet, *Hitchhiker's Guide* resists subscribing to this English 'fantasy image', because its imaginary disavowal of imminent destruction is seen as woefully inadequate when confronted by the brute realities of the Vogon fleet and its deadly weapons. In this sense, it pre-empts what we are later to see as the self-parodic tendency in English comedy, especially in the form discussed in Chapter 4. This is hardly a fantasy projection of England within the post-imperial era, but rather a tacit acknowledgement of the country's redundancy on the world stage (which was especially evident in the 1970s, when the original radio series of *Hitchhiker's Guide* was written). It is also a comically pessimistic envisioning of the nation's contemporary geopolitical positioning, as a pawn in the nuclear face-off between the USA and the Soviet Union: the pub landlord's suggestion that he and his patrons put paper bags over their heads to fend off the coming apocalypse, in fact, chimes with the quaintly optimistic tones of the 'Protect and Survive' public information material distributed during this period.

As much as this tone is achieved through self-mockery of cultural archetypes, though, it is also done through the way the series acknowledges its status *as television*. Notably for the contexts in which it was made, the series uses the resources of a primarily *cinematic* imaginary, in the form of special effects, in such a way as to make the televisual confines of the series all the more evident. This suggests that the show may be, to return to the earlier discussion, laughing at itself; but it is at once more understanding of the predicament of the television medium, and in a certain way generous to the power of cinematic special effects technologies. We cannot assume that *Hitchhiker's Guide* is taking aim at these increasingly dominant 'global' forms, since it draws on these for its own purposes. The Vogon fleet may allegorise nuclear destruction, but in more ways than one it also represents the emerging globalised currency of late twentieth-century science fiction film and television, dominated by spectacular special effects technologies, and what Susan Sontag, in a 1965 essay, famously called science fiction cinema's 'imagination of disaster'.[56]

Douglas Adams' Double Bind: *Hitchhiker's Guide* in Hollywood

If we follow the logic of the television show, the film version of *Hitchhiker's Guide* was always bound to be caught in a double bind. Within the terms of its own discourse, 'Hollywood' is the problem to which English sci-fi responds. At the very least, this begs the question of how a narrative like *Hitchhiker's Guide* would make sense as a Disney-produced blockbuster movie. As an economically resourceful medium, Hollywood sci-fi cinema does not need to laugh at itself or draw attention to disparities between the different media of film and television. The type of verisimilitude presumed to be beyond the reach of the earlier television show, and which therefore – supposedly – *determined* the form and content of the show itself, is entirely within the grasp of the *Hitchhiker's Guide* movie. Evidence would suggest though that the film was seen as a logical destination for Douglas Adams' narrative journey, a key target for Adams in the 20 years between the production of the television series and his early death. The success in 1997 of *Men in Black* had apparently convinced Hollywood of the potential for 'intergalactic, effects-filled sci-fi comedy', and when Disney subsequently put production into motion, Adams claimed (in a 1998 interview) to be 'highly delighted', adding that 'although it's been a long, long wait since the idea was first mooted, now is a much, much better time to make [the film]'.[57] The fact that the 1990s saw a significant advance in CGI technologies (showcased in films like *Men in Black*) presumably had some weight in this regard.

The dialogue between 'local' and 'global' contexts is less obvious in the film, for the simple reason that the film subsumes such oppositions within its inherent economic and technological character. As a Hollywood movie, albeit one that is significantly marked in many senses (crew, most of the cast, original source material) as 'culturally English', the film is inevitably over-determined by the financial logic of the modern blockbuster, which requires that movies need in advance to promise return on studio investment. Everything is consequently that much bigger than in the television series: Slartibartfast's planetary workshop, for instance, the 'Deep Thought' computer, the destruction of the Earth, the movement and mutations of Zaphod's space ship *Heart of Gold*, are all rendered in forms of photo-realistic CGI, their 'videological' and spectacular value competing with their narrative function.

The film of *Hitchhiker's Guide* is also significantly shaped by the demands of a more 'classical' narrative structure. The relationship in the film between Arthur and Trillian, the girl he meets at a party in Islington before Zaphod Beeblebrox whisks her away to his ship, is given much more prominence. Notably – and incongruously, given the supposed urgency of the world's imminent destruction – the conversation in the pub between Arthur and Ford is interrupted by a flashback scene illustrating in detail Arthur and Trillian's meeting at the party. The significance of this meeting to the overall structure of the film is highlighted by the way Arthur's everyman charm is seen eventually to win Trillian back from the less-than-reliable and egomaniacal Zaphod. More importantly, the film is also determined by the aesthetic conventions of contemporary mainstream cinema, as characterised by intensified continuity style,[58] an aesthetic which, as noted in the analysis of *Hot Fuzz*, is marked by a much more accelerated speed of editing, a tendency towards mobile camerawork, and a more pronounced emphasis on the close-up. The impact of this style on *Hitchhiker's Guide* is far from incidental, as its use across the board in the film nullifies much of the sense of spatial difference or nuance that might otherwise exist in it. The particularly distinctive rhythms and sounds of English village life or London are overwhelmed here by the pace, fragmentation and orchestrally-scored nature of the first parts of the film, to the extent that there is little perceptual difference between Arthur's terrestrial and cosmic experiences.[59]

To put a more productive spin on this, it makes more sense to think of the *Hitchhiker's Guide* film as exploring, in a parodic mode, the conventions of contemporary sci-fi cinema itself; and as such, everything and everyone within the film are incorporated into the signifying properties of the modern sci-fi blockbuster. In these terms, the film is not about anything but its own provenance, and modern sci-fi itself becomes the source of estrangement. The frenetic and often hyperbolic rhythms and impressions of intensified continuity style, especially within the effects-driven world of sci-fi cinema, are here actually well-suited to the task, given their propensity towards self-parodic excess, and their exhaustively inter-textual efforts to outdo previous representations.

The destruction of the Earth in the film of *Hitchhiker's Guide*, for instance, could be seen as a reflection on the available technologies of filmmaking, in dramatic distinction to the prior limitations of the television show; but it is also an acknowledgement of the more obviously global coverage and standardised forms of contemporary global film. Whereas the earlier series gave us an entirely local perspective (and the quaintly Imperialist impression, in the ensuing demolition sequence, that a solitary Vogon ship chose exclusively to speak to England), the film cuts quickly between a series of aerial tracking shots from three of the world's major cities, each one accompanied by screaming at slightly different varieties of tone and pitch, before finishing on a shot of sheep running away in a field. This sequence has a similar sense of planetary sweep to, and clearly seems intended to evoke, end-of-the-world films such as *Independence Day* and *Armageddon*, both of which feature pan-national montages of hope and defiance, though here there is a very different tone of global ineffectuality and impotence. As we return to Arthur and Ford, whose special electronic thumb is sending a beam up towards the overhanging Vogon demolition craft, a series of staggered jump cuts following the beam reveals the enormous depth and scale of the ship bearing down on England. Cued to the rhythmic bursts of Joby Talbot's orchestral score, which consistently threatens to reach a climax only to return once more, these cuts then reveal more encroaching ships, until, finally, we see a shot of the whole of the Earth surrounded by square-like blocks. There is then a pause in both the score and the jump cuts, before the planet disintegrates in a quietly muffled explosion.

This sequence of destruction may be clearly read as parodic on a number of levels. Underpinning the scene is the fact that it is already an over-saturated staple of science fiction cinema, familiar from films such as *Independence Day*, of course, but also similar sequences in *When Worlds Collide* and *Star Wars* (the destruction by the Death Star of Princess Leia's planet Alderaan). The aesthetics of the sequence work through comic techniques of exaggeration (the staggered revelation of ships to the point of overwhelming scale) and misdirection (the false climaxes), as well as inversion (the panicked global population as a series of fly-by snapshots; their symbolic reduction to sheep). The film's quotational genre parody is maintained in the subsequent title sequence. As the Earth disintegrates, leaving only its outline in the form of the Vogon fleet, we hear the famil-iar, though orchestrally rearranged, opening notes of the television series' theme music. As the camera tracks upward into open space, a shadowy, vast and smooth rectangular form emerges into view, at the very centre of the frame, eventually occupying its whole width in a striking abstract composition. This seems a very deliberate allusion to the black mono-lith that appears throughout *2001*, most notably at the beginning of the 'Jupiter' sequence, into which the surviving astronaut, Dave Bowman, is sent along with the viewer on an intense, psychedelic, special-effects domi-nated journey (the vertical camera movement in *Hitchhiker's Guide* from the demolished planet to the rectangular shape replicates a very similar sequence from this point in Kubrick's film). Again, though, the conception of the image in *Hitchhiker's Guide* flips its meaning in a moment of comic *peripeteia*. As the horizontal form moves across the screen, it gradually turns and reveals itself – and, in turn, the title of the film – as a copy of *The Hitchhiker's Guide to the Galaxy*.

This beautifully-rendered sequence embodies much of the film's com-plexity. At once referencing prior texts and seeming to parody them, mainly by inverting their narrative significance, the film is also partici-pating in the spectacular display of cinematic special effects, a point that is underscored by its insistence on both marking the connections to the

6.2 This is the way the world ends: the Earth, about to go out with a whimper, in the film of *The Hitchhiker's Guide to the Galaxy* (2005)

earlier television show, but also indicating its distinction in terms of scale and technology. From one perspective we might argue that *Hitchhiker's Guide* disavows its function within the economies of science fiction cinema, apparently distancing itself through parody from what it is actually a proponent of. As with the earlier discussions, though, this is too technologically leading and reductive, insisting that, like the television series, *Hitchhiker's Guide* must be obliged to renounce its technological bases. Here, it is less technology itself that is an issue, but its narrative uses.

One of the ideological paradoxes of Hollywood special effects-driven sci-fi, with the apocalyptic disaster movie being no exception, is that is often marked within the terms of human mastery and technology. Narratively, movies like *Independence Day* and *Armageddon* tend to reiterate the idea of a global community led by America; while the special effects themselves serve as markers of Hollywood's technological prowess. Narrative and technology therefore combine to extend the US 'military-industrial complex' to the realm of mass entertainment. To assume then that the destruction of the Earth in the film of *Hitchhiker's Guide* pokes fun at the conventions of the sci-fi- or apocalyptic disaster movie is only half the story, as the sequence works through an extended and accumulative use of comic *peripeteia* that consistently defamiliarises the form and motifs that are its generic points of reference. Bound as it inevitably still is within the terms of technologically-driven sci-fi, its exaggerations and misdirections undermine much of the latter's ideological connotations. The significant point at which the Earth actually disintegrates is itself a type of comic inversion, its silent implosion a bathetic and incongruous demise, though one that finds a quite suitable analogy for the same point in Adams' novel: 'There was a terrible ghastly silence. There was a terrible ghastly noise. There was a terrible ghastly silence'.[60]

Paul: The Inverted Logic of Science Fiction Cinema

As our analysis of the *Hitchhiker's Guide* film suggests, the technological and aesthetic tendencies of sci-fi can be exploited both to affective and critical effect. As I've suggested here, parody can sustain science fiction's 'estranging' function even through the parodic exposure of convention. We can also see, though, the extent to which such texts walk a fine line; between the presumed disruption of genre and their maintenance of those same genres through reiteration. Contemporary English sci-fi, poised as it is between the demands of global exportability, budgetary constraints and (in theory) the sustaining of a national identity, inevitably finds itself ambivalently positioned. As we have seen throughout this book, a type of popular English cinema has sought a way to incorporate the influence and local perception of a dominant Hollywood imaginary, to produce exportable kinds of genre cinema, that are also reflections on national identity in relation to these same genres.

In *Paul*, the two stars of *Hot Fuzz*, Simon Pegg and Nick Frost, turn their attention as writers and performers to the sci-fi genre. In a similar way to *Hot Fuzz*, *Paul* makes the consumption of genre film and television central to its narrative and aesthetic, working around allusions to, and comic inversions of, wider tropes of Hollywood sci-fi film and television. The Paul of the title is a stranded alien, resident on Earth for half a century, who, while the object of fascination and paranoia on the part of the secret services, has also secretly been shaping the look and content of American science fiction culture. Pegg and Frost here play Graeme and Clive, a science fiction artist and writer duo who run into Paul during their personal sci-fi homage: a road trip of the American west, starting from San Diego Comic-Con, taking in the landmarks and sights both of America's history of alien conspiracy theory, and of the sci-fi cinema that, in films such as *Close Encounters of the Third Kind* and *E.T.: The Extra-Terrestrial* (1982), itself played with narratives and iconography of alien invasion and governmental conspiracies. The climax of the film eventually takes place near Devils Tower, the Wyoming landmass that is used so dramatically as the alien landing site in *Close Encounters*.

Paul is very much a postmodern science fiction film in its recognition that the genre is as much about the reproduction and recycling of images as it is the representation of anything 'real' as such. Hence Paul himself, with his child's body, huge head and almond-shaped eyes resembles, but then repudiates, the image science fiction culture has created for it (Paul, voiced by Seth Rogen, is exceptionally foul-mouthed, lewd and fond of beer and cigarettes). As a comedy about genre, the film's most obvious predecessor is *Galaxy Quest*, in which the crew of the titular sci-fi television show (transparently modelled on *Star Trek*) find themselves called upon to fight a very real galactic battle, in a real space ship modelled on the television version, for an alien race who have misread transmissions of the show as historical documents.

Paul's sporadically frattish and 'gross-out' mode of comedy often detracts from its most interesting central observation; that the two historical narratives of, on one side, sci-fi film and television, and on the other, Midwest America's fascination with alien life and UFOs, are inter-related. *Paul* is essentially a road movie that wends its way from California through the western states, and therefore shares with many road movies a type of documentary effect. It has a distinct cinematic feel for the empty spaces, physical isolation and landscapes that inform the American sci-fi imaginary and give it not just its sites, but its shape. Indeed, *Close Encounters* proves less a passing reference than a central structuring text, as *Paul* re-enacts a similar journey to the one made by Roy Neary (Richard Dreyfuss) in the earlier film, culminating in the Wyoming landing.

As Spielberg's biographer Joseph McBride points out, *Close Encounters* was made during the 1970s revival of interest in UFOs, after the first major wave of fascination in the 1950s:[61] not coincidentally, the two eras which saw the emergence and then triumphant re-emergence of sci-fi as a dominant cinematic form. It is an indication of sci-fi's postmodern associations, especially in terms of postmodernity's 'weakening of historicity',[62] that its films and television shows so prevalently appropriate historical narratives within their own science-fictional plots. We can identify this in key sci-fi texts such as *Doctor Who* and, as the most obvious reference for *Paul*, *The X-Files*, both of which often use alien intervention as a means of fiction- ally 'explaining' historical and political contexts. A stringent ideological critique of sci-fi would consequently highlight its capacity to provide not only diverting spectacle, but paradoxically *reassuring* counter-narratives of alien invasion, conspiracy and cover-up. The *X-Files* especially, across several television seasons and two films, spun an alternate chronicle of American history which, from a Jamesonian point of view, can only really represent the 'waning of affect' that is for him a feature of postmodern culture: the point at which generic narratives 'spread out and colonise […] reality itself'.[63] This is not to say for a moment that, as much as it implores us to 'believe', many viewers take *The X-Files* for reality, but this is not to under-estimate the impact of sci-fi on our imaginary, and our cognitive frameworks for interpreting and describing the world.[64]

Paul's simple central conceit is both to literalise and flip Hollywood sci-fi's over-arching conspiracy narrative. In this instance, sci-fi is not the occult narrative of history's hidden truths: instead, a banal truth of his- tory is depicted as the generator of so many *fictions*. Paul, as he himself puts it, resembles the clichéd representation of extra-terrestrial life because he was the model for it; just as, by his own claim, he gave American film and television its best sci-fi ideas ('Agent Scully – she was *my* idea!'). One sequence has Paul, in the middle of a vast, shadowy warehouse of wooden crates – a clear visual allusion to the end of *Raiders of the Lost Ark*, and the US government's occult storeroom – discussing over a phone with 'Steven' how to improve his alien protagonist by giving him healing powers. If the character of Paul is himself an example of parodic inversion, the rest of the film carries this through in various sequences. Paul's arrival on a Wyoming farm in 1947, preceded by orange light and the rapt gaze of a watching dog, ends with the dog getting squashed (via a sound bridge across the cut into the title credits) by a mechanically failing flying saucer. A similar type of bathetic comedy occurs at the film's climax, when the secret service chief is unceremoniously flattened by the arrival of Paul's mother ship. Such delib- erately corrupting strategies undermine the potential for its spectacle to function, at least in the way Hollywood has aimed to exploit it.

For all its conceptual strengths, *Paul* was a critical and commercial disappointment after Pegg and Frost's notable achievements in *Shaun of the Dead* and *Hot Fuzz*, and is a key example of the problems involved in discussing 'English' cinema in the global marketplace. Though considerably more expensive than *Shaun of the Dead* and *Hot Fuzz* (imdb.com puts its budget at approximately $40m), it shares the same production and distribution support (Working Title and Universal, respectively), besides the obvious impact of Pegg and Frost, whose performances as English geeks abroad marks their national identity in ways their earlier films do not require them to. Despite debunking many of the conventions and cultural or ideological characteristics of the science fiction genre, though, *Paul* seems structurally in thrall to the demands of wider generic frameworks. It also has an ending that somewhat straight-facedly mimics that of *E.T.*, as Paul flies off home, in much the same way that its opening sequence, with alien orange glow bursting through the cracks in the doorframe, is directly borrowed from the scene in *Close Encounters* where the little boy is taken by the aliens. A willingness to disrupt the system of spectacle is always balanced, then, by a tacit acknowledgement of the same spectacle, just as the gentle critique of alien representation requires that Paul still speaks English, the *lingua franca* of dominant global entertainment. Moreover, the distance between a fannish appropriation of Hollywood material and the contexts in which it is used (*Hot Fuzz*'s use of the action movie in an English provincial context, most notably) is here collapsed, both in terms of its actual American locations, but also in the way the film makes industrial marketing sites such as Comic-Con central to its story. *Paul*, in this sense, and in a self-publicising way, promotes the very same institutions that Hollywood studios use to promote films like *Paul*.[65]

Overall, then, the film demonstrates Harries' view that an increasingly ironic film culture is able to parody and reaffirm in the same gesture:[66] in the absence of a 'high-cultural' canon, or any obvious evaluative criteria, there is no effective difference between the parody and its subject. As we have seen, this was more or less the same point made in *Hot Fuzz*, though as I argued, the intent in that earlier film is more dialogically engaged with particularities of identity and context. *Paul* is at once too subservient to the prevailing mode of re-affirmative parody in Hollywood cinema, and too much in thrall of its notional targets, to work effectively as a piece of 'national' cinema, at least in the ways I've described. But it does, neverthe-less, hint towards the pertinence of more parodic modes as an alternative to the dominance of big-budget 'event' sci-fi; and as importantly, towards the possibilities of comic sci-fi as a form of science-fictional engagement in itself.

Again, Sam: Reproduction as Alienation in *Moon*

Both the tragic *and* comic potential of science fiction, and its reliance on dramatic *peripeteia*, are exemplified in *Moon*; a relatively low-budget ($5m) British production, distributed by Sony Pictures Classics, and directed by Duncan Jones, who also wrote the original story (the screenplay is by Nathan Parker). Thirty minutes into the film, the protagonist, Sam Bell (American actor Sam Rockwell), through an accidental sequence of events, comes face to face with a double. Up to this point we have seen Sam in his work as the sole engineer on a moon base, co-ordinating the mining and conveyance to Earth of a renewable energy source called Helium 3, for a multi-national company called Lunar Industries. It turns out that Sam and the 'new' Sam double are both clones of an 'original' Sam. These Sams are in fact a renewable source of short-term labour with built-in obsolescence, whose compliance with Lunar is maintained (in an inter-textual nod to the Replicant Rachel, built by the Tyrell Corporation, in *Blade Runner* [1982]) through their possession of long-term memory and expectation of a future life beyond their three-year contract (or rather, life-span).

In terms of the film's narration, this moment of protagonist perceptual revision is analogous to our own process of perception and reading. We see Sam being revived and woken after, disturbed by an apparent hallucina-tion, he has crashed his buggy into one of the huge lunar harvesters under his control. Following as it does a blackout and dissolve, and following the conventional grammar of film narrative, we might assume in the context of the film that this waking Sam is the same Sam as before. This error, and hence the reality concealed by the film's opening section, is only revealed in retrospect when this Sam (henceforth Sam Two) discovers his cloned 'self' (Sam One) still alive in the lunar buggy.

Needless to say, there is nothing particularly novel about such reversals in science fiction. From one point of view the estranging capacities of this kind of *peripeteia* are central to the ways the genre works. Any number of science fiction films – *2001*, *Alien* (1979), the original and 'director's cut' (1992) of *Blade Runner*, both Andrei Tarkovsky's and Steven Soderbergh's films of *Solaris* (1973, 2002), all work through climactic or late moments of reversal which, relying as they do on restricted narration, shift our reading of events in line with the protagonists'. Or when they employ more omniscient modes of narration, for example in *The Truman Show* (1998) or *The Matrix* (1999), an emphasis is placed on the central protagonist's process of emerging discovery and self-realisation.

Moon's emphasis on alienated labour, and on the work of global corporations to 'discipline' the working body to the demands of capital, makes it a film in the dystopian-political tradition:[67] one that includes films like *THX 1138* (1971), *Alien* and *Outland* (1981). Jameson locates the structurally political aspect of science fiction *peripeteia* in Brian Aldiss's 1957 novel *Non-Stop* (*Starship* in the US), something of an ur-text for the later science fiction films. We learn near the end of the novel that the starship believed to have been adrift in space for centuries, off-target in its intended course for Earth, has in fact been held in the Earth's orbit all along, maintained in an effective quarantine. For Jameson, in answering the question of where the ship is headed, secondary and overriding questions come into play, namely, what are they doing there in the first place? The cosmological questions, for Jameson, therefore give way to a more urgent political fable about ideology and consciousness.[68]

Moon's reversal may superficially echo those of its cinematic predecessors, though the more subtle effect is closer in spirit to Aldiss's own orbital narrative. In both *Alien* and its first sequel *Aliens* (1986), or in the hierarchical deep-space mining colony in *Outland*, alienation is narratively seen to occur when the protagonists' expendability is revealed: for example, when we realise that the crew of the Nostromo in *Alien* are sacrificial, used merely to help bring home a specimen creature. But they are also obviously and visibly alienated from the start: hence in *Alien*, the sweaty mechanics 'below deck' are marked by being in turn 'white trash' or black. The novelty of *Moon* is that – from a certain perspective – there is here no deception at all, no conspiracy or corporate machination. Nor is there any hidden motive informing the work: as far as we can see, however much it is also lining the pockets of Lunar's shareholders, the Helium 3 that Sam farms really is feeding the planet's energy needs. Sam's alienation, therefore, derives largely from the fact that, once his clone status is revealed, his working routine now constitutes the extent and horizon of his existence. In this sense, *Moon* makes estrangement out of the very stuff of quotidian working routine, eschewing the more hyperbolic aspect of works such as *Blade Runner*, or the obvious spatial division between 'inauthentic' and 'real', such as we see in *The Truman Show* or *The Matrix*.

If we share Sam's perceptual shift through the film's narrative reversals, then we also, by this same token, saw nothing untoward in the first section; even if retrospectively this is clearly not the case. This begs the question of what it is that maintains both the film's and the diegetic world's sense of unreliable normality. This is the point where parody comes in, as *Moon*'s perceptual qualities turn on its particular use of *other films* as part of its narrative process. While from one point of view the film looks backwards for its vision of the future, the film turns out to be both innovative and subtly reflexive in identifying the tendencies toward recycling in the sci-fi film. Its distinction is in the way it exploits these tendencies to a specific science-fictional effect.

The potential 'problem' of *Moon*, both in terms of design and (to some extent) narrative, is its indebtedness to a range of New Hollywood science fiction motifs. Jones has actually spoken of his desire to make a film in this vein:[69] hence the very liberal allusions to films such as *2001*, especially in *Moon*'s use of a soft spoken, all-seeing and controlling robot called GERTY. *Moon* also owes a lot to both *Silent Running* (1972) and the two versions of *Solaris*, mainly in their respective focus on solitude and qualities of art design (sterile whites, hexagonal corridors, the space station as study and workshop). Sam's initial appearance in full beard and unkempt hair also evokes the grungy trippiness of *Dark Star*, about three astronauts so adrift in space they no longer know why they are there or for how long they have been journeying.

Moon would in this sense exemplify Jameson's critique of a postmodern work 'without a vocation', a 'pastiche': 'a neutral practice of [...] mimicry, without any of parody's ulterior motives, amputated of the satiric impulse'.[70] Set in a notional future, Sam's initial appearance is nevertheless more in line with the film's main visual frames of reference, namely the late 1960 and 1970s. As Sobchack and Adam Roberts have both observed, this nostalgic tendency is one of the genres more paradoxical characteristics,[71] especially apparent in Hollywood's post-classical period; be it in the retro-futurism of *Star Wars* or the return to a form of unadulterated 'nature' in *Close Encounters of the Third Kind*. This begs the question of what *Moon* actually does, beyond reiterate in a form of homage the other films of which it is so respectful.

Roberts makes the point that science fiction has in some sense shaped the way we narrate developments in science *fact*, rather than the other way around. The idea that science fiction texts actually provide the template for our experience is perhaps – and in fact, a reiteration of Roberts' point – the stuff of science fiction. But Roberts makes the related point that not much critical work on science fiction from the viewpoint of postmodernity actually focuses on the media of reproduction – television, computers and so on – most typically associated with the postmodern.[72] Roberts may seem here to ignore the impact of critical works such as Scott Bukatman's *Terminal Identity*, in which the interface of the computer terminal becomes the defining core of postmodernity. Science fiction's role within postmodernity, as Bukatman consequently puts it, is 'to repeatedly narrate a new subject that can somehow directly interface with – and master – the cybernetic technologies of the Information Age'.[73] The subtle implication in Roberts' argument, though, is that such approaches may fail to include these science fiction texts *themselves* within their postmodern paradigms of the human and technological interface. Are other sci-fi texts transparent representations of this 'terminal identity', or do they create more layers of disruption and misperception?

The distinction in *Moon* from a more obvious mode of pastiche is that this 'weakened' historicity in the film, the result of its inter-textuality, has a narrative and interpretive function absent from other films, and contemporary science fiction films in particular. Above all, *Moon* operates around a sense of temporal dislocation. It is not merely the isolation from any tangible family or community that sets Sam adrift, but the representational sense that he is not anchored in any specific place or time. Like the broader inter-textual mode of the film, his clothes are a mishmash of various retro items (baseball caps and sweatpants in the colours of the New York Cosmos soccer team; what look to be 'Hi-Tech' training shoes favoured by British schoolboys of the 1980s), while specific cultural allusions are disorientating in their incongruous specificity, most notably, the way Sam wakes up to Chesney Hawkes' 1991 hit, 'The One and Only'. Sam's apparent fondness for 1960s American television comedies – we see him watch *Bewitched* and *The Mary Tyler Moore Show* – only adds to this sense of historical dislocation, this feeling of a free-floating cultural space and time. Where the plethora of pop-cultural artifacts in films like *Reservoir Dogs* (1992) and *Pulp Fiction* (1994) cohere in a type of alternate American time and space, and are the perennial subjects of their characters' devotion and conversation, here they have neither a specific frame of reference nor coherence.

If *Moon* offers a kind of 'banal' dystopia, then, its intrinsic pleasures of inter-textuality are a constituent part of this same dystopian construction. If 'dystopia' literally means 'bad place', the more nuanced characteristic of the dystopian text is that it is also at once an ideal place; a fact that brings it much closer to the utopian than we might often think. Dystopia shares with utopia its original connection to states and forms of government (the word 'utopia' was coined by Thomas More in his same-titled political treatise of 1516), and the dystopian novel or film more or less by definition depicts societies and their particular political configurations. State power, in Louis Althusser's terms, cannot be maintained without the manufacture of consent; in other words, the complicity of citizens to be ruled.[74] This, argues Althusser, is why complicity must be gained through ideology, the construction of belief. As soon as the state reveals itself as repressive (for example, through the use of military force), belief can no longer be maintained.

Dystopias, therefore, if they are to work at all, cannot be recognised as dystopias. There is always therefore the risk that a cinematic representation of dystopia fails by virtue of its very transparency, its obviousness. As Michael Ryan and Douglas Kellner point out, 'the rhetorical strategy of many technophobic [dystopian] films […] is to establish a strong opposition between terms (liberty vs. equality) that does not permit any intermediation. The elimination of the middle ground is an essential operation of this ideology'.[75] This is in fact one of the main limitations of George Lucas' *THX 1138*, the famous use in which of identical white clothes and shaven heads, along with its incessant focus on audio-visual surveillance, while aesthetically striking, renders the dramatic tension between the technocratic society and the individualist will of the titular hero all too apparent and schematic.

While a film like *The Matrix* gets round this problem by making its tech-nocratic state resemble our own everyday experience (the 'dream' world of those humans plugged into the Matrix), it is ultimately no less schematic in the way it separates its 'real' world – the dark wasteland of machine rule and its system of human batteries – from the dream world of ideology. *The Matrix* may be the film that launched a thousand dissertations on contemporary postmodern society and the 'simulacrum',[76] but what dis-cussions of the film often miss is their inherent paradox: that the replace-ment of reality by simulacra or spectacle is in the film made totally obvious, thereby disproving its actual relevance to contemporary society. As J. P. Telotte puts it, 'utopian and dystopian films […] which powerfully visual-ize what could be in a fully imagined and convincing diegetic world […] potentially undermine the critical effect of such a vision by dislocating this distinctly imagined world from our own'.[77] In such films, dystopia as a form of spectacle may in fact work to maintain ideology instead of critiquing it: 'such fantastic constructions, much like any culture's dominant ideology, can easily distract us from what [should] be done'.[78] Or most extremely in *The Matrix*, which ends with the apparently radical injunction to put on dark glasses, criticism elides into a form of pseudo-political posture that is in truth a kind of acquiescence, and one that avoids the social and political altogether.

One of the ways *Moon* deals with this problem is to render its dysto-pian vision banal to the point of indifference. This banality of electronic interaction is representative of the transformed ideology of technology over recent decades; from the technophobia of much 1970s and 80s cin-ema, often opposing technological rationality to a notion of 'nature' and social cohesion,[79] to the commercial technophilia of our present age and the computer's central, rather than peripheral, role within work and lei-sure. The robot is a related index of the human-technological interface in SF, and this is exemplified in *Moon*. On one side, the ubiquity of GERTY in the film suggests a domestication of technology, or its harmonisation with mankind's labour; exemplified by the various droids in the *Star Wars* series, or the helpful gardening robots Huey and Dewey in *Silent Running*. Yet the more obvious allusion, as noted, is to the HAL 9000 computer in *2001*. As Sobchack has argued, the mellifluous economy of HAL's speech, compared to the laconic blandness of the astronauts' in Kubrick's film, underscores a distance between our advanced technology and our limited language;[80] an irony that underpins the film's evolutionary struggle between human intelligence and AI.[81] The more optimistic subtext of the film is nevertheless that humans might learn from their own technological achievements, and evolve accordingly.

Moon plays with this Darwinian narrative to suggest that banality is not an obstacle to the realisation of a human-technology interface, but its possible *culmination*. This explains GERTY's reduction of human interaction to a series of screen-displayed emoticons and repetitious, solicitous requests, typically revolving around Sam's food intake. The detail of having yellow post-it notes stuck around GERTY's screen also reflects common workplace practice, our own quasi-intimate and dependent relationship to the computer terminal, and its organisation of our communications, business and leisure. But by banalising technology, the outcome of the evolutionary struggle is muddied: is this harmonisation, human mastery, or simply the point at which the machine has us exactly where it wants us? Unlike the more obviously troubling HAL with its all-seeing eye, GERTY's cuteness and apparent benevolence conceals the more corporate agenda behind his actions (in this instance, his concealing from Sam his real nature as a clone); but also the idea that surveillance is best achieved through the unknowing compliance of its subjects. Indeed, this sense of complicity with technology's own instrumental ends is typified by our contemporary relationship to internet search engines: technology that at once enables and speeds up our internet browsing, at the same time as collating these searches as data, converted into stored user information and, via algorithms, into user-directed advertisements – and more disturbingly, into forms of self-engineered surveillance.

Reference points in *Moon* to other cinematic texts, in this instance *2001*, are therefore knowing nods which simultaneously work to conceal a very pointed agenda. Parodying HAL in *Moon* makes *2001*'s autocratic electronic eye seem cute by comparison. But the fact that GERTY is made to seem normal and familiar is precisely the point of *Moon*'s ideological concerns. And because *Moon* is almost entirely made up of quotation, this becomes a paradigm for the whole film's depiction of time and space. *Moon* situates its protagonist, and in turn its audience, within a space of all-pervasive reproduction, but our possible awareness of the film's inter-texts is not shared by its protagonist. Sam's experience is, as Jameson might put it, cut off from history, left free to go round and round (the film, after all, is named after a satellite, which might as well be Sam himself) with no sense of linearity or progression. The joke, to this extent, is on him; though Sam's fate is not exactly funny. The fact that Sam's place within the organisation of labour is maintained largely through the assistance of media, through the use of communications and entertainment, is here as disturbing as any overt form of physical repression, precisely for the reason that he is so blandly acquiescent. This then becomes acutely problematic when it is revealed that Sam is a clone, because his own condition (his alienation, his subjection to what Michael Hardt and Antonio Negri describe as 'bio-power'[82]) does not wholly proceed from any repressive labour structure, but from his own willing participation in postmodern culture.

Conclusions: I Think I Am a Clone, Therefore I Am (Not)

The main rhetorical point in *Moon*, then, is that 'estrangement' is not produced by some overwhelming visualisation of our alienation, in the vein of *THX 1138* or *The Matrix*. Rather, estrangement is a condition of 'ordinary', 'everyday' life itself: life in its condition as reproduction, pastiche and temporal dislocation.

What we also see here, again, is that the question of economic and visual expenditure, and the film's distinctions from big-budget sci-fi, do not reduce merely to self-conscious recognition of difference, or even self-parody. For one thing, *Moon's* relatively small budget and use of practical miniature work (here, the shots of the lunar buggy and harvesters) belies its high-technological investment; most obviously, in the digital compositing used to represent the two Sams simultaneously on screen, but also in the variety of realistic CGI effects of light and lunar dust, GERTY's robotic arms and in some instances its body – that could be, and in some critical responses clearly have been, taken as practical effects. But more importantly, the question is not the self-conscious limitation of special effects technologies, but their specific use and aim. In this instance, if anything is targeted by the film's choice of focus and representation, it is the hyperbolic character of mainstream science fiction cinema, in terms of its tendency toward both spectacle and conservatism. But there is also a more pointed targeting here of Hollywood's tendencies toward individual-oriented narrative, exemplified for instance by *The Matrix* and its Christ-like story of Neo/'The One', and his ultimate ascension over and beyond the mundane human matrix. That Sam in *Moon* is in fact *not* 'The One and Only', and is forced to acknowledge his status as reproduction, seems in this respect much more than a knowing pop-cultural joke.

To suggest then that *Moon*'s aesthetic is merely a default representation born out of financial necessity, or is reducible to some kind of national cinematic character, would miss the point that *Moon* is adopting a specifically dialogic position towards the traditions of cinematic sci-fi, one that is only partially to do with the economics and cultural politics of English film, and as much to do with wider global concerns. That *Moon* seems to explicitly undermine the individualist and super-heroic thrust of contemporary sci-fi links up, for example, with a broader ecological concern also present in *Hitchhiker's Guide*. The satire of the latter is directed implicitly at the failings of humanity to check their drive towards 'progress', wherein the construction of a bypass is simply one element in the long-term imposition on planetary space and resources. Interestingly, the ending of the *Hitchhiker's Guide* film offers a form of fantastical, possibly ironic, though ideologically reassuring compensation in the idea of a second Earth, albeit one that is exactly the same as before. The ending of the television series is equally fatalistic in its circularity, though in a very different way: Arthur and Ford end up, in an inverted take on *Planet of the Apes* (1968), on a prehistoric, prelapsarian Earth, waiting its several millennia before being destroyed once more. But the circularity in both texts, like the fixation with repetition in *Moon*, rejects the more typically unilinear sense of time and physical movement in much sci-fi, which frequently draws on a frontier myth in its depiction of galactic adventure.[83] From its main narrative focus, *Moon* is less interested in extending the reach of (one) man into space than it is in considering how to deal with life precisely *as* repetition and circularity.

Moreover, where the theme of duplicated humans is frequently treated within the terms of the uncanny, or as threat, *Moon* is more interested in exploring its potential for *comedy*. By placing the two Sam clones together

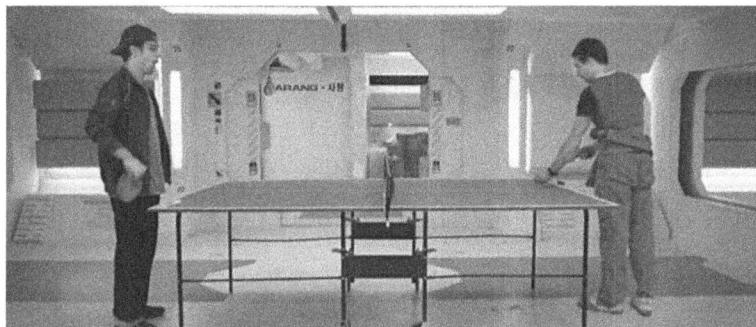

6.3 Not the One and Only: Sam plays himself at table-tennis in *Moon* (2009)

in the confined space of the lunar base, the film focuses on the challenge to identity and uniqueness; but in this instance such characteristics are not the source of narrative anxiety but the location for comic drama, as the two Sams try and frequently fail to get along. Indeed, by splitting the protagonist literally down the middle, *Moon* problematises the individualist dynamic of much narrative cinema. This comic tension reaches its apogee at the point where the two Sams face off in a symmetrically-orchestrated game of table tennis, the two opponents sending the ball back and forth at ridiculous velocity until the 'new' Sam cracks. But the tone here is above all one of bathos and slapstick; and in the traditions of such comedy the failure to work harmoniously is more related to individual failings (here, narcissism and incompetence) than it is to some external obstacle.

But the film's inter-textual nature also assumes a more prominently narrative and thematic significance. *Moon*'s narrative of concealment and *peripeteia*, in which the unique is revealed as copy, is doubly represented at the level of design and generic motifs. Sam's failure to recognise his cloned status is also a failure to recognise he is in a sci-fi film. We've all been here before: this is the point of the film, the source of its comic drama. *Moon*'s awareness of this fact as its own source of estrangement makes it distinctive amongst recent sci-fi cinema. Similarly, what makes the film of *Hitchhiker's Guide* so distinctive as a sci-fi text is the way it inverts the dominant forms of the genre itself as a means of estranging our perspective, and in turn, potentially, our mainly anthropocentric view of the world, if not the universe. *Paul*, meanwhile, for all its possible limitations, also uses the motifs and structures of Hollywood sci-fi in order to tease out some of the stranger realities these films often conceal. In all these respects, while working very much within the frameworks of cinematic sci-fi, these films, with their cultural aspects of Englishness at work in them, forge for themselves a specific and distinct identity, as well as encouraging us to rethink the conceptual boundaries of the genre.

Epilogue: James Bond, Runner Beans
and Jumping Queens

On 27 July 2012, nearly one billion television viewers worldwide saw the opening ceremony for London's Olympic Games. 'Isles of Wonder' was overseen and jointly devised (with writer Frank Cottrell-Boyce) by screen and stage director Danny Boyle, best known for his work on the films *Trainspotting* (1996) and the Oscar-winning *Slumdog Millionaire* (2008), but also a filmmaker who has diversified into low-budget horror (*28 Days Later* [2002]) and high-budget transnational science fiction (*Sunshine* [2007]). Boyle's fondness for socially and culturally marginal subjects, combined with his populist style, as well as his willingness to embrace a more global type of narrative and theme, made him an interesting choice to helm what would be the most widely-viewed display of British cultural creativity ever produced.

Unsurprisingly, Boyle made use of the ceremony, segueing as it did between recorded material and the live action in the Olympic Stadium, as a media event, not just the transmission of a staged work. Inserted film and edited live performance joined up therefore in a continuous flow of narrative, sound and image. Most striking in this respect was the entrance of Queen Elizabeth II to officially open the games. A short film begins with a specially invited guest making his way into Buckingham Palace. Elsewhere in the building, a group of schoolchildren notice this famous visitor through the window. Turning out to be none other than James Bond (as played by Daniel Craig), Britain's top secret agent is subsequently introduced, via shots of rolling Corgis, to Her Majesty, before the two make their way out onto the grounds and on board a helicopter. After flying eastwards over London to reach the Stadium, Bond is surprised to see his traveling companion throw herself out of the chopper, to the burst of Bond's famous theme, and in a clear allusion to the similar moment in *The Spy Who Loved Me* (described earlier in this book), a live shot from below shows us the Queen coming down to earth, held aloft by a Union Jack parachute.

This match-up was no mere opportunist throwing-together of two prominent British, indeed English, icons. In this instance, the London Olympics arrived at a stupidly good time, as if fated by the stars rather than the International Olympic Committee. James and Elizabeth's first public outing together was, in fact, no more than the visible manifestation of a stroll they have been taking together throughout their professional lives. After all, 007 epitomises an alternate and aspirational lifestyle for the second Elizabethan age partly because he so unerringly coincides with it. Bond did not introduce himself to the world in 1952, but Ian Fleming chose that year to write *Casino Royale*, which was subsequently published in 1953, the year of Elizabeth II's coronation. If the novels appeared throughout the 1950s' decade of austerity, the films, starting with *Dr No* in 1962, play out various phases in the correlating fortunes and moods of English life and the English film industry: the punchy transatlantic pop-cultural confidence of the 1960s, the troughs and excesses of the 1970s and 1980s, the return to confidence and cool in the 1990s, the more globally-conscious political realism and pragmatism of the 2000s.

With *Skyfall* due to appear in the autumn of 2012, the Olympic ceremony film was also well timed to chime with, and provide free publicity for, this imminent release. *Skyfall* also represented Bond's Golden (Screen) Anniversary, just as the Olympics followed on the heels of the Queen's Diamond Jubilee the previous month. *The Spy Who Loved Me* was itself aware of its national contexts, made as it was in the Silver Jubilee year of 1977. In reviving this image for another set of anniversaries, the creators of Isles of Wonder showed their knowledge and awareness of these interlinking histories. But it is also significant that the homage is inverted here: 'the Queen' acknowledges Bond's jubilee, rather than the other way around, suggesting here that English global significance is perhaps as much relatable now in terms of fictional screen icons, than it is on real-life symbols of a faded Empire

Later in the ceremony, Rowan Atkinson's appearance in the guise of Mr Bean – as discussed in the first chapter, one of the most successfully exported English film and television characters – added to this trinity of global English media figures. In another blending of live and recorded action, Bean is found playing the repetitive synthesiser note in a rendition of Vangelis's famous theme for *Chariots of Fire* (1981) (another British Oscar winner, focusing on two British runners from different cultural and religious backgrounds at the 1924 Paris Olympics). Daydreaming, Bean projects himself into the film's opening beach sequence of training athletes, jostling his co-runners out of the way, and going on – before conductor Simon Rattle rudely awakens him from his reverie – to 'win' the imaginary race in his head.

What is striking about both these sketches is the way they are at once so confident in their display of English media icons, and at the same time, so apparently confident about not taking them too seriously. Even *Chariots of Fire* – a film specifically celebrating British multicultural sporting achievement, and whose American success heralded at the time a presumed (though short-lived) renaissance for British film production – does not escape irony's wicked grip: a film about the Olympic spirit being parodied in the Olympics itself! And yet, everyone comes out of this unscathed: no less so than Craig's Bond, whose Sam Mendes-directed *Skyfall* would go on to crush all existing box-office records for the series.

That this parodic gambit at the Olympic ceremony worked may owe something to the expectations of what a British or English event might be like, as if somehow a specific type of 'Englishness' permeated the performance. As I have argued throughout this book, though, what we might misleadingly refer to as English character ahistorically fixes what is contingent and circumstantial, born not of some pre-existent essence, but as the product of various global forces, and the consequent projection outward of a constructed idea. The most obvious precedent for the 2012 Olympic Games, the 1951 Festival of Britain, was not characterised by irony and self-parody, but rather a mostly forward- and future-thinking projection of national ambition, and of cultural and scientific achievement, after the austere post-war period. Its instructive aims were, as Becky Conekin's study of the Festival has shown, to project 'progress and modernity' as the way forward 'to build a better Britain'.[1] What, then, is at stake in the 2012 opening ceremony, and what, if anything, can its uses of parody tell us about contemporary English culture?

Like the 1951 Festival, much of the media build-up around the 2012 opening ceremony placed it in the context of economic austerity, harking back in nostalgic turn to the wartime injunction to Keep Calm and Carry On: the mid-century Home Front slogan now re-functioned through its 'ubiquitous [use] in British media and marketing'.[2] As Conekin notes, if self-parody was not an obvious feature of the Festival itself, much contemporary media did poke fun at its pretensions, rebranding its ethos of 'Britain Can Make It' as 'Britain Can't Have It'.[3] For some commentators in the run-up to 2012, perhaps those ready to sniff out a 'typically English' disaster story, one of the challenges of the London event was to follow Beijing's extraordinary display of 2008. Beijing's hugely expensive spectacle, also coordinated by a film and theatre director in the form of Zhang Yimou (whose most recent films included the martial-arts extravaganzas *Hero* [2002] and *The Curse of the Golden Flower* [2006]), mobilised its massive cast into sumptuously choreographed presentations, simulating amongst other things native arts of woodblock printing and scroll painting in a panoramic tour of China's creative history.

In considering London's strategy as a response to Beijing, we risk a racially-inflected essentialising of national character that should, needless to add, be avoided. Just as we should see Boyle's ceremony both in relation to his own work elsewhere and also as strategic within its own specific terms, Zhang's work for the 2008 ceremony is no less consistent with his own wider output. As William Costanzo notes, the Chinese director's use, since the late 1990s, of international funding structures and transnational casts, as well as his move toward the more globally exportable martial-arts (*wuxia*) action spectacle, has led some commentators to question the 'Chinese' identity of his films.[4] Not only does the supposed political correctness of such questioning limit the idea of Chinese cinema to a prescribed and seemingly incommunicable notion of national culture; it also overlooks the way performances of the 'imagined' China of Zhang's work,[5] extending to the Olympic ceremony, play a part in shaping and even discussing Chinese identity at the intersection of tradition, history and an increasingly globalised, diasporic and technologised Chinese community. Such 'Chinese cinema' is in this sense not a strict representation of China at all, but necessarily, as a global, diasporic cinema, 'a projection of the imagination'.[6]

As this book has explored, English film and television, both as domestic and intentionally global products, frequently look to comedy, and more specifically parody, for reasons that are at once politically conscious, as well as aesthetically and economically strategic. But like the Chinese example, to think of such film or television as a representation of 'England' in any literal sense is largely to miss its point, and to underestimate its function as a globally-strategic imaginary projection. At the same time, to fall into the trap of thinking that the London ceremony was having a laugh at its own (lack of) expense overlooks its highly organised construction, conceptual polish and – indeed – expense, which while not quite in the Beijing league, called into question the 2012 Olympics' connotation as the new 'Austerity Games' (the opening ceremony alone cost £27m to produce). The fact that the ceremony incorporated aspects of self-deriding humour might suggest, superficially, that the type of skepticism only prevalent in the media in 1951 had seeped into representation itself. But while this does suggest a different, revisionist type of attitude towards ideology and national myth – a shift this book has explored at various points – we need to be careful how we position this attitude within the terms of a high-cost mass-media global presentation like the one under discussion here.

As we have seen, the films and television series analysed in this book are marked not so much by their economic disparity from Hollywood's dominant products (even though this disparity, to a large extent, does exist), but by a sense of product differentiation. Consistently, though, such differentiation can hardly be founded on any *essential* difference, questionable as this would be. Rather, it is the cultural precedents through which ideas of England and Englishness have been historically constructed – most prominently, films themselves, but also literature, narratives of history and various national myths – that become the source material for such parodic explorations of English identity. The Arthurian legend, the spirit of music hall and Northern comedy, Boy's Own adventure and war movies, the aesthetics of heritage, Gothic horror and science fiction: this material becomes at once the form through which this strain of English comedy establishes its distinctiveness, its cultural specificity – at the same time as distancing itself from the problematic connotations of its sources and inspirations, through the incongruities and excesses of its references and quotations. Such approaches to filmmaking and subject matter allow both domestic and international audiences to laugh at, but also enjoy, such manifestations of an imagined England, though one clearly marked as construction, as history, as fiction.

Boyle's willingness to play so pointedly with mediatised figures and events of national history, both real and invented, showed a canny awareness of this parodic tradition, and the increasing centrality of parody as a mode and practice of twenty-first-century media. As a ceremony informed by its consciousness of nation and history as cultural memory and construction – refracting centuries of history through fragments of literary, filmic and musical quotation and allusion – nothing, and especially not the crowned Head of State, was allowed too much respect. But such lack of 'serious' respect is only commensurate with their own status as figure(head)s: as *images* through which the imagined nation is constructed.

But finally, let us not fall into the concluding trap of placing Bond and Bean on the commercially disinterested pedestal of self-reflective national critique (a task I will leave to other writers on the subject). We should be wary of giving too much political headway to a show 'which took place in a thoroughly corporatized, securitized commercial environment'.[7] As its status as pre-publicity for *Skyfall* indicates, such shows are also clearly *showcases*: and in this instance, the Olympic ceremony serves at once to joke about English history and perception (of itself, and that of others towards it), but also to display this defining character as a marker of what the country's creative industries can specifically sell to the world. Such performances within the globalised twenty-first century inevitably represent the reciprocal movement between the global and the local and back again.[8] Like many of the texts explored in this book, the ceremony was a manifestation of Englishness seen anew through the global circuit of screen cultures, and then re-projected strategically out into the world. The notional enclosure of the local consequently opens out to the aesthetic and commercial strategies of the glocal, in a move we have seen on numerous occasions throughout this study. Like many of the works we have considered, then, Boyle's ceremony, with its jumping Queen and running Bean, offered a parody of Englishness that was also, in its same gesture, a confident expression of what Englishness means in a global media context. Funny it most certainly was: a joke, at the expense of national self-perception and global significance, it most certainly was not.

Notes

Preface

1 The film version of *The Trip to Italy* was premiered at the Sundance Festival in January 2014 prior to a limited worldwide release. The television version was first screened over six weeks on BBC2, April–May 2014.

Introduction

1 While much of the production background of *Father Ted* places the show within the terms of Irish television, its writers (Graham Linehan and Arthur Matthews) have played down its 'ethnic' qualities, acknowledging its location within the traditions of Anglo-Irish culture. See Ben Thompson, *Sunshine on Putty: The Golden Age of British Comedy from Vic Reeves to The Office* (London, 2004), pp. 193–5.
2 On the relationship of personal viewing experience to the reading of *Spaced*, see Neil Archer, *Studying Hot Fuzz* (Leighton Buzzard, 2015).
3 Dan Harries, *Film Parody* (London, 2000), p. 6.
4 Brett Mills, *The Sitcom* (Edinburgh, 2009), p. 83.
5 Linda Hutcheon, *A Theory of Parody: The Teachings of Twentieth-Century Art Forms* (New York, 1985), p. 32.
6 Ibid.
7 Ibid., p. 87.
8 Harries, *Film Parody*, pp. 43, 55, 62, 71, 77, 83.

9 Wes Gehring, *Parody as Film Genre: Never Give a Saga an Even Break* (Westport, CT, 1999).

10 Geoff King, *Film Comedy* (London and New York, 2002).

11 Margaret A. Rose, *Parody: Ancient, Modern and Post-Modern* (Cambridge, 1993), p. 28.

12 Ibid.

13 Harries, *Film Parody*, p. 6.

14 Simon Dentith, *Parody* (London and New York, 2000), p. 9.

15 Dan Harries, 'Film Parody and the Resuscitation of Genre', in Steve Neale (ed), *Genre and Contemporary Hollywood* (London, 2002).

16 Tim Bergfelder, 'Popular European Cinema in the 2000s: Cinephilia, Genre and Heritage', in Mary Harrod, Mariana Liz and Alissa Timoshkina (eds), *The Europeanness of European Cinema: Identity, Meaning, Globalization* (London and New York, 2015), pp. 33–57.

17 Dentith, *Parody*, p. 155.

18 Fredric Jameson, *Postmodernism; Or, The Cultural Logic of Late Capitalism* (Durham, NC, 1991), p. 17.

19 Harries, 'The Resuscitation of Genre'.

20 Harries, *Film Parody*, p. 31.

21 Ibid., p. 3.

22 Linda Hutcheon, *The Politics of Postmodernism* (London and New York, 1989).

23 Dentith, *Parody*, p. 161.

24 Ibid.

25 Mathijs, Ernest and Jamie Sexton, *Cult Cinema* (Chichester, 2011), p. 225.

26 Ibid., p. 47.

27 Ibid.

28 Ibid.

29 Ibid., p. 46.

30 Ibid., p. 23.

31 Andy Medhurst, *A National Joke: Popular Comedy and English Cultural Identity* (London and New York, 2007), p. 1.

32 Ibid., p. 31.

33 Ibid., p. 33.

34 Benjamin R. Barber, *Jihad vs. McWorld: Terrorism's Challenge to Democracy* (London, 2003); George Ritzer, *The McDonaldization of Society*, 6th edition (Thousand Oaks, New Delhi, London and Singapore, 2011).

35 Medhurst, *A National Joke*, p. 33.

36 Andrew Higson, *Film England: Culturally English Filmmaking since the 1990s* (London and New York, 2011).

37 Ibid., p. 4.

38 Ibid., p. 25.

39 Andrew Spicer, 'The Reluctance to Commit: Hugh Grant and the New British Romantic Comedy', in Phil Powie, Ann Davies and Bruce Babbington (eds), *The Trouble with Men: Masculinities in European and Hollywood Cinema* (London and New York, 2004), p. 77.

40 Andrew Higson, *Waving the Flag: Constructing a National Cinema in Britain* (Oxford, 1995), p. 6.

41 Roland Robertson, *Globalization: Social Theory and Global Culture* (London, Thousand Oaks and New Delhi, 1992).

42 Ulrich Beck, *What Is Globalization?* (Cambridge, 2000), p. 46.

43 Ibid., p. 47, my emphasis.

44 Tom Shone, *Blockbuster: How the Jaws and Jedi Generation Turned Hollywood into a Boom Town* (London, 2004), p. 246.

45 Medhurst, *A National Joke*; I.Q. Hunter and Larraine Porter (eds), *British Comedy Cinema* (London and New York, 2012); Thompson, *Sunshine on Putty*.

46 Robert Shail (ed), *Seventies British Cinema* (Basingstoke, 2008); Sue Harper and Justin Smith, *British Film Culture in the 1970s: The Boundaries of Pleasure* (Edinburgh, 2012).

Chapter 1: Cricklewood vs. Hollywood

1 King, *Film Comedy*, p. 161.

2 Ibid., p. 162.

3 Medhurst, *A National Joke*, pp. 65–6.

4 Andy Medhurst, 'Music Hall and British Cinema', in Charles Barr (ed), *All Our Yesterdays: 90 Years of British Cinema* (London, 1986), p. 172.

5 King, *Film Comedy*, pp. 37–8.

6 Ibid., p. 38.

7 Higson, *Waving the Flag*, p. 149.

8 Medhurst, 'Music Hall and British Cinema', p. 174.

9 Ibid.

10 Higson, *Waving the Flag*, p. 154.

11 Ibid.

12 Medhurst, *A National Joke*, pp. 68–71.

13 Ibid., p. 132.

14 Ibid., p. 133.

15 Harries, *Film Parody*, p. 132.

16 Medhurst, 'Music Hall and British Cinema', p. 183.

17 Graham McCann, *Morecambe and Wise* (London, Fourth Estate, 1998), pp. 154–60.

18 Ibid., p. 252.

19 Higson, *Waving the Flag*, pp. 163–4.
20 Peter Waymark, 'From Telly Laughs to Belly Laughs: The Rise and Fall of the Sitcom Spin-Off', in Hunter and Porter (eds), *British Comedy Cinema* (London, 2012).
21 McCann, *Morecambe and Wise*, pp. 168–9.
22 Ibid., p. 179.
23 King, *Film Comedy*, p. 35.
24 McCann, *Morecambe and Wise*, p. 190.
25 John Fitzgerald, *Studying British Cinema: 1999–2009* (Leighton Buzzard, 2010), pp. 28, 33.
26 Ibid., p. 29.
27 Laurence Napper, '"No Limit": British Class and Comedy of the 1930s', in Hunter and Porter (eds), *British Comedy Cinema*, p. 42.
28 Ibid., p. 41, emphasis in the original.
29 Higson, *Film England*, p. 35.
30 Fitzgerald, *Studying British Cinema*, pp. 32–3.
31 Andrew Higson, 'The Heritage Film and British Cinema' in Andrew Higson (ed), *Dissolving Views: Key Writings on British Cinema* (London and New York, 1996), pp. 232–48.
32 In Fitzgerald, *Studying British Cinema*, p. 33.
33 Nicholas J. Cull 'The Man Who Made *Thunderbirds*: An Interview with Gerry Anderson', in John R. Cook and Peter Wright (eds), *British Science Fiction Television: A Hitchhiker's Guide* (London and New York, 2006).
34 Fitzgerald, *Studying British Cinema*, pp. 27–35.
35 Fitzgerald notes that the budgets for *Chicken Run* and *The Curse of the Were-Rabbit* were $42m and $80m respectively (*Studying British Cinema*, pp. 30–1).
36 Jonathan Gray, *Watching with The Simpsons: Television, Parody and Intertextuality* (New York and London, 2006), p. 66.

Chapter 2: Silly, Really

1 Steve Neale and Frank Krutnik, *Popular Film and Television Comedy* (London and New York, 1990), pp. 196–208.
2 Ibid., p. 196.
3 'Monty Python: And Now For Something Rather Similar': broadcast on BBC One, 29 June 2014.
4 In Justin Smith, 'Making *Ben-Hur* Look Like an Epic: Monty Python at the Movies', in Hunter and Porter (eds), *British Comedy Cinema*, p. 175.
5 See Smith, 'Making *Ben-Hur* Look Like an Epic'; also Michael Palin, *Diaries 1969–1979: The Python Years* (London, 2006).
6 Neale and Krutnik, *Popular Film and Television Comedy* (London and New York, 1990), p. 198.

7 Smith, 'Making *Ben-Hur* Look Like an Epic'.
8 Palin, *Diaries*, pp. 166–80.
9 Sue Harper and Justin Smith, *British Film Culture in the 1970s: The Boundaries of Pleasure* (Edinburgh, 2012), p. 182.
10 Smith, 'Making *Ben-Hur* Look Like an Epic'.
11 Justin Smith, *Withnail and Us: Cult Films and Film Cults in British Cinema* (London and New York, 2010), pp. 120–1.
12 Smith, 'Making *Ben-Hur* Look Like an Epic'.
13 Harper and Smith, *British Film Culture in the 1970s*, p. 179.
14 Ibid., p. 180.
15 Palin, *Diaries*, pp. 163–4.
16 Ibid., pp. 189–90.
17 Ibid., p. 190.
18 Harper and Smith, *British Film Culture in the 1970s*, p. 180.
19 Smith, 'Making *Ben-Hur* Look Like an Epic', p. 175.
20 Harper and Smith, *British Film Culture in the 1970s*, p. 180.
21 Robert Burgoyne, *The Hollywood Historical Film* (Oxford, 2008), p. 8.
22 Ibid.
23 Ibid., p. 9.
24 Ibid., pp. 8–9.
25 Rick Altman, 'A Semantic/Syntactic Approach to Film Genre', *Cinema Journal* 23/3 (1984).
26 Colin MacCabe, 'Theory and Film: Principles of Realism and Pleasure', *Screen* 17/3 (1976), p. 12.
27 Ibid.
28 Colin MacCabe, 'Realism and the Cinema: Notes on Some Brechtian Theses', *Screen* 15/2 (1974).
29 Raymond Williams, 'A Lecture on Realism', *Screen* 18/1 (1977), p. 65.
30 Ibid.
31 Comolli, Jean-Luc and Paul Narboni, 'Cinema/Ideology/Criticism', *Screen* 12/2 (1971), p. 32.
32 Robert Stam, *Subversive Pleasures: Bakhtin, Cultural Criticism, and Film* (Baltimore and London, 1989), p. 111.
33 Burgoyne, *Hollywood Historical Film*, pp. 1–2.
34 Harries, *Film Parody*, p. 77.
35 Smith, 'Making *Ben-Hur* Look Like an Epic', p. 174.
36 Alexander Walker, *Hollywood, England: The British Film Industry in the Sixties* (London, 1974), p. 374.
37 Thomas Malory, *Le Morte D'Arthur*, Volume One (London, 1969), p. 178.
38 Smith, *Withnail and Us*, pp. 120–1.
39 Malory, *Le Morte D'Arthur*, p. 162.
40 This failed attempt became the subject of a 2002 documentary, *Lost in La Mancha*.

41 Anthony Close, *Don Quixote* (Cambridge, 1990), p. 14.
42 Robert Stam, *Literature through Film: Realism, Magic and the Art of Adaptation* (Oxford, 2005), p. 26.
43 Mikhail Bakhtin, *The Dialogic Imagination: Four Essays* (Austin, TX, 1981), p. 23.
44 Simon Dentith, *Bakhtinian Thought: An Introductory Reader* (London and New York, 1995), p. 50.
45 Burgoyne, *The Hollywood Historical Film*, p. 2.
46 Benedict Anderson, *Imagined Communities: Reflections on the Origin and Spread of Nationalism* (London and New York, 1991).
47 As indicated most recently by the very popular BBC series *Merlin* (2008–12), which distilled much of the Arthur legend into a pre-watershed Saturday evening entertainment.
48 This war is the main focus of the anonymous *Death of King Arthur*, written at the end of the 14th century, and one of the precedents for Malory's later work.
49 Bruce Babington and Peter William Evans, *Biblical Epics: Sacred Narrative in the Hollywood Cinema* (Manchester and New York, 1993), p. 100.
50 Harries, *Film Parody*, p. 122.
51 Palin, *Diaries*, p. 473.
52 Vivian Sobchack, '"Surge and Splendor": A Phenomenology of the Hollywood Historical Epic', *Representations* 29 (1990), p. 24.
53 Ibid., p. 26.
54 Burgoyne, *The Hollywood Historical Film*, p. 1.
55 Ibid., pp. 1–2.
56 Sobchack, 'Surge and Splendor', p. 28.
57 Ibid., p. 25.
58 Whissel, Kristen. 'The Digital Multitude', *Cinema Journal* 49/4 (2010), p. 92.
59 Ibid.
60 On the crucifixion in cinema see Pamela Grace, *The Religious Film* (Oxford, 2009).

Chapter 3: History and Hysteria

1 See for example Roger Wilmut, *From Fringe to Flying Circus: Celebrating a Unique Generation of Comedy, 1960–1980* (London, 1980).
2 Sue Harper, 'Keynote Lecture, Don't Look Now: British Cinema in the 1970s Conference, University of Exeter, July 2007', in Paul Newland (ed), *Don't Look Now: British Cinema in the 1970s* (Bristol and Chicago, 2010), p. 24.
3 Dominic Sandbrook, *Seasons in the Sun: The Battle for Britain, 1974–1979* (London, 2012), p. 77.
4 In ibid., p. 81.
5 Walker, *Hollywood, England*, pp. 287–9.

6 Robert Shail, 'Introduction: Cinema in the Era of "Trouble and Strife"', in Robert Shail (ed), *Seventies British Cinema* (Basingstoke, 2008), p. xiv.
7 Justin Smith, 'Glam, Spam and Uncle Sam: Funding Diversity in 1970s British Cinema', in Shail (ed) *Seventies British Cinema*, p. 69.
8 Harper, 'Keynote Lecture', p. 24.
9 Ruth Barton, 'When the Chickens Came Home to Roost: British Thrillers of the 1970s', in Shail (ed), *Seventies British Cinema*, p. 50.
10 Ibid., p. 51.
11 Ibid., p. 46.
12 Harper, 'Keynote Lecture', p. 23.
13 Ibid., p. 25.
14 Ibid.
15 James Chapman, 'Action, Spectacle and the Boy's Own Tradition in British Cinema', in Robert Murphy (ed), *The British Cinema Book* (London, 2009), p. 86.
16 Ibid., p. 85.
17 http://www.bbc.co.uk/programmes/b03zqgk1 accessed 6 April 2014. The programme, 'Alexander Armstrong's Real Ripping Yarns', was screened on BBC4 on 3 April.
18 Palin, *Diaries*, p. 509.
19 George MacDonald Fraser, *Royal Flash* (London, 1970).
20 There is an intriguing contextual overlap here, insofar as Woodfall was originally run by Harry Saltzman, the British producer who would go on in the 1960s, also with the partnership of United Artists, to create the James Bond franchise.
21 Walker, *Hollywood, England*, p. 361.
22 Richard Maltby, *Hollywood Cinema* (Malden, MA and Oxford, 2003), pp. 165–7.
23 Mark Connelly, *The Charge of the Light Brigade* (London and New York, 2003), pp. 60–6.
24 Smith, 'Glam, Spam and Uncle Sam', p. 77.
25 Ibid., p. 69.
26 Higson, *Waving the Flag*, p. 273.
27 Ibid.
28 Ibid., p. 41.
29 Robert Hewison, *The Heritage Industry: Britain in a Climate of Decline* (London, 1987).
30 See especially Claire Monk, 'The British Heritage-Film Debate Revisited', in Claire Monk and Amy Sargeant (eds), *British Historical Cinema* (London and New York, 2002), pp. 176–98.
31 Dominic Sandbrook, *State of Emergency: The Way We Were: Britain, 1970–1974* (London, 2010), pp. 196–8.
32 Ibid.

33 See Sarah Street, 'Heritage Crime: The Case of Agatha Christie' in Shail (ed) *Seventies British Cinema*, pp. 105–16.

34 Sandbrook, *State of Emergency*, p. 202.

35 In ibid.

36 Robert Shail, ' "More, Much More…Roger Moore": A New Bond for a New Decade', in Shail (ed), *Seventies British Cinema*, pp. 150–8.

37 Ibid.

38 Ibid., p. 156.

39 James Chapman and Nicholas J. Cull, *Projecting Empire: Imperialism and Popular Cinema* (London and New York, 2009), pp. 170–1.

40 Ibid., pp. 175–6.

41 Ibid., pp. 144–5.

42 Ibid., p. 144.

43 Ibid., pp. 147–8.

44 Thompson, *Sunshine on Putty*, pp. 325–7.

45 Derek Paget, 'Popularising Popular History: *Oh What A Lovely War* and the Sixties', *Critical Survey* 2/2 (1990), 117.

46 Ibid., p. 118.

47 George MacDonald Fraser, *Flashman* (London, 1969), p. 13.

48 Andrew Sanders, 'Introduction', in Thomas Hughes, *Tom Brown's Schooldays* (Oxford, 1989), pp. xxiv–xxv.

49 Ibid., p. ix.

50 Connelly, *Charge of the Light Brigade*, p. 57.

51 Hughes, *Tom Brown's Schooldays*, p. 110.

52 Ibid., p. 112. Indeed, the Monty Python team in *The Meaning of Life* (1983) explicitly links militarism with rugby in a striking graphic-match cut, where a young player's mud-spattered face becomes the same muddied face on the battlefields of World War I.

53 Ibid., p. 111.

54 Connelly, *Charge of the Light Brigade*, p. 15.

55 Ibid., pp. 5–6.

56 Neil Sinyard, *Richard Lester* (Manchester and New York, 2010), p. 46.

57 Walker, *Hollywood, England*, p. 264, my emphasis.

58 Connelly, *Charge of the Light Brigade*, p. 60.

59 Ibid.

60 See ibid., pp. 40–1.

61 Fraser, *Royal Flash*, pp. 9–10.

62 Ibid., p. 10.

63 Ibid., p. 110.

64 Sinyard, *Richard Lester*, p. 112.

65 Ibid., p. 116.

66 Ibid., p. 112.

67 Hutcheon, *A Theory of Parody*, p. 32.
68 Andrew Higson, 'Re-Presenting the National Past: Nostalgia and Pastiche in the Heritage Film', in Lester D. Friedman (ed), *Fires Were Started: British Cinema and Thatcherism* (London and New York, 2006), p. 99.
69 Chapman and Cull, *Projecting Empire*, p. 149.
70 *The Life and Death of Colonel Blimp* begins with its main character, the ageing General Clive Candy, being surprised when his war-game training begins before the appointed hour: an event that gives way to the film's wider reflection on 'total war', and the anomalous traditional British values of 'fair play'.
71 Palin makes various references in his *Diaries* to contemporary British cinema, though without mentioning either *The Eagle Has Landed* or *The Thirty Nine Steps*. He does, nevertheless, reserve a particular ire for *The Spy Who Loved Me*, describing it as 'most unpleasant' and 'mindless garbage' (*Diaries*, p. 428).
72 Harries, *Film Parody*, p. 105.
73 Ibid.
74 Ibid., p. 104.

Chapter 4: "The Shit Just Got Real"

1 Harries, 'The Resuscitation of Genre'.
2 James Leggott, *Contemporary British Cinema: From Heritage to Horror* (London and New York, 2008), p. 56.
3 Andrew Higson, *Waving the Flag*; Andrew Higson, 'The Limiting Imagination of National Cinemas', in Mette Hjort and Scott Mackenzie (eds), *Cinema and Nation* (London and New York, 2000), pp. 63–74; Higson, *Film England*.
4 Higson, *Waving the Flag*, pp. 4–5.
5 Ibid., p. 4.
6 John Hill, *British Cinema in the 1980s: Issues and Themes* (Oxford, 1999).
7 In Higson, 'The Limiting Imagination of National Cinemas', p. 71.
8 Higson, *Waving the Flag*, p. 5.
9 Higson, 'The Limiting Imagination of National Cinemas', p. 66.
10 Ibid., p. 71.
11 Hutcheon, *A Theory of Parody*.
12 Harries, *Film Parody*, p. 6.
13 King, *Film Comedy*, p. 107.
14 Ibid., p. 109.
15 In ibid., p. 112.
16 Arjun Appadurai, *Modernity at Large: Cultural Dimensions of Globalization* (Minneapolis, 1996), p. 33.
17 Ibid., p. 42.

18 Marc Augé, *Non-Places: Introduction to an Anthropology of Supermodernity* (London and New York, 1995).

19 Hill, *British Cinema in the 1980s*, pp. 34–8.

20 Ibid., p. 46.

21 Imdb.com puts *Revolution*'s budget at an estimated $28,000,000. Its theatrical gross in the US was just $346,761.

22 Maltby, *Hollywood Cinema*, p. 388.

23 Harries, *Film Parody*, p. 125.

24 Ibid., p. 121.

25 Gray, *Watching with The Simpsons*, pp. 43–68.

26 Ibid., p. 66.

27 Brett Mills, 'Comedy Vérité: Contemporary Sitcom Form', *Screen* 45/1 (2004), p. 65.

28 Paul Wells, *Understanding Animation* (London and New York, 1998), p. 6; quoted in Gray, *Watching with The Simpsons*, p. 66.

29 Kim Edwards, 'Moribundity, Mundanity and Modernity: *Shaun of the Dead*', *Screen Education*, 50, 2008, pp. 99–103.

30 David Bordwell, *The Way Hollywood Tells It: Story and Style in Modern Movies* (Berkeley, Los Angeles and London, 2006).

31 Harries, *Film Parody*, p. 35.

32 Ibid., p. 16.

33 Harries (ibid.) gives as a similar example the use of dislodged frames in the animated film *Duck Amuck* (1953), while another form of cinematic time-suspension, the 'bullet time' most famously employed in *The Matrix* (1999), is parodied in *Scary Movie* (2000)

34 Ibid., pp. 62–76.

35 Thompson, *Sunshine on Putty*, p. 346, emphasis in the original.

36 Ibid.

37 Appadurai, *Modernity at Large*, p. 31.

38 Justin Wyatt, *High Concept: Movies and Marketing in Hollywood* (Austin TX, 1994).

39 Dyer, *Pastiche*, p. 46.

40 Higson, *Film England*, p. 26.

41 Ibid., p. 29.

42 Ibid., pp. 78–9.

43 Ibid., p. 70.

44 Roland Robertson, *Globalization: Social Theory and Global Culture* (London, 1992).

45 Higson, *Waving the Flag*, p. 9.

46 Thomas Elsaesser, *European Cinema: Face to Face with Hollywood* (Amsterdam, 2005), p. 71.

Chapter 5: From Distance to Difference

1 Siobhan O'Flynn, 'Epilogue', in Linda Hutcheon with Siobhan O'Flynn, *A Theory of Adaptation* (London and New York, 2013), p. 191.

2 Henry Jenkins, *Convergence Culture: Where Old and New Media Collide* (New York, 2006), pp. 150–1.

3 Cornish and Wright collaborated on the script for Steven Spielberg's *The Adventures of Tintin* (2011), and Wright was executive producer for Cornish's film *Attack the Block* (2011); Buxton also has a supporting role in *Hot Fuzz*.

4 Jenkins, *Convergence Culture*, p. 136.

5 In ibid., p. 143.

6 Dyer, *Pastiche*, p. 37.

7 Jenkins, *Convergence Culture*, p. 143.

8 Dyer, *Pastiche*, p. 47.

9 Ibid.

10 O'Flynn, 'Epilogue', p. 192.

11 Dentith, *Parody*, p. 161.

12 Chris Jenks, *Culture* (London and New York, 2005), p. 23.

13 Ibid., p. 21.

14 Theodor Adorno, *The Culture Industry: Selected Essays on Mass Culture* (London and New York, 1991).

15 Michel De Certeau, *The Practice of Everyday Life* (Berkeley, Los Angeles and London, 1984).

16 Stuart Hall, 'Encoding, Decoding', in Simon During (ed), *The Cultural Studies Reader*, (London and New York, 1999), pp. 507–17.

17 Raymond Williams, *Culture and Society, 1780–1950* (Nottingham, 2013).

18 Smith, *Withnail and Us*, p. 7.

19 Ibid., p. 5.

20 Scott McCracken, *Pulp: Reading Popular Fiction* (Manchester and New York, 1998), p. 5.

21 Ibid., p. 128.

22 Ibid.

23 Smith, *Withnail and Us*, pp. 97–119.

24 Dyer, *Pastiche*, pp. 36–7.

25 Harries, 'The Resuscitation of Genre'.

26 Ibid., p. 283.

27 Harries, *Film Parody*, p. 134.

28 Ibid., pp. 120–34.

29 David Pirie, *A New Heritage of Horror: The English Gothic Cinema* (London and New York, 2008), pp. 81–2.

30 David Pirie, *A Heritage of Horror: The English Gothic Cinema 1946–1972* (London, 1973), p. 165.

31 Ibid., p. 167.
32 Steve Chibnall and Julian Petley, 'The Return of the Repressed? British Horror's Heritage and Future', in Steve Chibnall and Julian Petley (eds), *British Horror Cinema* (London and New York, 2002), pp. 4–6.
33 Pirie, *A Heritage of Horror*, p. 165.
34 Ibid., p. 155.
35 Timothy Corrigan, *A Cinema Without Walls: Movies and Culture after Vietnam* (London, 1991), p. 81.
36 Ibid., p. 84.
37 Ibid., p. 98.
38 Smith, *Withnail and Us*, p. 14.
39 Corrigan, *A Cinema Without Walls*, p. 85.
40 Smith, *Withnail and Us*, p. 15.
41 Ibid., p. 16.
42 Ibid., p. 17.
43 Rick Altman, 'A Semantic/Syntactic Approach to Film Genre', p. 14.
44 Harries, 'The Resuscitation of Genre', p. 286.
45 Jameson, *Postmodernism*, p. 16.
46 Bergfelder 'Popular European Cinema in the 2000s', p. 42.
47 James Herbert, *Lair* (London, 1979), p. 253.
48 Ibid., p. 247.
49 See for example I. Q. Hunter, *British Trash Cinema* (London, 2013).
50 Steve Chibnall 'A Heritage of Evil: Pete Walker and the Politics of Gothic Revisionism', in Chibnall and Petley (eds), *British Horror Cinema*, p. 162.
51 Harries, *Film Parody*, p. 121.
52 Peter Hutchings, 'The Amicus House of Horror', in Chibnall and Petley (eds), *British Horror Cinema*, p. 139.
53 Ibid.
54 Geoff King, *Spectacular Narratives: Hollywood in the Age of the Blockbuster* (London and New York, 2000), pp. 91–6.
55 See Ernest Mathijs, 'They're Here!: Special Effects in Horror Cinema of the 1970s and 1980s', in Ian Conrich (ed), *Horror Zone: The Cultural Experience of Contemporary Horror Cinema* (London and New York, 2010), pp. 153–72.
56 '"You've Got to be Fucking Kidding!" Knowledge, Belief and Judgement in Science Fiction', in Sean Redmond (ed), *Liquid Metal: The Science Fiction Film Reader* (London and New York, 2004), pp. 11–16.
57 McCracken, *Pulp*, p. 131.
58 Smith, *Withnail and Us*, p. 109.
59 Thompson, *Sunshine on Putty*, p. 444.
60 Ibid., p. 445.

Chapter 6: Where No Joke Has Gone Before

1 See for example Peter Biskind, *Easy Riders, Raging Bulls* (London, 1998); Shone, *Blockbuster*.
2 King, *Film Comedy*, p. 128.
3 Gehring, *Parody as Film Genre*, p. 5.
4 Ibid., p. 17.
5 Christine Cornea, *Science Fiction Cinema* (Edinburgh, 2007), p.91.
6 Vivian Sobchack, *Screening Space; The American Science Fiction Film* (New Brunswick, NJ, 1987), pp. 165–9.
7 King, *Film Comedy*, p. 109.
8 Gehring, *Parody as Film Genre*, p. 3.
9 Ibid., pp. 7–8; Harries, 'The Resuscitation of Genre', p. 283; King, *Film Comedy*, p. 112.
10 Neale, *Genre and Hollywood*, pp. 29–39.
11 King, *Film Comedy*, p. 108–11.
12 Cornea, *Science Fiction Cinema*, p. 5.
13 In ibid.
14 Ibid.
15 Barry Keith Grant, 'Sensuous Elaboration: Reason and the Visible in the Science Fiction Film', in Annette Kuhn (ed), *Alien Zone II: The Spaces of Science Fiction Cinema* (London and New York, 1999), pp. 23–4.
16 Ibid., p. 28.
17 Robert Scholes, *Structural Fabulation: An Essay on the Fiction of the Future* (Notre Dame, IN, 1975).
18 Darko Suvin, *Metamorphoses of Science Fiction: On the Poetics and History of a Literary Genre* (New Haven, CT, 1979), p. 64.
19 Derek Johnston, 'The BBC Versus "Science Fiction": The Collision of Transnational Genre and National Identity in Television of the Early 1950s', in Tobias Hochscherf and James Leggott (eds), *British Science Fiction Film and Television* (Jefferson, NC, and London, 2011), p. 44.
20 Ibid., pp. 41–2.
21 Ibid., p. 44.
22 Ibid., p. 45.
23 See ibid.; also James Chapman, '*Quatermass* and the Origins of British Television SF', in Cook and Wright (eds), *British Science Fiction Television*, pp. 21–51.
24 Johnston, 'The BBC versus "Science Fiction"', p. 44.
25 Cornea, *Science Fiction Cinema*, p. 31.
26 Tom Gunning, 'The Cinema of Attractions: Early Film, its Spectator and the Avant-Garde', in Thomas Elsaesser (ed), *Early Cinema: Space, Frame, Narrative* (London, 1990), pp. 56–62.

27 Cornea, *Science Fiction Cinema*, p. 250.

28 Chapman, '*Quatermass* and the Origins of British Television SF', p. 31

29 Ibid.

30 Tobias Hochscherf and James Leggott, 'Introduction: British Science Fiction Beyond the TARDIS', in Hochscherf and Leggott (eds), *British Science Fiction Film and Television*, p. 4.

31 imdb.com puts the film's budget at $50m.

32 M.J. Simpson, 'Counterpointing the Surrealism of the Underlying Metaphor in *The Hitchhiker's Guide to the Galaxy*', in Cook and Wright (eds), *British Science Fiction Television*, p. 219.

33 Ibid., p. 223.

34 Ibid., p. 224.

35 In John Tulloch and Manuel Alvarado, *Doctor Who: The Unfolding Text* (London, 1983), p. 302.

36 James Chapman, *Inside the TARDIS: The Worlds of Doctor Who* (London and New York, 2013), p. 177.

37 Tulloch and Alvarado, *Doctor Who*, p. 302.

38 Nicholas J. Cull, 'Tardis at the OK Corral: *Doctor Who* and the USA', in Cook and Wright (eds), *British Science Fiction Television*, p. 58.

39 Ibid., pp. 55–6.

40 Ibid., p. 58.

41 Ibid., p. 55.

42 Chapman, *Inside the TARDIS*, p. 177.

43 John R. Cook and Peter Wright, '"Futures Past": An Introduction to and Brief Survey of British Science Fiction Television', in Cook and Wright (eds), *British Science Fiction Television*, p. 15.

44 Mark Bould, *Science Fiction* (London and New York, 2012), p. 114.

45 Ibid., pp. 106–7.

46 Lincoln Geraghty, 'Visions of an English Dystopia: History, Technology and the Rural Landscape in *The Tripods*', in Hochscherf and Leggott (eds), *British Science Fiction Film and Television*, p. 105.

47 Jerry Palmer, *The Logic of the Absurd: On Film and Television Comedy* (London, 1987).

48 Douglas Adams, *The Hitchhiker's Guide to the Galaxy* (London, 1979), p. 1.

49 Harries, *Film Parody*.

50 Ibid., p. 33.

51 Adams, *Hitchhiker's Guide*, p. 28.

52 Cook and Wright, 'Futures Past', p. 16.

53 Garrett Stewart, 'The "Videology" of Science Fiction', in George Slusser and Eric S. Rabkin (eds), *Shadows of the Magic Lamp: Fantasy and Science Fiction in Film* (Carbondale, IL, 1985), p. 159, my emphasis.

54 Cornea, *Science Fiction Cinema*, pp. 85–9.

55 Bould, *Science Fiction*, p. 170.

56 Susan Sontag, *Against Interpretation* (London, 2001).

57 M. J. Simpson, *Hitchhiker: A Biography of Douglas Adams* (London, 2003), p. 312.

58 Bordwell, *The Way Hollywood Tells It*, pp. 121–38.

59 The film's eventual worldwide box office return was $104m (boxofficemojo. com): a reasonable but not overwhelming return on its budget, and an indication perhaps of the film's awkward 'fit' within the frameworks of contemporary film sci-fi.

60 Adams, *Hitchhiker's Guide*, p. 30.

61 Joseph McBride, *Steven Spielberg: A Biography* (London, 1997), pp. 264–6.

62 Jameson, *Postmodernism*.

63 Ibid., p. 371.

64 Adam Roberts, *Science Fiction* (London and New York, 2006), p. 28.

65 Neil Archer, *Studying* Hot Fuzz (Leighton Buzzard, 2015), p. 108.

66 Harries, 'The Resuscitation of Genre'.

67 Michael Ryan and Douglas Kellner, *Camera Politica: The Politics and Ideology of Contemporary Hollywood Film* (Bloomington, IN, 1988), pp. 244–57.

68 Fredric Jameson, *Archaeologies of the Future: The Desire Called Utopia and Other Science Fictions* (London and New York, 2005), p. 261.

69 Lewis Wallace, '*Moon*: Duncan Jones' Homage to Classic Sci-Fi', *wired.co.uk*, 12 June 2009.

70 Jameson, *Postmodernism*, p. 17.

71 Sobchack, *Screening Space*; Roberts, *Science Fiction*.

72 Ibid., pp. 124–5.

73 Scott Bukatman, *Terminal Identity: The Virtual Subject in Postmodern Science Fiction* (Durham, NC, 1993), p. 2.

74 Louis Althusser, *Lenin and Philosophy and Other Essays* (London, 1971).

75 Ryan and Kellner, *Camera Politica*, p. 247.

76 Jean Baudrillard, *Simulacra and Simulation* (Ann Arbor, MI, 1993).

77 J. P. Telotte, 'The Problem of the Real and *THX 1138*', *Film Criticism* 24/3 (2000), p. 46.

78 Ibid., p. 45.

79 Ryan and Kellner, *Camera Politica*, pp. 245–50.

80 Sobchack, *Screening Space*, pp. 176–8.

81 Andrew Utterson, *From IBM to MGM: Cinema at the Dawn of the Digital Age* (London, 2011), pp. 92–112.

82 Michael Hardt and Antonio Negri, *Empire* (Cambridge, MA, 2000).

83 See especially King, *Spectacular Narratives*.

Epilogue

1 Becky E. Conekin, *The Autobiography of a Nation: The 1951 Festival of Britain* (Manchester and New York, 2003), p. 4.

2 Anita Biressi and Heather Nunn, 'The London 2012 Olympic Games Opening Ceremony: History Answers Back', *Journal of Popular Television* 1/1 (2013), p. 114.

3 Conekin, *The Autobiography of a Nation*, p. 50.

4 William V. Costanzo, *World Cinema through Global Genres* (Chichester, 2014), pp. 86–7.

5 Ibid., p. 71.

6 Ibid., p. 87.

7 Biressi and Nunn, 'History Answers Back', p. 118.

8 Manfred B. Steger, *Globalization: A Very Short Introduction* (Oxford, 2013), p. 7.

Bibliography

Adams, Douglas, *The Hitchhiker's Guide to the Galaxy* (London, 1979).

Althusser, Louis, *Lenin and Philosophy and Other Essays* (London, 1971).

Altman, Rick, 'A Semantic/Syntactic Approach to Film Genre', *Cinema Journal* 23/3 (1984), pp. 6–18.

—*Film/Genre* (London, 1999).

Anderson, Benedict, *Imagined Communities: Reflections on the Origin and Spread of Nationalism* (London and New York, 1991).

Appadurai, Arjun, *Modernity at Large: Cultural Dimensions of Globalization*, (Minneapolis, 1996).

Archer, Neil, *Studying Hot Fuzz* (Leighton Buzzard, 2015).

Augé, Marc, *Non-Places: Introduction to an Anthropology of Supermodernity* (London and New York, 1995).

Babington, Bruce and Peter William Evans, *Biblical Epics: Sacred Narrative in the Hollywood Cinema* (Manchester and New York, 1993).

Bakhtin, Mikhail, *The Dialogic Imagination: Four Essays* (Austin, TX, 1981).

Barber, Benjamin R., *Jihad vs. McWorld: Terrorism's Challenge to Democracy* (London, 2003).

Barton, Ruth, 'When the Chickens Came Home to Roost: British Thrillers of the 1970s', in Shail (ed), *Seventies British Cinema*, pp. 46–55.

Baudrillard, Jean, *Simulacra and Simulation* (Ann Arbor, 1993).

Beck, Ulrich, *What is Globalization?* (Cambridge, 2000).

Bergfelder, Tim, 'Popular European Cinema in the 2000s: Cinephilia, Genre and Heritage', in Mary Harrod, Mariana Liz and Alissa Timoshkina (eds), *The Europeanness of European Cinema: Identity, Meaning, Globalization* (London and New York, 2015), pp. 33–57.

Biressi, Anita and Heather Nunn, 'The London 2012 Olympic Games Opening Ceremony: History Answers Back', *Journal of Popular Television* 1/1 (2013), pp. 113–20.

Biskind, Peter, *Easy Riders, Raging Bulls* (London, 1998).

Bordwell, David, *The Way Hollywood Tells It: Story and Style in Modern Movies* (Berkeley, Los Angeles and London, 2006).

Bould, Mark, *Science Fiction* (London and New York, 2012).

Bukatman, Scott, *Terminal Identity: The Virtual Subject in Postmodern Science Fiction* (Durham, NC, 1993).

—'The Artificial Infinite: On Special Effects and the Sublime', in Kuhn (ed.), *Alien Zone II* (London and New York, 1999), pp. 249–75.

Burgoyne, Robert, *The Hollywood Historical Film* (Oxford, 2008).

Chapman, James, '*Quatermass* and the Origins of British Television SF', in Cook and Wright (eds), *British Science Fiction Television* (London and New York, 2005), pp. 21–51.

Bibliography

—'Action, Spectacle and the Boy's Own Tradition in British Cinema', in Robert Murphy (ed), *The British Cinema Book* (London, 2009), pp. 85–95.

—*Inside the TARDIS: The Worlds of Doctor Who* (London and New York, 2013).

Chapman, James and Nicholas J. Cull, *Projecting Empire: Imperialism and Popular Cinema* (London and New York, 2009).

Chibnall, Steve, 'A Heritage of Evil: Pete Walker and the Politics of Gothic Revisionism', in Chibnall and Petley (eds), *British Horror Cinema* (London, 2002), pp. 156–71.

Chibnall, Steve and Julian Petley (eds), *British Horror Cinema* (London and New York, 2002).

Chibnall, Steve and Julian Petley, 'The Return of the Repressed? British Horror's Heritage and Future' in Chibnall and Petley (eds), *British Horror Cinema*, pp. 1–9.

Close, Anthony, *Don Quixote* (Cambridge, 1990).

Comolli, Jean-Luc and Paul Narboni, 'Cinema/Ideology/Criticism', *Screen* 12/2 (1971), pp. 145–55.

Conekin, Becky E., '*The Autobiography of a Nation': The 1951 Festival of Britain* (Manchester and New York, 2003).

Connelly, Mark, *The Charge of the Light Brigade* (London and New York, 2003).

Cook, John R. and Peter Wright, ' "Futures Past": An Introduction to and Brief Survey of British Science Fiction Television', in Cook and Wright (eds), *British Science Fiction Television* (London and New York, 2005), pp. 1–20.

—(eds), *British Science Fiction Television: A Hitchhiker's Guide* (London and New York, 2006).

Cornea, Christine, *Science Fiction Cinema* (Edinburgh, 2007).

Corrigan, Timothy, *A Cinema Without Walls: Movies and Culture after Vietnam* (London, 1991).

Costanzo, William V., *World Cinema through Global Genres* (Chichester, 2014).

Cubitt, Sean, *The Cinema Effect* (Cambridge, MA, 2004).

Cull, Nicholas J., 'Tardis at the OK Corral: *Doctor Who* and the USA', in Cook and Wright (eds), *British Science Fiction Television* (London and New York, 2005), pp. 52–70.

—'The Man Who Made *Thunderbirds*: An Interview with Gerry Anderson', in Cook and Wright (eds), *British Science Fiction Television* (London and New York, 2005), pp. 116–130.

De Certeau, Michel, *The Practice of Everyday Life* (Berkeley, Los Angeles and London, 1984).

Debord, Guy, *Society of the Spectacle* (Detroit, 1983).

Dentith, Simon, *Bakhtinian Thought: An Introductory Reader* (London and New York, 1995).

—*Parody* (London and New York, 2000).

Dyer, Richard, *Only Entertainment* (London and New York, 1992).

—*Pastiche* (London and New York, 2007).

Edwards, Kim, 'Moribundity, Mundanity and Modernity: *Shaun of the Dead*', *Screen Education*, 50, 2008, pp. 99–103.

Elsaesser, Thomas, *European Cinema: Face to Face with Hollywood* (Amsterdam, 2005).

Fitzgerald, John, *Studying British Cinema: 1999–2009* (Leighton Buzzard, 2010).

Fraser, George MacDonald, *Flashman* (London, 1969).

—*Royal Flash* (London, 1970).

Gehring, Wes, *Parody as Film Genre: Never Give a Saga an Even Break* (Westport, CT, 1999).

Geraghty, Lincoln, 'Visions of an English Dystopia: History, Technology and the Rural Landscape in *The Tripods*', in Hochscherf and Leggott (eds), *British Science Fiction Film and Television* (Jefferson, NC and London, 2011), pp. 104–16.

Bibliography

Grace, Pamela, *The Religious Film* (Oxford, 2009).

Grant, Barry Keith, 'Sensuous Elaboration: Reason and the Visible in the Science Fiction Film', in Kuhn (ed), *Alien Zone II* (London and New York, 1999), pp. 16–30.

Gray, Jonathan, *Watching with The Simpsons: Television, Parody and Intertextuality* (New York and London, 2006).

Gunning, Tom, 'The Cinema of Attractions: Early Film, its Spectator and the Avant-Garde', in Thomas Elsaesser (ed), *Early Cinema: Space, Frame, Narrative* (London, 1990), pp. 56–62.

Hall, Stuart, 'Encoding, Decoding', in Simon During (ed), *The Cultural Studies Reader*, (London and New York, 1999), pp. 507–17.

Hardt, Michael and Antonio Negri, *Empire* (Cambridge MA, 2000).

Harper, Sue, 'Keynote Lecture, Don't Look Now: British Cinema in the 1970s Conference, University of Exeter, July 2007', in Paul Newland (ed), *Don't Look Now: British Cinema in the 1970s* (Bristol and Chicago, 2010), pp. 21–8.

Harper, Sue and Justin Smith, *British Film Culture in the 1970s: The Boundaries of Pleasure* (Edinburgh, 2012).

Harries, Dan, *Film Parody*, (London, 2000).

—'Film Parody and the Resuscitation of Genre', in Steve Neale (ed), *Genre and Contemporary Hollywood* (London, 2002), pp. 281–293.

Hewison, Robert, *The Heritage Industry: Britain in a Climate of Decline* (London, 1987).

Higson, Andrew, *Waving the Flag: Constructing a National Cinema in Britain* (Oxford, 1995).

—'The Heritage Film and British Cinema', in Andrew Higson (ed), *Dissolving Views: Key Writings on British Cinema* (London and New York, 1996), pp. 232–48.

—'The Limiting Imagination of National Cinemas', in Mette Hjort and Scott Mackenzie (eds), *Cinema and Nation* (London and New York, 2000), pp. 63–74.

—'Re-Presenting the National Past: Nostalgia and Pastiche in the Heritage Film', in Lester D. Friedman (ed), *Fires Were Started: British Cinema and Thatcherism* (London and New York, 2006), pp. 91–109.

—*Film England: Culturally English Filmmaking since the 1990s* (London and New York, 2011).

Hill, John, *British Cinema in the 1980s: Issues and Themes* (Oxford, 1999).

Hochscherf, Tobias and James Leggott (eds), *British Science Fiction Film and Television* (Jefferson, NC and London, 2011).

Hochscherf, Tobias and James Leggott, 'Introduction: British Science Fiction Beyond the TARDIS', in Hochscherf and Leggott (eds), *British Science Fiction Film and Television* (Jefferson, NC and London, 2011), pp.1–9.

Horton, Andrew, *Comedy/Cinema/Theory* (Berkeley and Los Angeles, 1990).

Hughes, Thomas, *Tom Brown's Schooldays* (Oxford, 1989).

Hunter, I.Q., *British Trash Cinema* (London, 2013).

Hunter, I.Q. and Larraine Porter (eds), *British Comedy Cinema* (London and New York, 2012).

Hutcheon, Linda, *A Theory of Parody: The Teachings of Twentieth-Century Art Forms* (New York, 1985).

—*The Politics of Postmodernism* (London and New York, 1989).

Hutcheon, Linda with Siobhan O'Flynn, *A Theory of Adaptation*, 2nd edition (London and New York, 2013).

Bibliography

Hutchings, Peter, 'The Amicus House of Horror', in Chibnall and Petley (eds), *British Horror Cinema*, pp. 131–42.

Jameson, Fredric, *Postmodernism: Or, The Cultural Logic of Late Capitalism* (Durham, NC, 1991).

—*Archaeologies of the Future: The Desire Called Utopia and Other Science Fictions* (London and New York, 2005).

Jenkins, Henry, *Convergence Culture: Where Old and New Media Collide* (New York, 2006).

Jenks, Chris, *Culture* (London and New York, 2005).

—*Textual Poachers: Television Fans and Participatory Culture* (London and New York, 2013).

Johnston, Derek, 'The BBC Versus "Science Fiction": The Collision of Transnational Genre and National Identity in Television of the Early 1950s', in Hochscherf and Leggott (eds), *British Science Fiction Film and Television* (Jefferson NC and London, 2011), pp. 40–9.

King, Geoff, *Spectacular Narratives: Hollywood in the Age of the Blockbuster* (London and New York, 2000).

—*Film Comedy* (London and New York, 2002).

Kuhn, Annette (ed), *Alien Zone II: The Spaces of Science Fiction Cinema* (London and New York, 1999).

Leggott, James, *Contemporary British Cinema: From Heritage to Horror* (London and New York, 2008).

MacCabe, Colin, 'Realism and the Cinema: Notes on Some Brechtian Theses', *Screen* 15/2 (1974), pp. 7–27.

—'Theory and Film: Principles of Realism and Pleasure', *Screen* 17/3 (1976), pp. 7–28.

McCann, Graham, *Morecambe and Wise* (London, 1998).

McCracken, Scott, *Pulp: Reading Popular Fiction* (Manchester and New York, 1998).

Malory, Thomas, *Le Morte D'Arthur, Volume One* (London, 1969).

Maltby, Richard (2003), *Hollywood Cinema* (Malden MA and Oxford, 2003).

Mathijs, Ernest, 'They're Here!: Special Effects in Horror Cinema of the 1970s and 1980s', in Ian Conrich (ed), *Horror Zone: The Cultural Experience of Contemporary Horror Cinema* (London and New York, 2010), pp. 153–72.

Mathijs, Ernest and Jamie Sexton, *Cult Cinema* (Chichester, 2011).

McBride, Joseph, *Steven Spielberg: A Biography* (London, 1997).

Medhurst, Andy, 'Music Hall and British Cinema', in Charles Barr (ed), *All Our Yesterdays: 90 Years of British Cinema* (London, 1986), pp. 168–88.

—*A National Joke: Popular Comedy and English Cultural Identity* (London and New York, 2007).

Mills, Brett, *The Sitcom* (Edinburgh, 2009).

—'Comedy Vérité: Contemporary Sitcom Form', *Screen* 45/1 (2004), pp. 63–78.

Monk, Claire, 'The British Heritage-Film Debate Revisited', in Claire Monk and Amy Sargeant (eds), *British Historical Cinema* (London and New York, 2002), pp. 176–98.

Napper, Laurence, '"No Limit": British Class and Comedy of the 1930s', in Hunter and Porter (eds), *British Comedy Cinema* (London, 2012), pp. 38–50.

Neale, Steve, *Genre and Hollywood* (London and New York, 2000).

—'"You've Got to be Fucking Kidding!" Knowledge, Belief and Judgement in Science Fiction', in Sean Redmond (ed), *Liquid Metal: The Science Fiction Film Reader*, London and New York, 2004), pp. 11–16.

Bibliography

Neale, Steve and Frank Krutnick, *Popular Film and Television Comedy* (London and New York, 1990).

O'Flynn, Siobhan, 'Epilogue', in Linda Hutcheon with Siobhan O'Flynn, *A Theory of Adaptation* (Abingdon and New York, 2013), pp. 179–206.

Paget, Derek, 'Popularising Popular History: "Oh What A Lovely War" and the Sixties', *Critical Survey* 2/2 (1990), pp. 117–27.

Palin, Michael, *Diaries 1969–1979: The Python Years* (London, 2006).

Palmer, Jerry, *The Logic of the Absurd: On Film and Television Comedy* (London, 1987).

Pirie, Donald, *A Heritage of Horror: The English Gothic Cinema 1946–1972* (London, 1973).

—*A New Heritage of Horror: The English Gothic Cinema* (London and New York, 2008).

Ritzer, George, *The McDonaldization of Society*, (Thousand Oaks, New Delhi, London and Singapore, 2011).

Roberts, Adam, *Science Fiction* (London and New York, 2006).

Robertson, Roland, *Globalization: Social Theory and Global Culture* (London, Thousand Oaks and New Delhi, 1992).

Rose, Margaret A., *Parody: Ancient, Modern and Post-Modern* (Cambridge, 1993).

Ryan, Michael and Douglas Kellner, *Camera Politica: The Politics and Ideology of Contemporary Hollywood Film* (Bloomington, IN, 1988).

Sandbrook, Dominic, *State of Emergency: The Way We Were: Britain, 1970–1974* (London, 2010).

—*Seasons in the Sun: The Battle for Britain, 1974–1979* (London, 2012).

Scholes, Robert, *Structural Fabulation: An Essay on the Fiction of the Future* (Notre Dame, IN, 1975).

Shail, Robert, (ed), *Seventies British Cinema* (Basingstoke, 2008).

—'Introduction: Cinema in the Era of "Trouble and Strife"', in Shail (ed), *Seventies British Cinema*, pp. xi–xix.

—'"More, Much More…Roger Moore": A New Bond for a New Decade', in Shail (ed), *Seventies British Cinema*, pp. 150–58.

Shone, Tom, *Blockbuster: How the Jaws and Jedi Generation Turned Hollywood into a Boom Town* (London, 2004).

Simpson, M.J., *Hitchhiker: A Biography of Douglas Adams* (London, 2003).

—'Counterpointing the Surrealism of the Underlying Metaphor in *The Hitchhiker's Guide to the Galaxy*', in Cook and Wright (eds), *British Science Fiction Television*, pp. 219–39.

Sinyard, Neil, *Richard Lester* (Manchester and New York, 2010).

Smith, Justin, 'Glam, Spam and Uncle Sam: Funding Diversity in 1970s British Cinema', in Shail (ed), *Seventies British Cinema*, pp. 67–80.

—*Withnail and Us: Cult Films and Film Cults in British Cinema* (London and New York, 2010).

—'Making *Ben-Hur* look like an epic: Monty Python at the movies', in Hunter and Porter (eds), *British Comedy Cinema* (London, 2012), pp.171–183.

Sobchack, Vivian, *Screening Space: The American Science Fiction Film* (New Brunswick, NJ, 1987).

—'"Surge and Splendor": A Phenomenology of the Hollywood Historical Epic', *Representations* 29 (1990), pp. 24–49.

Sontag, Susan, *Against Interpretation* (London, 2001).

Spicer, Andrew, 'The Reluctance to Commit: Hugh Grant and the New British Romantic Comedy', in Phil Powrie, Ann Davies and Bruce Babington (eds), *The Trouble with*

Men: Masculinities in European and Hollywood Cinema (London and New York, 2004), pp. 77–87.

Stam, Robert, *Subversive Pleasures: Bakhtin, Cultural Criticism, and Film* (Baltimore and London, 1989).

—*Literature through Film: Realism, Magic and the Art of Adaptation* (Oxford, 2005).

Steger, Manfred B., *Globalization: A Very Short Introduction* (Oxford, 2013).

Stewart, Garrett, 'The "Videology" of Science Fiction', in George Slusser and Eric S. Rabkin (eds), *Shadows of the Magic Lamp: Fantasy and Science Fiction in Film* (Carbondale, IL, 1985), pp. 159–207.

Street, Sarah, 'Heritage Crime: The Case of Agatha Christie' in Shail (ed), *Seventies British Cinema*, pp. 105–16.

Suvin, Darko, *Metamorphoses of Science Fiction: On the Poetics and History of a Literary Genre* (New Haven, CT, 1979).

Telotte, J.P. (2000), 'The Problem of the Real and *THX 1138*', *Film Criticism* 24/3, pp. 45–60.

Thompson, Ben, *Sunshine on Putty: The Golden Age of British Comedy from Vic Reeves to The Office* (London, 2004).

Tulloch, John and Manuel Alvarado, *Doctor Who: The Unfolding Text* (London, 1983).

Utterson, Andrew, *From IBM to MGM: Cinema at the Dawn of the Digital Age* (London, 2011).

Wallace, Lewis, '*Moon*: Duncan Jones' Homage to Classic Sci-Fi', *wired.co.uk*, 12 June 2009, available at www.wired.co.uk/news/archive/2009-06/12/moon-duncan-jones%E2%80%99-homage-to-classic-sci-fi (accessed 14 May 2015).

Walker, Alexander, *Hollywood, England: The British Film Industry in the Sixties* (London, 1974).

Waymark, Peter, 'From Telly Laughs to Belly Laughs: The Rise and Fall of the Sitcom Spin-Off', in Hunter and Porter (eds), *British Comedy Cinema* (London, 2012), pp. 141–53.

Wells, Paul, *Understanding Animation* (London and New York, 1998).

Whissel, Kristen, 'The Digital Multitude', *Cinema Journal* 49/4 (2010), pp. 90–110.

Williams, Raymond, 'A Lecture on Realism', *Screen* 18/1 (1977), pp. 61–74.

—*Culture and Society, 1780–1950* (Nottingham, 2013).

Wilmut, Roger, *From Fringe to Flying Circus: Celebrating a Unique Generation of Comedy, 1960–1980* (London, 1980).

Winder, Simon, *The Man Who Saved Britain* (London, 2006).

Wyatt, Justin, *High Concept: Movies and Marketing in Hollywood* (Austin, TX, 1994).

Index

Index

Index

Cinema and Society series

General Editor: Jeffrey Richards

Acting for the Silent Screen: Film Actors and Aspiration between the Wars
Chris O'Rourke
The Age of the Dream Palace: Cinema and Society in 1930s Britain
Jeffrey Richards
Banned in the USA: British Films in the United States and their Censorship, 1933–1960
Anthony Slide
Best of British: Cinema and Society from 1930 to the Present
Anthony Aldgate & Jeffrey Richards
Beyond a Joke: Parody in English Film and Television Comedy
Neil Archer
Brigadoon, Braveheart and the Scots: Distortions of Scotland in Hollywood Cinema
Colin McArthur
Britain Can Take It: British Cinema in the Second World War
Tony Aldgate & Jeffrey Richards
The British at War: Cinema, State and Propaganda, 1939–1945
James Chapman
British Children's Cinema: From the Thief of Bagdad to Wallace and Gromit
Noel Brown
British Cinema and the Cold War: The State, Propaganda and Consensus
Tony Shaw
British Film Design: A History
Laurie N. Ede
Children, Cinema and Censorship: From Dracula to the Dead End Kids
Sarah J. Smith
China and the Chinese in Popular Film: From Fu Manchu to Charlie Chan
Jeffrey Richards
Christmas at the Movies: Images of Christmas in American, British and European Cinema
Edited by Mark Connelly
The Classic French Cinema 1930–1960
Colin Crisp
The Crowded Prairie: American National Identity in the Hollywood Western
Michael Coyne
The Death Penalty in American Cinema: Criminality and Retribution in Hollywood Film
Yvonne Kozlovsky-Golan
Distorted Images: British National Identity and Film in the 1920s
Kenton Bamford
The Euro-Western: Reframing Gender, Race and the 'Other' in Film
Lee Broughton
An Everyday Magic: Cinema and Cultural Memory
Annette Kuhn
Family Films in Global Cinema: The World Beyond Disney
Edited by Noel Brown and Bruce Babington
Femininity in the Frame: Women and 1950s British Popular Cinema
Melanie Bell

www.ingramcontent.com/pod-product-compliance
Lightning Source LLC
Chambersburg PA
CBHW071417290326
41932CB00046B/1903